SCOLDING

Why It Hurts More Than It Helps

SCOLDING

Why It Hurts More Than It Helps

ERIK SIGSGAARD

Translated by Dorte Herholdt Silver

Teachers College, Columbia University
New York and London

Published by Teachers College Press, 1234 Amsterdam Avenue, New York, NY 10027

Originally published in Danish as *Skældud*, Copyright © 2002 by Erik Sigsgaard and Hans Reitzel's Forlag A/S

Preface and English translation Copyright © 2005 by Teachers College, Columbia University

Library of Congress Cataloging-in-Publication Data

Sigsgaard, Erik.
  [Skældud. English]
  Scolding: why it hurts more than it helps / Erik Sigsgaard / translated by
    Dorte Herholdt Silver
      p. cm.
  ISBN 0-8077-4580-4 (cloth : alk. paper) — ISBN 0-8077-4579-0 (pbk. : alk. paper)
  1. Discipline of children. 2. Discipline of children—Psychological aspects. I. Title.

HQ770.4.S535 2005
649*.64—dc22   2005041702

ISBN 0-8077-4579-0   (paper)
ISBN 0-8077-4580-4   (cloth)

Printed on acid-free paper

Manufactured in the United States of America

12 11 10 09 08 07 06 05   8 7 6 5 4 3 2 1

Contents

Similarities and Differences Between the United States and Denmark

In every cry of every Man,
In every Infant's cry of fear,
In every voice, in every ban,
The mind-forg'd manacles I hear
—William Blake

SCHOOLS AND PRESCHOOL PROGRAMS

The Danish term for *teaching* applies only to schools. Teachers teach and educate the students, whereas early childhood educators (*pædagogs* in Danish)* look after the younger children, who develop with their care and support. In practice, however, many Danish preschool activities are very similar to the corresponding American activities. This similarity will probably become even more pronounced after the passing in 2004 of a law requiring binding education plans for all preschool programs for children up to the age of 6.

The cultural differences between schools and preschool facilities will continue to be pronounced for generations. To ask for "order in the class" is commonplace in schools, while no one would propose discipline as a key goal in preschool programs. In school the children *receive* education, in preschool programs they *develop*. In school everybody typically engages in the same activity at the same time, while preschools and kindergartens often display a cacophony of widely different but simultaneous activities that coexist and collide, and whose participants come and go. In school the children are usually divided into groups according to age, which prevents them from learning from older children or caring for the younger ones.

Preschool programs, by contrast, have a moderate or strong degree of integration across age groups. This may mean that a 4-year-old can choose

---

* Throughout the book, we have used *early childhood educator* for *pædagog*, which has no direct English translation. In a few cases where the Danish term is more exact, we have left *pædagog*.

to join the early childhood educator as he or she changes the baby's diaper, thus preparing for later parenthood, perhaps the most important learning possible. But it may also mean that older and younger children are unable to engage in age-appropriate interests in peace, but instead are always stuck with each other. In an earlier survey, 6-year-old kindergartners were asked about kindergarten, "What is the worst thing?" They replied, "When we have to *help* the younger ones" (Sigsgaard, 1993a; emphasis added).

The current trend in Danish schools is an increase in the use of teaching teams, with a team of teachers being in charge of a class; during theme weeks, the lesson plan is broken up. However, in the majority of cases and most of the time, schools divide the day into 45-minute lessons and 10-minute breaks. During the lessons, one teacher usually handles 20 to 30 students alone. On normal schooldays students and teachers spend the breaks apart, and even young children are unable to get hold of their class teacher if they need to. In preschool programs, the children are never without adult supervision (but rarely close to the adults), the day is only roughly structured into indoor and outdoor periods, and the specific content of the day depends on the inclination and enthusiasm of the adults. In some places, the adults are the source of inspiration and initiative; in others, they play a more passive role as monitors.

School is mainly a *must*-culture, while preschool programs are characterized by a *can*-culture. Locally, there are efforts to increase the *can*-aspect of school, with less discipline, calmer work conditions, less teacher-directed learning, more teamwork (often with the participation of early childhood educators), less homework, and more self-selected assignments, perhaps with self-selected partners. These trends are in accordance with current legislation. However, other forces are pushing for preschool programs with more centralized control, a stronger emphasis on narrowly subject-related skills, more testing, an earlier introduction of traditional school activities, and a strengthening of elements that provide more direct school preparation.

In educational journals, esteemed American professors recommend that we change the school and bring it closer to the kindergarten format. Current political practice has the opposite goal of moving preschool programs closer to the traditional school approach.

NOT ALL PRESCHOOL PROGRAMS ARE THE SAME

It would be somewhat misleading to compare school and preschool cultures directly, as a direct comparison might obscure the fact that some preschool programs have strong leanings toward the school culture, while some schools are characterized by typical preschool values. This should be evident from the final chapter of this book.

A Danish-American book on day-care centers in the Nordic countries today (Wagner & Wagner, 2003) states:

> In Denmark, for example, preschool children routinely climb trees, carry stacks of porcelain dishes, cut apples with sharp knives, and use saws and drills for woodworking. They play in "pillow-rooms," which are off-limits to adults. Up to the point of fisticuffs, when adults typically step in, children are left to resolve their own disputes because pædagoger (early childhood teachers) are confident that children can and (usually) will do so.

This is not untrue, of course. Children do these things in many Danish institutions. But in many places they need to ask permission first, never knowing whether they will be turned down or by whom. In other places, there are no knives within reach, and the children's attempts to resolve their own conflicts are hampered by the heavy-handed discipline imposed by the adults. No one knows how many institutions use the former approach and how many make the children suffer under the latter.

It is not a misrepresentation when "egalitarianism, emancipation, and a good childhood" are held forth as key concepts in the Nordic discourse within the field—along with democracy and children's rights—but they are certainly not the only factors that determine practice, and an analysis of contemporary political decision-making patterns would reveal that they are under threat.

Like their American counterparts, Danish preschool programs vary a great deal in quality, from outstanding to rather inferior facilities without public supervision and with untrained staff. Furthermore, many years of heavy cutbacks have undermined the staff's ability to spend time with the children, which is a core value for many Danish *pædagogs*; this has caused some highly skilled early childhood educators to leave the profession.

Nevertheless, it is still easy to find high quality programs all over Denmark. Despite the fact that these—oversubscribed—institutions have no knowledge of each other, they have amazingly similar values: freedom, equal opportunities for development, respect for children's competence and right to be heard, and respect for children's right to a childhood with unscripted play and autonomy.

FACTS ABOUT PRESCHOOL PROGRAMS IN DENMARK

Children up to the age of 6 may attend a variety of preschool programs under public management and supervision as well as subsidized private ones with a bare minimum of regulation and supervision. The area falls under the administrative auspices of the Ministry of Social Affairs and the local municipalities. The municipalities typically guarantee preschool placement for families that request it. Parents must cover approximately a third of the cost. When the children are around 6, 98% enter preprimary classes that prepare the child for school. Preprimary classes are fully funded.

Today 90% of the 3- to 6-year-olds and 50% of children under the age of 3 are receiving some form of this institutionalized care. From the 1970s to the 1990s, the rise in institutionalization was virtually explosive. The main reason for this development is that a family with two adults and a couple of children now has to work at least 70 hours a week—compared with 50 hours in the 1950s—to maintain the current average standard of living. Thus, there has been a steep increase in the number of hours that parents work outside the home, especially since 1970. Today, no other group in Denmark spends as many hours on the job as parents with young children.

Naturally, single parents—a growing group—are unable to work 70 hours a week. Hence, they are not able to achieve the normal standard of living for their family. This is a contributing factor to the economic, social, and cultural polarization that in the past decade has more and more come to characterize the previously so-egalitarian Danish society.

The workload shouldered by parents of young children is the main reason why quite a few children have to spend 10 hours or more a day in institutions, which typically stay open from 6:30 A.M. to 5:00 P.M. There is no restriction on the number of hours a child may spend in an institution per day.

Nursery schools and kindergartens typically have an enrollment of 20 to 85—the average is growing. The children are usually divided into groups of 20 to 22. The groups may segregate children by age or integrate children of different ages. Two or three adults are assigned to each group. About two-thirds of the staff have a degree based on 3½ years of educational training, while some staff members have received only brief basic educational training.

Each year, the institution will draw up a plan on the basis of the focus areas pointed out by the municipality for that year and the regulations laid down by the minister of social affairs under a mandate from the Danish Parliament.

THE EXTENT OF INSTITUTIONALIZATION

In a typical group of parents today, about half will have attended kindergarten; 25 to 30 years from now, that will be nine out of ten. Today, one in four in a typical group of early childhood educators will have attended a preschool program themselves; 25 to 30 years from now, that number will be approximately three in four. What impact are these changes likely to have on the pedagogical approach?

Most of today's adults had secret forts and hideouts as kids, smoked cigarettes and kissed on the sly, played with older and younger children without adult supervision, and battled with the children from neighboring streets; 25 to 30 years from now, few will have had such experiences. Will this make early childhood educators and parents demand more latitude for the children in institutions, or will the fact that they themselves never experienced such "wild" things instead make them expand the scope of adult supervision in institutions?

The fact that children have gradually been removed from the streets, fields, parks, shops, and local communities to be placed in social and educational institutions probably represents the single most important change, for better or worse, in childhood conditions for almost two centuries. Childhood is not what it used to be, to put it mildly. We may justly speak of the institutionalization of childhood. And no other country has taken this development as far as Denmark has.

Let us look at the institutionalization in terms of numbers: Around 1960, a typical Danish child would spend 7,000 to 8,000 hours of his or her childhood in school, and for the vast majority, there was no additional institutionalization. Today, children spend more time in school, and nursery schools, pre-primary classes, and after-school programs have emerged. Today's child is institutionalized for some 25,000 hours of his or her childhood, or more than three times as many as yesterday's child.

Almost all Danish children are institutionalized to the same great extent. In the United States, conditions vary more. Some big cities will have levels similar to Denmark's. In rural or depressed areas and in some inner-city areas, the level will often be considerably lower. But the trend, the increasing institutionalization of childhood, remains the same.

Some studies have discussed whether children benefit from attending kindergarten or whether it is better for them to stay at home until they begin in school, but hardly any studies have looked at the price that children have to pay as institutional life expands and "civilian" life is eroded. It is in this light that the Scolding Project, which forms the basis for this book, should be seen. We have good reason to study the effect of adult scolding in institutions, for everywhere in the world scolding is the worst thing a child knows, and everywhere in the world the institutionalization of children's lives is growing. It seems only natural that the first specific scolding project should be carried out in the country that has taken the institutionalization of children's lives the farthest.

DANISH AND AMERICAN VIEWS OF THE TASKS OF
KINDERGARTEN AND EARLY CHILDHOOD EDUCATORS

In 1989, a study was published — which was later followed up — of the view of kindergarten and its tasks in three different countries: the United States, China, and Japan (Tobin, Wu, & Davidson, 1989). It included a questionnaire survey of early childhood educators, parents, administrators, and educational professionals. The survey included a total of 750 respondents, almost evenly distributed among the three countries.

Two of the questions in the American survey were later put to Danish parents of 6-year-olds and to early childhood educators from 11 institutions (Sigsgaard, 1993a).

One question was "What characterizes a good early childhood educator?" Both Danish and American (as well as Chinese and Japanese) parents and early childhood educators agreed that the most important requirement is for early childhood educators to be kind and warm and to truly like children. The discrepancy between this degree of agreement on the one hand and the very widespread use of verbal sanctions on the other is striking.

The second question was "What is the most important thing to learn in kindergarten?" Both Danes and Americans put "self-reliance/self-confidence" first. Chinese and Japanese respondents rated it fourth, which is still reasonably high.

"Cooperation and how to be a member of a group" was ranked second in all four countries. There are big differences in the ranking of "sympathy/empathy/concern for others," which was seen as one of the top three qualities by 80% of the Japanese respondents. Only 20% of the Chinese and 39% of the U.S. respondents placed it in the top three. Danish early childhood educators resembled the Japanese respondents, with 80% placing it in the top three, while only 40% of Danish parents agreed with this.

"Beginning reading and math skills" was rated last by the Japanese and Danish respondents; 22%–23% of the American and Chinese respondents had this as a top priority, which puts it in seventh place.

Over the past twenty years, parents have been spending less and less time with their children, and more and more parents now see the pedagogical — but not yet the academic — aspects as essential aspects of preschool programs.

The growing emphasis on preschool programs and schools as institutions of learning may lead to more intense institutionalization with stricter demands, increased control, and more scolding, following the logic that "since schools and preschool programs are where kids learn, we have to make sure that they spend a lot of time there, so that they can learn a lot." It may also, however, lead to a more critical view of the use of sanctions. The logic here would be as follows: Maybe the teacher in the old-fashioned school was insensitive and tough, but at least the kids got off at 1:00 or 2:00 in the afternoon, which left them free to spend time with and learn from adults outside the classroom. Today, many children spend up to ten hours a day with professional caregivers and educators. This implies increased opportunities for excessive discipline and even abuse, and therefore parents, school boards, and the media must keep a keen eye on the use of sanctions, including scolding.

In summary, the similarities among Chinese, Japanese, and American perceptions are more striking than the differences, and the Danish results resemble them. Such similarities across different cultures may be related to the fact that all the national studies revolved around institutionalized children. The impact of this common feature on thinking, mind-set, and ideology may outweigh any cultural differences.

There is, however, a tendency for the Japanese to stand out. Preschool socialization is freer in Japan.

The differences between the United States and Scandinavia (Denmark) are not insignificant, as we have seen, and they must be taken into consideration when studies done in one context are presented in another. But Tobin and colleagues' (1989) study, here with added Danish respondents, does suggest that the similarities outweigh the differences. Most of the limited amount of scolding research has been carried out in Denmark, the United States, and Japan. In both Denmark and the United States institutionalization is on the rise, the children's life outside of school is being eroded, and their freedom in it is dwindling. This poses major new problems for socialization. Institutional scolding is one of the symptoms. However, verbal sanctions are also one of the inherent manifestations of institutionalization. If exacerbation of the clashes between adults and children caused by increased institutionalization is to be avoided, the form of institutionalization must be carefully considered and adjusted to match the new conditions.

Briefly put, a de-institutionalization of institutions is required both in the United States and in Denmark.

THE EFFECTS OF THE SCOLDING PROJECT

All over Denmark, the past two years have seen development projects inspired by the Danish edition of this book on the Scolding Project. Below are a few examples:

Preschool Action Plan

One preschool has written a 16-page plan for 2004, with two pages dedicated to the eradication of scolding. An excerpt:

> We have focused on "less scolding," not because we think that we scold the children all the time, but because we see it as an opportunity to improve our ability to read the children's signals and acknowledge and respect their expressions in words and actions. . . . To that end, we will employ the following methods:
> - Limiting scolding and being especially aware of body language and tone of voice.
> - Focusing on the children, doing things together with them, talking with them, and leaving practical chores till later . . . this causes less trouble and fewer conflicts among the children.
> - Being especially mindful of the fact that we operate on the basis of guidelines that may be changed as the need arises, not fixed rules or "restrictions."
> - Ensuring, as far as possible, that the same adults are always with the children, while temps take care of practical chores.

After just a few months, the amount of scolding had decreased, perhaps mainly due to the critical focus on verbal sanctions.

Bullying by Teachers

Most schools—probably in both Scandinavia and the United States—have launched initiatives to counter the widespread problem of bullying. Some places have drawn up anti-bullying plans; Sweden in particular has been successful with such measures. Most anti-bullying plans, however, do not mention bullying by teachers. This makes bullying a problem that is exclusively the child's "fault." This means missed opportunities for addressing bullying as part of classroom activities and the way that classes are organized.

That is not the case in the Danish school "Skolen ved Sundet" ("The School by the Sound"). The school's action plan (Skolen ved Sundet, 2003) states:

> If a student is bullied by an adult:
> - If an adult discovers that a student is being bullied by another adult, that adult is obliged to approach the bully and/or pass on this knowledge to the school's management, which then has to inform the student's parents and take up the specific incident with the student.

- The student may discuss the bullying with his or her parents, who may then contact the school's management, and/or
- The student may discuss the bullying with a teacher that he or she trusts or with the school's management. The school's management will then contact the bully and the student's parents before confronting the student with the bully.
- If necessary, the management will involve the teaching team, parent representatives, the school psychologist, and/or the school nurse assigned to the class.
- The management is to approach the bully/bullies in question and seek to resolve the problem.

This is unusual in Denmark. The guidelines state unambiguously that adults in fact sometimes do abuse the children entrusted to their care. This is not to be hushed up, as it has been so often in the past. Instead, the problem is to be addressed and resolved. In recognition of the fact that it is hard for a child to file a complaint against a teacher, the action plan describes several paths that the child may take and also specifies that any of the bullying teacher's colleagues are obliged to act rather than simply turning a blind eye.

As illustrated by the two examples, the situation may in fact improve through a sharper focus on rough and insensitive treatment and verbal sanctions meted out to children by adults. This may lead to a certain de-institutionalization of our institutions—to the benefit of children as well as adults. Yes, the adults will benefit, too! As this book will demonstrate, it is liberating for adults to lift the taboo that precludes us from addressing the issue of scolding, bringing it into the light and examining it closely. Making it a public issue is the most important step forward.

Erik Sigsgaard
May 2004

CHAPTER 1

Introduction

The current focus on bullying is clearly justified. But nothing suggests that the discomfort and pain related to scolding are any less severe. So why is bullying on the agenda, while scolding tends to be hushed up? Could it be that bullying can be addressed as something that takes place exclusively among the children and has nothing to do with the teachers' or early childhood educators' methods and views?

Putting scolding on the agenda implies an inescapable focus on the adult.

> An adult (*A*) is helping a 5-year-old boy (*C*) put on his gumboots; he is going outside to play.
> **A:** Come on now, you have to stick your foot in yourself. At 5, you can do that!
> **C:** When are you gonna have a day off?
> **A:** What do you mean?
> **C:** You need it!
> **A:** What do you mean?
> **C:** You are always scolding us.

THE BACKGROUND FOR THE SCOLDING PROJECT

In the early 1990s, two kindergartens, which I would rate as some of the best and friendliest in the country, took part in the project "What is a good life for a 6-year-old?" (Sigsgaard, 1993b).

One day, something surprising happened. At one of the kindergartens, the children and I were discussing the difference between their kindergarten and home. Mette said that the kindergarten is bigger and that there are more adults and more children. Then, the usually rather quiet Anders said, hesitantly: "Err, they scold you more in kindergarten." Mette and Anna agreed.

The children in the other kindergarten made similar statements. No child stated the opposite. This was hard to forget, and the children's state-

1

ments played a significant part in making scolding the key topic in the Scolding Project, the combined development and research project described in this book.

Another element in the Scolding Project was an emerging new view on children and relationships: Children are people with rights (Qvortrup, 1994), they have many competencies (Stern, 1995), and they need to enter into appreciative relationships with others (Bae & Waastad, 1992).

How should one understand the growing interest in developing "appreciative relationships" and viewing children as "competent"?

When these views began to emerge, the notion that childrearing was about "setting boundaries" had prevailed almost completely. Children with various difficulties were commonly described as "boundary-testing." Problems with juvenile delinquents, drug addicts, or other afflicted children of parents from the "flower-power generation" were typically ascribed to a lack of firm boundaries. In this context, children's need for "boundaries" refers to their need for adults who demand things of them, tell them what to do, and prohibit certain activities. The alternative was portrayed as indifference or a laissez-faire attitude.

The long-standing tradition of democratic childrearing and education, of making decisions with the children rather than for them, of doing things with the children rather than making them do things, of seeing childhood as valuable in itself rather than merely as a preparation for adulthood, had been under threat, first from "structured" educational methods in the 1970s and early 1980s and then from the focus on "boundaries" in the late 1980s and 1990s. This latter view gained momentum when its core content was described in new concepts and a new view of the child and of child–adult relations ("the competent child," "appreciative relations"). Sociologists' emerging interest in children as members of society in their own right, not just as objects of childrearing and education, also played a role.

Parents and educators were able to use these new concepts to tackle the new socialization conditions rather than simply fending for themselves with firm boundaries and restrictions.

The new context made it natural to take a critical look at the relations between children and adults as they had developed toward the end of the 20th century. In the 1990s, it was common to criticize or even to fire early childhood educators who were not sufficiently able or willing to impose boundaries, but now the atmosphere was changing, and it was possible to take a more critical look at the use of boundaries. The seemingly boundary-testing child, who was "testing" the adults, might now instead be viewed as a human being protesting against forced institutionalization, loss of autonomy, and abuse.

The third element that influenced the Scolding Project was a new awareness of the rapid growth in institutionalization. In Denmark, where the institutionalization of children's lives is the most extensive, a typical child spends 25,000 hours of his or her childhood in preschool, school, and after-school programs. And the institutionalization continues to expand and intensify: the "schoolification" of preschool, mandatory pre-primary classes, more lessons in the early grades, a younger age of starting school, and a growing emphasis on theoretical subjects. Thus, institutionalization is on its way to becoming the single most important factor in the child's socialization, almost outweighing even parental influence.

INSTITUTIONS AND INSTITUTIONAL NORMS

But does it make sense to talk about the educational approaches of institutions in general, when schools and other institutions are as different as they are?

In this context, the term *institution* is used to mean an organization that has an independent physical setting and that is intended to perform an externally defined task, typically a public service. This excludes the "institutions" of marriage or family, for example. But prisons, hospitals, army barracks, schools, nursing homes, and nurseries are included.

It has often caused astonishment that life on the "inside" appears to differ so much from life on the outside.

In the institution, newcomers may be doused with water balloons; outside the institution, they receive help to settle in.

On the inside, the organizational structure is hierarchical. In many hospitals, the doctor still does daily rounds in ceremonial style, marching in with a group of nurses in tow, headed by the chief nurse. The doctor is in command: "Please, can I stay another day? I feel so poorly." "No, Mrs. Schmidt, others are waiting, and we need to reduce those waiting lists!" Life outside the institution is based on networks: Our lives are intertwined with the lives of friends, neighbors, and family. Trust is the basis. Message on the Internet: "I need a transmission belt for my old Opel. Can anyone help?"

Outside of educational institutions, children are typically free to go outside and play whenever they want to. In preschool and especially in school, certain times are allotted for indoor and outdoor activities, respectively.

In a family, a child may normally move from the living room to the bedroom without asking permission. In school, it would normally be un-

heard of for a student to get up in the middle of math class and walk out
in order to drop by the art class in Room 4B.

What is the source of these fundamental differences? Might these differences be the defining characteristics of the institution, the pillars that it
rests on?

If soldiers were to throw off their uniforms and stop walking in step,
would the barracks still constitute a military institution? If the residents in
a nursing home are able to come and go as they please, does the nursing
home cease to be a nursing home and begin to resemble a real home?

What causes these defining assumptions, these self-evident "truths"
(self-evident to the staff, at least), these unquestionable routines, and this
special institutional logic? (It is not the individual acts or routines that
distinguish the institution from the surrounding world, but the *system* of
acts and routines; in civilian life, too, some children are doused with water
balloons; some mothers—like the chief doctor—have more say than dad,
who has to toe the line; and some teenagers wear uniforms—but the op-
erative word here is *some: some* children, *some* mothers, *some* teenagers.)

How do these basic differences, these assumptions operate? May we
assume that they are not installed once and for all but are constantly re-
created in an ongoing interactive process to constitute what we perceive
as institutions?

Is it perhaps the case that different institutions owe their overall similarity to the fact that the basic processes at play are the same, so that one
may claim that the nursery school, the 9th grade classroom, the nursing
home, and the hospital resemble each other, despite the differences in
their tasks, settings, and functions?

THE SCOLDING PROJECT

This book is based on the Scolding Project, which took place under the
umbrella program "Childhood and the Welfare Society," financed by the
Danish Research Councils under the overall research area "Children's Living Conditions and Welfare." The grant was provided in 1997 as part of a
government program to launch new research initiatives concerning children and childhood.

The project examined the basic processes that may fall under the term
sanctions, which according to institutionalization researchers such as Foucault and Goffman help constitute any type of institution.

The sanction that we assume is the most widespread today is scolding, *skældud, reprensiones*, or *Schimpfen*—whatever the term may be in various languages.

The purposes of the study was:

- To learn about the extent, subjective impact, and harmful effects of scolding
- To analyze processes of change in institutions
- To attempt to define what in fact makes up an institution

The study has three parts. One is a case study of a kindergarten that undertook a 2-year development project concerning the adults' use of scolding. This project clarified and changed several aspects concerning scolding. Because the project was well documented and researchers were able to follow it closely, it allowed for a number of process analyses, which can tell us something about the nature of scolding and the way it helps provide the kindergarten with the common institutional character that it shares with all institutions as well as the specific character of the individual kindergarten.

The second part of the study is a survey that examines what others have said or thought about scolding in families, preschool facilities, and schools. Considering the importance of the subject, there are remarkably few such works and studies, and none of them have scolding as their main topic.

The third part of the study consists of extensive data collection from preschool programs, schools, and other institutions that, in a variety of ways, have taken a critical approach to child–adult relations and, directly or indirectly, to scolding. These data enabled us to outline a counterweight to the institutionalization approach, which may be referred to as the appreciative culture.

In addition, the book presents some historical perspectives.

THE SCOLDING PROJECT—PURPOSE AND FOCUS

The institution is, by virtue of its status as institution, characterized by sets of opposite forces (chaos vs. order, adult planning vs. spontaneity, staff vs. alumni, *must* vs. *want*). An examination of these opposite forces may therefore be the best way to understand the institution, particularly in situations where they clash. Therefore, these opposite forces are the focus of the study, and scolding incidents offer particularly good case material.

The book focuses on scolding because it appears to be such a widespread type of sanction and because an analysis of scolding may be expected to provide salient insights into the true nature of institutionalization.

However, the book also offers a perspective of change. Previous projects have shown that children often feel intense discomfort and pain when they are scolded. If this book is able to suggest a way toward a form of institutionalization with less—and less severe—scolding, it may allow both children and adults to have a better time together and may make childhood—and thus life—brighter for many children.

ACKNOWLEDGMENTS

We thank all the participating schools and preschool facilities. Most of all, we thank the Vognmandsparken Kindergarten in Roskilde, which was involved throughout the entire process (7 years), and in particular director Lillian Gregersen and deputy director Gitte Guldager, as well as Malene Borup, who carried out most of the interviews.

Special thanks go to the Scolding Team: Karin Pharés, Tine Ødorf, Mie Simonsen, and Søren Pedersen. Most joined the team as students and have since graduated as early childhood educators and begun to gather experience. They have contributed with stories, discussions, observations, and critical participation. Thanks are also due to associate professor, Henning Kopart, MA (in psychology), early childhood educator Pernille Hedegaard, and Thomas K. Hansen, a student of early childhood education. Librarian Birthe Christiansen contributed valuable data, and managing clerk Bente Gravesen acted as project secretary.

Sanne Gudmann, educational consultant in Elsinore Municipality, provided the first story in this introduction. Many others have contributed with stories and comments during the process. Some of these stories have been included in the book.

Finally, I wish to thank the Danish publisher, Hans Reitzels Forlag, for its commitment, competent collaboration—and angelic patience.

CHAPTER 2

The Development Project

In January 1995 Vognmandsparken Kindergarten, named after its local neighborhood, took part in a lecture and seminar by the Norwegian researcher Berit Bae. The theme was "appreciative relations." For a number of years the kindergarten had been engaged in developing child–adult relations with the aim of helping the adults adopt a more appreciative attitude—after a number of years with a structured pedagogical approach characterized by adult control.

The kindergarten decided to take part in a development project with the author of this book as a consultant. The description below is based on the kindergarten's report *Skældud er ikke bare "skældud"* (*Scolding isn't just "scolding"*; Vognmandsparken, 1997).

First a verbal image of the institution:

> For some years now, we have tried to make the kindergarten resemble a private home as much as possible. In the lobby, there are pictures of the children and their families. The kindergarten has a small covered patio, old sofas and tables, a piano, a bathtub, rag rugs, chickens, and rabbits.
>
> For 7 or 8 years, we have had a group of children called "Group I." These are children who have chosen kindergarten over a pre-primary class. (p. 4)

The institution established the following pedagogical principles:

- It should be nicer to be here than not to be here.
- As adults, we need a good reason to say "no."
- We should see possibilities instead of limitations.
- Each child is special.
- Children must be taken seriously.
- The children should be given experiences that they would not otherwise have had.

From the outset, the staff recognized that they as adults have what Berit Bae refers to as "the power of definition," as they are the ones who define what is good or bad, acceptable or unacceptable. Bae (1996) says about "the power of definition":

Adults are in a position of power vis-à-vis children as regards their perception of themselves. The way that adults respond to children's communication, the way they verbalize their actions and experiences, what they respond to and do not respond to—these are the processes through which the power of definition is exercised. This power can be exercised in a way that promotes the children's independence, confidence, self-respect, and respect for others, but it can also be used in a way that undermines children's self-respect and independence. The problem with the abuse of the power of definition exists in all relationships where one party depends, in some way, on the other.

The staff believed that the communication process between child and adult affects the child's self-image and development "immensely." An appreciative attitude from the adults in their communication with the children helps foster "independence, self-respect, and confidence" in the child through the way that "we adults understand the child's intentions on the child's own terms and view all the child's actions as meaningful instead of judging or moralizing on the basis of our own mindset."

The concept of appreciative relations also comes from Berit Bae, who says, "Appreciation involves the ability to accept opposed and paradoxical perspectives. This, in turn, requires tolerance of the undefined and the ability to handle relations as a both–and phenomenon rather than an either–or phenomenon" (Bae & Waastad, 1992).

The both–and attitude became increasingly important as the development project progressed. Gradually, it became natural to view running in the hallway as something that is both permitted and forbidden: It depends. This might be confusing to parents: "But what is your attitude, is it allowed or not?" What makes sense to children and staff might appear wishy-washy to parents.

The staff chose to base their work on a number of texts and subsequent discussions about the concept of power. The dilemma and the initial stance are outlined in a statement from the report:

> We felt that we were leaving a great deal of power to the children, but the fact that we are adults means that in the end it is always up to us exactly how much power we are prepared to give up. And we find this okay. (p. 8)

But what should the specific topic be? It took 6 months of frustration and debate before the staff chose to focus specifically on scolding. This was in accordance with the fact that in the previous project—*What is a good life for a 6-year-old?*—many children had said that scolding was simply the worst, and some of the children had added that there was more scolding in kindergarten than at home. In the discussions about power, several statements of a similar type emerged:

Peter: I think you should stop scolding us—and then when we do something wrong, you should just tell our parents when they come to pick us up. (giggles, fools around a bit, and shuffles his feet)

Katrine: Can't we scold you at all, then?

Peter: Well, when we do something that is a little bit wrong, then you can scold a little, 'cause maybe we didn't know we were doing something wrong. But when we've done something very stupid—like hitting someone—then you should tell our parents, and then they decide whether they want to scold us or not.

When asked, "So, do you think we scold you too much?" Peter replied, "Yes, sometimes you do!"

The adults, for their part, did not think that they did much scolding. How could the adults and the children have such different perceptions of the same reality?

Thus, scolding became the topic for the development project.

CONTENT AND ASSUMPTIONS

The staff wanted to shed light on two issues:

- How do the children perceive us?
- How do we affect the children?

They also wanted to improve relations between children and adults and improve the adults' ability to listen to and talk with the children.

At a staff meeting, a set of assumptions were drawn up:

- We do more scolding of the children that we know the best.
- Children who are scolded often shut us out.
- Children do not respect the adults who do a lot of scolding.
- We do more scolding around mealtimes.
- We do more scolding when there are fewer adults.
- We do more scolding on outings.
- With experience, one becomes better at scolding.
- It is humiliating to be scolded, especially in front of others.
- Children are upset when they are scolded.
- Children think we stay angry with them after we have scolded them.
- Children and adults do not perceive scolding in the same way.
- Children mind it less if they are scolded by someone they know. (p. 11)

METHODS

So far, the adults had only discussed scolding among themselves. Now they had to hear what the children thought of the matter. This would be done through interviews. Generally, the methods developed as the project moved along.

The staff chose Malene, one of their colleagues, to be the interviewer. She had good, open, and direct rapport with the children, and the children would hopefully be able to open up to her, despite the fact that she represented the powerful adults. The questions below were used in what became two rounds of interviews. Most of the children were interviewed one-on-one in the staff room; the youngest children and some of the older ones who requested it were interviewed in pairs. They were told that it was okay to be completely frank and to take their time.

The questions for the first round of interviews:

- Are you scolded in kindergarten? If yes: Are you scolded a lot?
- Of the adults, who do you think does the most scolding?
- Which of the adults would you prefer to be scolded by? Why?
- How do you feel when you have been scolded?
- Do you think the adults stay mad at you after they have scolded you?
- Do you like it when other kids see you getting scolded?
- Why do you think adults scold?
- What do you think adults should do instead of scolding?

And in the second round:

- Can you tell me what is the worst scolding you have heard in this kindergarten?
- Can you tell me about a time when you were scolded?
- Are girls or boys scolded more?
- Do you sometimes feel sorry for the other kids when they are scolded?
- Could you try to explain how you can tell when an adult is angry? (pp. 12–13)

Later the question "Are kids allowed to scold adults?" was added.

During this period, the staff kept journals that focused partly on their own and other staff members' scolding. Everything was typed up, copied, handed out to the whole staff, and debated.

The All the Way Around (AWA) method (see p. 28) was developed during this part of the project. The purpose was for "everybody who is involved in a conflict to get the opportunity to present his or her side of the story." In practice, the procedure was as follows:

Whenever possible, as soon as a scolding began, another adult would begin to observe the situation and take notes on everything that was said by the adult and the child or children. If the scolding began in one room and continued to other locations, the observer would tag along.

The notes were to reflect the statements as precisely as possible. The child's direct reactions—such as tears, shutting of eyes, fingers in the ears, and so on—were also registered. Afterward, the child in question was asked a fixed set of interview questions. The adult was asked to write down his or her perception of the incident, reasons for intervening, mode of intervention, and reflections on his or her own behavior and subsequent thoughts and feelings.

Other adults and children who had witnessed the scolding were also involved—the children through interviews, the adults through their journal notes. Everything was put together in a compound "story." In total, some twenty All the Way Around incidents were recorded in this fashion.

Everyone gradually got used to observing and—the hardest part—being observed:

> To some adults, it may have been hard at times to be scolding someone, observed by, well, sometimes seven or eight kids, three or four adults, and a few parents, knowing that afterward everybody would give their own subjective version of what happened. It was tough knowing that you had to confront seven or eight people's opinion of what you had just done. But we learned to appreciate the approach. The method was useful. (p. 14)

No observation is ever objective. The observer is a subject with his or her own history, individuality, and opinions. If an observation states that the child was angry, that is an interpretation of a set of complex expressions that others might have interpreted differently. The advantage of the AWA approach, however, is that the combination of many different observations manages to reduce the subjectivity through diversity.

Everybody received a copy of the compound stories to read before the next staff meeting, where they were discussed (an example of an AWA story follows below; see pp. 29–34). The widely differing views were put into perspective. An example: "I did not feel that I was particularly angry." Another adult: "Boy, were you angry then!" The child who had been scolded: "I hate her!" (referring to the scolder).

The paperwork was fitted into the daily work.

Later, it was decided that everybody on the staff should also be interviewed one-on-one by Malene, the same way as the children had been.

INTERVIEWS WITH THE CHILDREN

It is clearly evident that the scolding is not evenly distributed. Half the children say that they are not scolded in kindergarten.

The half that is scolded is "emotionally deeply affected. We adults are not always aware of the consequences of scolding when we go in for the attack."

Here are some reactions:

> "I hurt inside."
> "I cry."
> "I feel like everyone is looking at me; it is embarrassing. I am also re-
> lieved, because now it's over."
> "A little bad—because there's been too much shouting."
> "Then I won't do it again."
> "Not very good—I get bored."
> "So that, er, . . . I am thinking: I wish they would stop. That's how I feel."
>   (pp. 16–17)

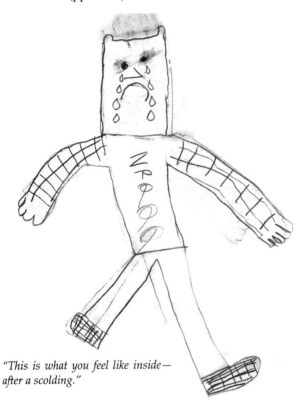

*"This is what you feel like inside—
after a scolding."*

> Look, I'm eating carrots. They taste good. She doesn't want to. And mom says you
> can't force little rabbits. How could they grow up, then, to be free and strong and
> good rabbits? You can never beat or pinch or pull on little rabbits. Then they grow
> quiet and silent and stop singing. No, you have to explain everything quietly and
> calmly at least a thousand times and have never-ending patience.
> —Ulf Nilsson and Eva Eriksson: *Lille Søster Kanin* (*Little Sister Rabbit*)

The interviews with the adults reveal that while adults are hardly ever scolded, and never by someone who is twice their size, they do not like being scolded any more than children do. If adults are scolded they typically kick themselves and think, "Ah, I'm so stupid!" "It's very demeaning. The feeling that someone else is not happy with what I do is hard to handle, and it takes time to regain confidence afterward." (From the adult interviews.)

The children's idea of an alternative is typically that the adults might "say it in a normal way":

> "I think they should just say that you're not supposed to do what you just
>   did, without scolding."
> "They could just say, 'Don't do that!'"
> "They could tell you that you can't do it, instead of scolding. Then you'd
>   learn it better, and you wouldn't get so upset."

When Jon says, "You'd learn it better" and "You wouldn't get so upset," is he expressing something that resembles the adults' "demeaning" and (indirectly) "undermining"?

Another important point is that "if children have to be scolded, they prefer to be scolded by the person they like the most." "I prefer to be scolded by you, Malene, because we're such good friends."

The children reply promptly to the question concerning who does the most scolding. The fact that they point to the director and deputy director leads to some discussion, as we shall see later. They distinguish between small-scale scolding ("when a kid has done something that is only a little bit wrong"), medium-scale scolding, and more severe levels.

One reply from a child led to questions to all the staff members. When asked whom he preferred to be scolded by, he said, "By you, Malene; you don't pull so hard!"

It turned out that all the adults would pull a child's arm from time to time, but this had never been discussed. Christina thought that adults do this only with children, because the adult is certain to come out on top. If we did it with other adults, we might risk getting punched.

Berit (adult) was being interviewed about this one day with 6-year-old Sanne sitting next to her, as Sanne said, "When is it my turn to be asked?" Of course, Sanne was interviewed at once. When she was asked if adults might scold each other, she laughed a little: "No way!" "Why not?" "Because if the other adult is stronger, then he'll just beat him up."

The adults agreed that pulling the child's arm was a sign of defeat—a sign that it seemed impossible to reach the child verbally.

Power relations were also on the agenda when Amin was asked, "Do kids get to scold adults?"

> *Amin*: Kids? No, they can't scold adults.
> *Malene*: How come?
> *Amin*: Because children are not bigger than adults.
> *Malene*: What could a child do if the child was mad at an adult?
> *Amin*: They should just leave the adult alone. (p. 24)

Other children, especially the older ones, and perhaps especially at a later stage in the development process, were able to imagine scolding the adults:

> *Malene*: Does a child get to scold an adult?
> *Malte*:Yeah, sure. What did Amin think?
> *Malene*: He said no. He doesn't think that children get to scold adults, because children are smaller than adults. [Actually, Amin did not say *get to*, but *can*.]
> *Malte (rolling his eyes)*: Aiiee, no. That's wrong. They do get to. I'm gonna go find Amin and tell him that kids do get to scold adults. (p. 24)

The big differences among the children and the strong impact of scolding made the staff decide on a restriction: "You can only scold a child that you have a warm and close relationship with."

Many children did not like it if anyone else was present when they were scolded, while others thought it was nice to have someone else there— "then you have someone to look at." As we shall see, the eyes are a problem: "She looks you, like, deep into the eyes, really, really deep!" one boy said about Christina. That makes it hard, then, if scolding is humiliating, while at the same time one likes Christina—but it might still be better than being scolded by an adult that one has a more distant relationship with.

Overall, the children have razor-sharp images of the scolding adult: "She stands like this, with her hands clenched down her side. (*M. makes fists.*) And then she looks you like deep, deep into the eyes." Another child: "If Lillian is very cross and angry, I am afraid to even walk past her; she might jump on you."

JOURNALS

The development project made the staff wonder why they did not interview the children occasionally as part of their normal work. The same
went for the journal, which we shall look at now. It also provided quality
input for the work with the children.

Everyone on the staff kept a journal. The notes were copied and discussed in staff meetings, which benefited from this specific case material
and became more rewarding than normal.

Gitte's journal from September 3:

> As for how I feel about the project, I think it is nice that we are now so focused
> that one can hardly raise one's voice without being confronted with a series
> of questions.
>
> I had a conflict with Emma in the kitchen, and I scolded her, in part be-
> cause she was crumbling her bread all over the floor. I want her to pick it
> up—and eventually, I take her hand and force it toward the bread, "helping"
> her pick it up. I do it twice and then go to the other side of the table to let her
> finish the job on her own. As I stand there—at a distance to Emma's crying—I
> hear Malene: "Berit, how do you actually feel about adults grabbing hold of
> children?"
>
> *There*—I just abused a child—one of the youngest in the kindergarten, too.
> (p. 26)

So Gitte's colleagues Malene and Berit were discussing Gitte's "abuse" in
both Gitte's and Emma's presence. Afterward, Malene went into the kitch-
en to question her about the incidence. This demonstrates, says the report,
"that we are engaged in each other, and that we want to help each other
improve our abilities to develop good relations with the children."

INTERVIEWS WITH THE ADULTS

The fully trained early childhood educators—in particular the director
and the deputy director (Lillian and Gitte)—feel that the others can be
somewhat too passive in conflicts. This was discussed extensively after the
adult interviews, approximately a year into the project.

> *Gitte*: We go in when no one else does. I can hear other adults around the
> place, and I'm waiting for someone to do something, but no one acts.
> We—Lillian and I—probably respond to more things.
> *Christina*: I still maintain that it is because you respond differently. . . . I am
> learning, but I do respond to the same things as you do.
> *Lillian*: Do I have a lower threshold?

Christina: Sometimes I am not sure which of us is going to intervene if we're both there.

Lillian: You expect me to act?

Christina: Maybe. Sometimes I think there are situations where you act sooner, because you know what you're going to do, while I have to think about it.

Lillian: But that shouldn't keep you from getting the time to respond or make me think that it's time I stepped in.

Berit: Because we expect Lillian to do it.

Lillian: As I am standing there, maybe I think that my way is the only proper way, and then I think: I'd better step in.

Kristian: Those situations, when someone intervenes, I don't see it as . . . well, maybe I do see it as a sort of criticism or, like, hey, you're supposed to do something here. But I also think it's kind of nice, 'cause then I know that now in this situation, I get to intervene.

Gitte: And that is the quick way to becoming the "bad cop," if you're always the first one there. And I think that maybe we see that in the interviews with the children, that Lillian gets mentioned a lot when it comes to which adults do the most scolding.

Lone (student): Yes, but it is also reassuring that you guys are there to intervene or support.

Malene: I see your point, but what I hear Gitte saying is that it can be annoying to have that role as "bad cop," and you're sitting there, waiting, and why the heck won't anyone else do something, then I guess you're already a little worked up, and maybe that would also be nice to avoid—getting so worked up.

Christina: I just think that if Gitte wanted me to respond to something that I wasn't responding to, if she would let me know afterward, then she would also get rid of some of her anger or irritation—right?

Lillian: Yes, directed at you instead of at the kids.

Christina: And I could actually learn from it.

Gitte: So, we could explain to each other why we each chose to respond or not to respond. (pp. 32–33)

The report highlights four aspects:

- The "veterans," who make up the management team, feel a special responsibility to preserve the spirit and the culture that they have helped create in the kindergarten. Consequently, they are very alert when something needs to be "addressed."
- In a kindergarten that has few formal rules, and which mostly operates on the basis of individual standards (which are exposed and debated as a result of the development project), it can be difficult for newcomers to know when to intervene. In case of doubt, they may tend to hold back and leave the scolding to others.

- It takes time to learn to scold in a way that does not make the child feel humiliated.
- Lillian does the most scolding because she is a skillful and high-profile leader with a strong personality who spends a great deal of time with the children. She "sets the norms for both children and staff," "emphasizes the mutual respect for our respective differences. She is the basis for the pedagogical approach here," "is demanding of her staff," and also "makes room for us to be the individualists that we are."

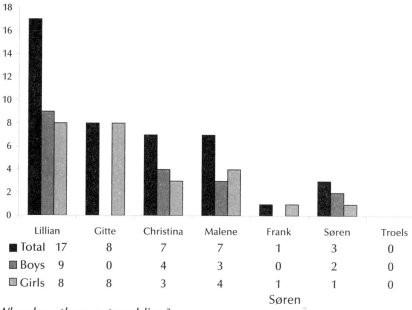

	Lillian	Gitte	Christina	Malene	Frank	Søren	Troels
■ Total	17	8	7	7	1	3	0
■ Boys	9	0	4	3	0	2	0
▫ Girls	8	8	3	4	1	1	0

Who does the most scolding?

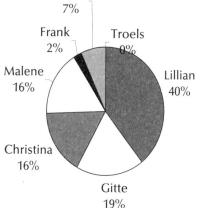

In the adult interviews, Malene used the following questions:

- Do you do any scolding at work? How do you define scolding?
- Do you think you scold often? How do you define *often*?
- Who among the adults do you think does the most scolding? Why?
- Are there, in your opinion, some children that you scold more than others? Have you considered why?
- Are there any children that you do not like to scold? Why?
- If you had to be scolded by an adult, whom would you prefer? Why?
- How do you feel after scolding someone?
- Do you stay slightly angry with the child afterward?
- Do you consider how the child feels afterward? And what do you do with the child afterward?
- Do you consider—in the situation—that other children are present, too? And how does that affect your scolding?
- What sorts of things can make you really angry?
- What do you think you do the most scolding over?
- Have you considered what you might sometimes do instead of scolding?
- What is your take on scolding? Do you think it's okay? (p. 30)

In a follow-up round, the adults were also asked about the act of grabbing a child's arm.

Like the children, the adults enjoyed being interviewed and taking the time to answer, but "we did notice that we didn't hold our heads as high as the kids did afterward!"

Maybe many of the children held their heads high after the interview because they felt good about letting the adults know how they feel about a pressing issue, something they have to endure, but for which they are not responsible. Maybe the mental posture of the adults expressed that they were not too happy about seeing themselves as scolders, despite their continued claim that scolding is in fact necessary.

Once everybody had been interviewed, the staff reviewed and discussed each other's replies. This took place on a Saturday; the discussion was taped and later transcribed.

At the outset of the project, the common perception had been that there was very little scolding in the kindergarten; now, by contrast, the staff felt that there was a considerable amount of scolding.

It was difficult to define exactly what constitutes scolding. One person says, "It is when I raise my voice, and I can tell that I am getting annoyed." Another says, "I only have to hand out a small reprimand before I see it as scolding. To me, this is where scolding begins, and then there are varying degrees upwards."

Everybody felt that they scolded "often," ranging from several times a day to about three times a week.

Scolding topics vary from person to person. In the report, the staff writes:

> One person scolds the children when they bang their knives and forks into the plates before lunch, another person gets angry if they run in the hallway, and a third person gets angry when they break branches off the trees.
>
> This made it easier for us to understand why the children felt that there was a lot of scolding. (p. 31)

Christina did not like to hear herself scolding the children for breaking branches off the trees because she could recall from her own childhood "the sensation of pulling leaves into the hand."

The staff agreed that it was necessary to maintain the individual assessment of the need for intervention. "But one has to be prepared to assume responsibility for the things one allows." The inherent risk might be that the children never feel safe; they never know what they might be scolded over.

In the public debate surrounding this development project and the subsequent research, many have tried to explain the children's perception of the large amount of scolding by saying that the children might in fact perceive ordinary directions and instructions as scolding. However, the analysis and discussion of the adults' interviews compared with the children's interviews made it clear that adults and children did perceive scolding in more or less the same way.

If adults are asked to imagine being scolded, they prefer it to be, on the one hand, clear and direct, and, on the other hand, done with intimacy and warmth—"emotionally, Malene would prefer to sit on the person's lap." This suggests that scolding should be handled by someone who is significant to the child and who cares about the child. "We prefer the ones where we know what we are up against."

The adult interviews revealed that "spontaneous scolding" had declined significantly: "The children are running in the hallway. What might I do instead of scolding? The hallway invites running. We could alter it, with mirrors in the floor, lines, and so on."

The report mentions that the early childhood educators often "see the unfortunate sides of scolding more clearly when observing a scolding colleague. Sometimes it may look very intense. One might think, 'It is okay for me to scold someone, but you really have to pull yourself together.'"

All adults feel bad after scolding, especially if it has been intense, and they spend a great deal of time and energy thinking about it afterward.

This means that scolding is a burden on both children and adults.

The staff agreed that the processing time after the scolding might be reduced if the adult clearly told the child that he or she was no longer angry and also asked how the child was feeling.

It is not that the adults stay angry with the child after scolding him or her, "but we may feel shocked. In a situation where a boy is lying on the ground and being kicked by other children, we may think: How on earth can they do that?"

WHEN SCOLDING BECAME PUBLIC

After completing an All the Way Around process, the staff concludes:

> Scolding used to be a right that the staff held, but at the same time it was also something private, something that we as adults could keep to ourselves— now it is openly discussed. What is reasonable? What is too much? The individual's use of scolding is questioned.
>
> In relation to the children, this enables us to see whether the children feel differently after a conflict than they express in the children's interview.
>
> The children now have an opportunity to tell another adult about the incident—and to express their thoughts and feelings. They discover that even if one adult is angry, that doesn't mean that all the adults are angry. (p. 40)

The right to scold is intact, but the adult is now held accountable. Did he or she go too far? Could he or she have done something else? Scolding has gone from being an individual early childhood educator's unquestioned and spontaneous reaction to acts or omissions that he or she disagrees with to being a conscious act in accordance with predetermined common guidelines based on the institution's overall pedagogical approach in combination with a personal assessment of the incident. In principle, scolding is public and open to discussion not only among the adults, but also among the children.

The staff adds that the approach is highly recommended for "promoting close relations within the staff group and between children and adults."

The unconditional and irrefutable right of adults to scold has been strongly modified and has become conditional. In practice, this has strengthened the children's rights—but still within the context of the basic institutional conflict and power relations between employees and children in forced placement.

CHANGES IN RELATIONS

In one of the closing chapters of the report, the staff attempts to define what "the ideal relationship" would be. The ideal relationship involves an adult who honestly seeks it and is truly interested in discovering "what

does the child want from me?" or "what is going on between those two
children right now?" The adult has to try to avoid being judgmental and
attempt to look behind the child's actions and statements. They write:

These are grand words, and everyone may feel that "that is exactly what I am
already doing" or "that is how I do things."

In actually saying it and doing it, we show understanding and care—
respect—to the same extent as we would with any other adult we took a
strong interest in.

Empathy is difficult—we are not children, we do not see things through
the eyes of a child—so we have to be aware of our own limitations in terms of
understanding. We have to be good at looking for explanations from the child
in order to understand and at asking advice from other adults—if we are to
avoid seeing everything only through the adult eyes. (p. 41)

The development work has led to "obvious changes in relations" overall.
The adults in the kindergarten have always tried to make each child feel
special and develop a strong sense of confidence and self-esteem. But now
they are experiencing more meaningful relationships. Why?

Of course, it makes a difference that we are so focused on relations, but the fact
that during the project we have allowed the children to answer questions concerning their perceptions of the adults—well, actually, they have had to express
whether they are happy with the way we interact with them—has probably
also had a major impact on the closer relationships that we enjoy now.

The staff members have ". . . touched on layers that, in our opinion, go
beyond simply letting the children decide whether they want to go to the
park or the swimming pool" (p. 42). An example:

We have always said that children must be taken seriously, but now this has
a very different ring to us.

We have never before asked the children, "What do you think of me?"
The children used to have a big say in deciding what to do, where to go on
excursions, how they would like the playground to look, what toys to buy,
and so on.

What they actually thought of us as individuals and the things we did to
them was never the focus of as much attention as it is now. (p. 54)

The staff take it one step further:

It is important for both children and adults to matter to each other. Seen in relation to all the new—politically popular—mega-institutions, it would seem
important to explore how many people can actually fit in if we want to maintain close relations! (p. 43)

And the final question:

> So, do you get to scold children? Our answer is, "Yes!" Yes, of course you do, and children also get to scold adults. It is the way it is done that is important—we should be able to say things without putting the child down, responding to the act, not the person. . . . Avoid being abusive and instead engage the child in dialogue. That is the greatest change in our daily work.

TEAMWORK

The fact that the staff had the courage to engage in a development project with such an explosive topic stemmed partly from the fact that topics like "How do I feel?" and "What do I want?" had frequently been on the agenda over the past ten years.

> If the topic "How do I feel?" is to be addressed, collegial supervision may be a possibility, as when Gitte tells Christina about a work-related problem. The other colleagues listen but are not allowed to interfere.
>
> Gitte asks follow-up questions but is not allowed to propose solutions. When Gitte thinks that she has heard enough, the other colleagues divide into two groups that take turns discussing and reflecting on Gitte's problem, while Gitte listens without commenting
>
> In conclusion, Christina and Gitte talk again and see if there are any new perspectives on Gitte's problem—and perhaps develop new ideas as to how Gitte may proceed.
>
> This is a lengthy process, and the goal is not for every single employee to take "the hot seat" in the course of an evening, but if anyone has a problem that they would like to address in this format, we take the time to do it.
>
> A staff meeting can be taxing, and therefore we often round off the evening by going to the music room to play, box, or give each other back rubs; not to say that all problems are now stowed away and forgotten, but because in our minds, teamwork is also about having fun together. (p. 44)

The rare use of the technical term *supervision* probably reflects the fact that working with mutually appreciative relationships is not a narrowly pedagogical project, but rather an expression of the character of the staff members' relationship to each other outside of school.

So, relations within the staff were already good. One of the key outcomes of the project was that relations improved, not least with regard to the direct interaction with the children. Here is an example:

Magnus and Frederik have had an altercation in the playground. Frederik comes in crying, and Lillian begins to deal with Frederik, who tells her that Magnus kicked him in the head.

Lillian and Christina briefly make eye contact, and Christina asks if she should go get Magnus. She does, and Lillian is now able to focus 100% on Frederik, who is shocked and upset. This gives Lillian an opportunity to teach Frederik to handle feelings of panic by taking deep breaths.

Christina finds Magnus, who is huddled in a corner of the playhouse. She tells him to come along, and Magnus gets up and follows her. Christina asks Magnus what happened, and Magnus says that Frederik would not get off the ship, although Magnus and Mads were playing there, and that Magnus then kicked Frederik in the head.

Christina listens to what Magnus tells her, without comment.

As Magnus enters the bathroom where Frederik and Lillian are, Frederik is still crying, and Lillian is checking to see if anything happened to Frederik's teeth. Lillian assures Frederik that his teeth are fine.

Magnus and Christina have been watching Lillian and Frederik for a while. Magnus looks uncomfortable. Christina asks if Lillian wants to speak to Frederik and Magnus. Lillian nods, so Christina leaves and shuts the door to the bathroom behind her. Frederik and Magnus now discuss what happened and sort out their problem.

> After the incident it occurred to us that the fact that two of us had cooperated on the conflict meant that Lillian had avoided the dual role of having to comfort one child while scolding another. Frederik had had the chance to tell Lillian what had happened, and Lillian was able to concentrate on listening and comforting. At the same time, Magnus was able to tell Christina what had happened. This gave the children and Lillian time to deal with the conflict that had arisen, and Frederik and Magnus were able to discuss the incident more calmly. (pp. 53–54)

It was not just the adults who found the time and space to think and act in accordance with their convictions. During and after the development project, it became clear that the children also need to be heard and understood. Because Magnus was seen and acknowledged in a new way, he has moved away from always (literally) plugging his ears when he is scolded and is now able to listen instead.

CONCLUSION

The Vognmansparken report's concluding section states:

> Before the development project, an adult might begin by scolding—and only afterward wonder if perhaps that had been a bit over the top. Now you think, "Wait a minute—count to ten—then find out what's going on!" . . .

> In hindsight we do see that the children were right when they said that we did too much scolding.
>
> This feeling ought to be reduced now, as we try to change scolding to dialogue, and we do see the children approach us in a different way. It is no rare occurrence, for example, that if we scold a child, one of the other children, who is otherwise not involved, will come up to us and say, "Hey, quit scolding already!" or "We don't want to listen to any more scolding now!" (p. 47)

Institutions have long been promoting learned helplessness in children. In this light, the improved social skills displayed by kindergartners as they intervene when an adult is scolding one of their friends may be one of the most important outcomes of the project.

Why did the children's social skills develop as a result of this process? Probably because the staff elevated the children's status by assigning the interviews with the children such a prominent role: They had the opportunity to talk about the adult power that they used to simply be subject to. The exercise of power became public and debatable.

The children's social skills are also expressed in situations that have nothing to do with scolding:

> Amalie asks Lillian if she will pour her a glass of milk. Lillian tells Amalie to give it a go herself. Amalie does not reach for the milk. She stays in her chair, waiting. Frederik, who has observed the exchange, takes the milk and pours Amalie a glass. Then Frederik looks at Lillian. Lillian looks at Frederik but says nothing, validating Frederik's own assessment of whether Amalie needed help. (p. 56)

Later in the report:

> There is a heightened focus on us as individuals and on our behavior, body language, facial expression, and tone of voice, which has enhanced our awareness of the way we come across. The focus is on the adults now—and not exclusively, as is commonly the case, on the children.

A comment about passing on the task of scolding:

> To an outsider, passing on the task of scolding may seem like a cop-out: "Oh, she just wants to be the nice one who never does any scolding."
>
> But that's not the case!
>
> What the reader should imagine is that in the course of a day, a given early childhood educator may have been on the same child's case several times— has counted to ten and had a dialogue, a skill that we have improved—but

the eleventh time you can just feel, "If I have to ask what's going on now, I have to admit that I won't be able to do a good job." So you find a colleague to take over for you.

To me this means that I can relax because I know that the conflict is addressed, and I don't have to respond inappropriately.

To my colleague it means that he or she is able to address the conflict without knowing that there have been numerous incidents throughout the day, and thus be more levelheaded about it.

In fact, we often see that if we are asked to take over a scolding, we address the situation without anger and are therefore better able to appreciate the child's point of view. To the child it means that he or she avoids being bawled out, and in many cases the conflict ends amicably. (p. 49)

The question now arises: When does a scolding cease to be a scolding? If the anger is gone, is it still a scolding? In what sense?

According to the conclusion of the development project, a "good" scolding has to live up to the following requirements:

1. One should say what needs to be said without putting the child down.
2. The adult should respond to the act, not to the individual.
3. The child should be allowed to take part in a dialogue.

What follows is the story about the time when Frederik nearly got a bad scolding but when the adult, fortunately, took the time to inquire, so that the end result, instead, was appreciation:

Frederik, who is 6½, is standing in the kitchen, looking at some cut-off pheasants' heads. The heads are on a plate; there is a female head and a male head.

Kristian and I are standing next to him, talking. Frederik is feeding the heads cranberries. Suddenly Frederik says to me, "This head is really neat, look at all the colors."

I turn around and see that he is holding the male head. I agree and begin to tell him that that is the general rule in the animal kingdom: The males have the brightest colors, the longest feathers, the biggest manes and so forth, while the females often look dull. In closing, I say that I'm not sure why that is, but in a way I think it is a little unfair.

Frederik looks at me and says, "Hmm!" He then goes back to feeding the heads. Kristian and I continue talking. A while later I look over at Frederik again and see that he is knocking the heads against each other.

My first impulse is to tell him, "Hey, stop that!" But luckily I don't. I look at his face and instead think, "I wonder what he is doing. Why is he doing it?"

So I ask him, "What are you doing, Frederik?"

He looks up, smiling: "I am passing some of the male pheasant's colors on to the female, so it's less unfair."

I am so glad that I didn't say something grumpy. After all, I'm the one who put those ideas into his head. Instead, I say that I think it's a good idea, and it is a good thing that there are people like him who try to make things fair. I also add that maybe he shouldn't do it so hard, as they may break. Frederik is still smiling; he nods and says, "Okay." (p. 57)

During the project, scolding has become something that everyone talks about. Two examples:

A parent overhears a child saying to Lillian, "You shouldn't scold me!" Lillian replies, "I am not scolding you, I am just telling you that you . . ."

Afterward, the parent hears the child saying to her friend, "Lillian was not scolding me, she was just telling me."

Here, Lillian uses her power of definition to "settle" the disagreement with the child over whether she was being scolded or not.

The parent addresses Lillian to say that it never occurred to her that one could simply put it like that.

Our kindergarten project has spread to the families at home. One morning, as she drops her child off in the kindergarten, a mother tells us that when she was in the middle of scolding her son, he confronted her with so many questions that she got all confused about why she was scolding him, and was completely baffled by the situation. (p. 54)

As already mentioned, no one had ever asked the children, "What do you think of me?" Thus, the children now have an influence on the adults' behavior. In the past, the adults could tell the children how to behave, but the reverse was unthinkable.

Making scolding more of a public issue increased the children's understanding of what the adults were thinking, as this story illustrates:

Frederik: Lillian! Can we go over to the playground with the yellow slide? (Lillian ponders this, and Frederik tries to read her mind.)

Frederik: Do you think we're gonna run off?

Lillian: No, I don't, why would you do that? But let's just figure out who should be responsible for getting all of you back here together.

The children discuss this among themselves, and Lillian hears their assessment that Magnus is too silly to be made responsible. In the end, the children pick Frederik, and they get permission to go to the other playground. (p. 56)

PROCESSES OF CHANGE

The process of change can be broken down into a number of stages:

1. The staff *focuses on relations* as the key to their work.
2. Relations between children and adults are seen as *power-based.*
3. There is a specific exploration of the power relations between children and adults—with an emphasis on *a critical look at scolding.*
4. *Gradual changes in practice* are carried out, and *scolding* is maintained as a pedagogical instrument.
5. Elimination or a radical *reduction in the amount of scolding* is seen as a possibility.
6. *Staff members intervene if children are scolded by other adults* in the public space (on outings).

At the outset of the development project, the staff felt: "We do not do very much scolding, but scolding can be necessary."

During the project: "We do a lot of scolding, and scolding is necessary and acceptable, but damages caused by scolding must be prevented."

At the conclusion of the project: "We still do a fair amount of scolding, but we do not humiliate the children, and they have a chance to present their case; it is necessary to scold, and we have the right to do it."

> *Lillian:* I have found a good way of doing it; I reflect, analyze and consider what I did and then use that in my future interactions.
> *Gitte:* I don't think I do as much severe scolding as before . . . and I take the time to consider if I could have acted differently and why I responded the way I did.

Throughout the process the children maintained that scolding is common and frequent, that being scolded is nasty, and that scolding—in many children's opinion—is unnecessary. There are also some statements that the adults are "better" at scolding now.

Toward the end of the project there were more and more cases in which the children intervened against scolding, including at home, and intervened in conflicts between adults. It seems that some of the children had learned *verbal self-defense* in the course of the project. Self-defense against scolding is a necessary skill today, as even the most severe scolding cannot, unlike physical abuse, be reported to the police (Elgin, 1980).

A few years after the completion of the development project, observations were carried out that revealed a number of pedagogical changes that probably help to preempt scolding. Lillian and Gitte now seemed to agree with the many children who had said that the adults did not need to scold the children, but instead ought to just "say it in a normal way." After the end of the project, new interviews had been carried out with the children and more All the Way Around descriptions had been made.

Thus, the development work continued after the formal end of the project, and important changes continued to take place several years after the project had ended.

Perhaps development projects that aim at in-depth changes ought to last no less than four to five years.

A CONFLICT—ALL THE WAY AROUND

As previously described, a variety of methods were used to collect data during the development project:

All the Way Around (AWA) is a combination of four methods—interviews with children, interviews with adults, observations, and journals—that AWA integrates to shed light on a given incident.

Often an incident is first addressed through one method and then through another. At one point all the children were interviewed one-on-one, then all the adults were interviewed, and later the children were interviewed again, and so forth. The methods offer valuable insights into the individual participants' view of certain sanctions (interviews and journals) or the way that specific scolding incidents are perceived and interpreted (observations and journals).

The AWA approach provides information about incidents, interpretations, and perceptions. Instead of discussing scolding on an abstract level, AWA addresses specific incidents as they are described by the involved parties and by observers, by the scolded as well as the scolder.

Where other approaches often leave us with one perception of an incident, one party's view, which cannot be taken as a full description of an actual event, the AWA approach may offer five, six, or seven points of view, which brings us closer to a balanced understanding that encompasses the inherent contradictions and contrasting points of view. Thus, the description of the conflict between Lone and Maja below is based on input from Lone, Maja, Malene, Christina, Martha, Gro, and Jan.

The AWA approach has no real practical application in research, as the method is too costly in man-hours. In the Lone–Maja incident, the researcher would also not have been present to record Maja's conversation with Lillian at the breakfast table a few days later.

Another reason the AWA approach is not applicable in research is that AWA incidents cannot be planned to fit into a researcher's schedule. Before the event, no one knew that Lone and Maja were going to have a major conflict. No one could have made sure that Malene would be so close for so long and be able to take the time to write down notes immediately afterward to provide a detailed account. The reason that she felt inspired to do so was the talk she had had with Lone about scolding the day before. Also, it would have been impossible to plan for Christina to be able to carry out three interviews with children in rapid succession and record her notes from these interviews.

Malene's and Christina's ability to almost spontaneously restructure their work depends on their colleagues' ability (and willingness) to jump in and take over the tasks they would otherwise have been handling. This requires a high degree of agreement among the staff about the importance of this project. Everyone must be prepared to take over if a colleague suddenly sits down to take notes. In fact, the AWA approach is so demanding that a full AWA process can never be a daily occurrence, but perhaps a monthly one. After the incident, the notes have to be typed up, copied, read, and discussed by all the staff.

But now, let us turn to the selected AWA incident, as it was recorded in writing by the staff members immediately afterward (they did not pick the headline, however).

Gro did it
or
Maja was scolded because she wouldn't do as she was told
or
?

A conflict between a child and an adult
as described by participants and witnesses
(Lone, Malene, Christina, and Jan are kindergarten staff).

Conflict with Maja, Lone's perspective, Friday September 9:

I am in the bathroom folding laundry. Gro and Maja (5-year-olds) are running in the hallway. I tell them to stop. A little later, I hear another adult tell them not to run in the hallway. When they run in the hallway a third time, now making even more noise than before, I get annoyed and tell them to put their shoes on and go outside if they want to run. Maja won't, because Gro was chasing her, and she maintains that she won't go outside. I ask her repeatedly, and at some point she tells me that I can't make her do that. I tell her that here, in the kindergarten, I can make her do that—and that right now I am ordering her to go. I squat down next to her locker where she is sitting and begin to put her shoes on. She is struggling, and I stop, because I am conflicted about whether to "force" her physically to put her shoes on and go outside.

At this point I give her the option of staying inside if she will stay in her group room, because she keeps refusing to go outside, and I don't know how to make her go outside, short of forcing her physically. I also ask her what she thinks I should say to her. She says that I can say whatever I feel like. I say that I think she should go outside. She refuses. I simply don't know what to tell her, and when she asks me to leave, I get up and go toward the office.

She says something to me, and I reply that now I have to talk to her again, as I couldn't hear what she said. She won't tell me what it was she said. I tell her that I will be in the bathroom folding laundry, and if she wants to talk to me, she can come see me.

Afterward, I am confused, because what I really wanted to do was simply grab her and put her outside, but I don't like engaging in the physical power struggles that this sort of action requires, because it makes me wonder if that is really the "right" way to solve a conflict. I was dealing with Maja, whom I have not had major conflicts with before, so I am not familiar with her reaction patterns, except that others tell me she can get really angry. I saw her as a stubborn girl, but she was really upset without shutting me out. Throughout the conflict I was conflicted as to the best way to handle this. In my own impression I was choosing several different approaches at once and made a mess of it. I am not sure if Maja understood what I wanted, and she ended up thinking I was stupid.

Malene observes, describes, and reflects on the conflict:

I hear Lone talking to Maja in a slightly louder and firmer voice than when I usually hear her voice. In fact, she sounds angry.

L: Go to the playground now. I am tired of you running up and
down the hallway.

M *(with tears in her voice):* No, I don't want to go outside.

L *(very firmly):* No, but you have to. Even if it means I have to put
your shoes on and carry you to the playground. I am tired of

you guys running. I heard Jan telling you to stop, and I have
also told you many times, and it isn't helping.

M *(tears in her voice):* I don't want to go outside!

L: But I don't want you running in here.

M: I don't want to go outside . . . I am not running anymore. *(crying)*

L: "Then what do you want me to say to you?"

M *(The crying stops; her voice turns angry/firm):* Say what ever you
feel like!

L: But I don't want all this running, and I also don't want to be so
angry, so what are we going to do about it?

M: I don't want to go outside.

L: No, but then, what . . . I just don't want to get so angry. Do you
think that you can remember not to run in here, if you're going
to stay inside?

M: I don't want to go outside.

L: No, I can hear that, but then what?

M *(angry now):* Go away!

L: So then what?

M: Go away already!

L: Okay . . . . *(walks away)*

M *(mumbling):* . . . don't you ever do that again . . .

L *(turns around):* What? . . . Now you're talking to me again, so I
have to talk to you, and you told me to go away. Now I am going
into the bathroom, and if you want anything or want to
talk to me, you can come out there.

Lone leaves.

Maja sticks her head into her locker and stays that way until Christina goes out there to interview her.

I note the episode because Lone's voice is angrier or firmer than I
have heard it in a long time.

And only yesterday I had a talk with Lone about scolding where
she told me that she often has more of a temper than she shows, and
that she feels like showing more of her self. So I'm thinking, "That was
quick, already the next day she springs into action!" Considering that
she is dealing with Maja, the matter is not straightforward; Maja is a
slightly "complicated" child in my view. With Maja you can really have
a big conflict.

At first, Lone is firm and unambiguous, but when Maja responds
with tears and sulking, she softens a little, and Maja grabs this chance
to sneak up on her and "be her equal"; at least her fear of getting
kicked outside subsides. And now Maja is angry.

Christina interviews Maria, who observed the conflict between Lone and Maja:

    C: What happened?

    M: I didn't really see what happened; I was only there a small part of the time.

    C: Was Lone angry?

    M: No, she wasn't:

    C: How can you tell if an adult is angry?

    M: It's 'cause they got angry eyes and happy eyes, so I can tell the difference.

    C: Are there other things you can see?

    M: I don't know.

    C: Do you think it's right or wrong for an adult to scold someone?

    M: It is okay.

    C: What do you think that Lone and the other adults could have done instead of scolding?

    M: They could just tell the kids to stop instead of scolding them.

Christina interviews Anne, who also observed the conflict:

    C: Did you see what happened?

    A: I just saw Lone scolding her.

    C: Did you think Lone looked angry?

    A: Yes, I did.

    C: How can you tell that an adult is angry?

    A: I don't know.

    C: Is it something in their face that lets you know they're angry?

    A: It's like a wide face.

    C: Is it okay for an adult to scold someone?

    A: Mmh. *(Meaning "Yes." A. nods.)*

    C: What should the adults do instead of scolding?

    A: I don't know.

    C: Couldn't the adults just talk in a normal way?

    A: No." *(shakes her head a little)*

Christina interviews Maja ten minutes after the incident:

    C: How do you feel now?

    M: I am a little upset.

    C: Do you think that Lone is still angry with you?

    M: Yes, she is still angry with me.

    C: Do you get scolded often here in kindergarten?

    M: I don't know.

C: Do you think that it's okay that you were scolded?

M: No, because Gro was chasing me.

C: Do you think any of the other children saw you being scolded, and was it okay for you that they saw it?

M: It's okay that the others were watching.

C: Would you have preferred if it had been another adult scolding you?

M: No.

C: What do you think Lone should have done instead of scolding you?

M: Lone should have told Gro not to chase me.

C: What do you think of Lone right now?

M: I don't feel so good, and I am angry with Lone.

Jan's journal, September 3:

Lone has told Maja several times not to run in the hallway, and that if she doesn't stop she will have to go outside. Eventually, Lone has had enough, and she scolds Maja. During the scolding Lone repeatedly tells Maja to put her shoes on and go outside; she even begins to put Maja's shoes on. Maja begins to cry and promises not to run in the hallway anymore, as she does not want to go outside. Eventually Maja manages to make Lone go away without Lone having accomplished what she wanted.

My opinion: Lone should have stuck to her guns and sent Maja outside. If she is not willing to make good on her "threat" she should not have issued it, but instead chosen a different approach.

I think that Lone handled the situation okay; it was a tough one. It has made some sort of impression on Maja, and she is not running in the hallway anymore. If I had been put on the spot, I think she would have wound up in the playground, because many children get reprimands . . . where the adult tells the child in a normal voice . . . the child says, yeah, yeah and forgets/doesn't care . . . I don't think that children should be scolded . . . but they have to learn to listen.

Afterwards, Lone is looking a little beat. Now, 15 minutes later, Maja looks cheerful; she is having a good time and playing Memory.

Maja talks to Lillian three days later:

M: Lillian, do you know who is the boss here in the kindergarten?

L: No.

M: I do; you are.

L: Yes.

M: So do you know who is my favorite among the adults?

L: Yes, I do; you like Gitte best.

M: Yes.

L: Which one of the adults does the most scolding?

M *(thinks long and hard):* . . . Can't you ask me something else?
   This is too difficult.

Comments on the Process

According to Lone, the conflict revolves around running in the hallway. A few years earlier, the staff had written in their report, "The children are running in the hallway. What might I do instead of scolding? The hallway invites running. We could alter it with mirrors in the floor, lines, etc."

Apparently the hallway has not been altered; it still invites running. Lone has not considered what she might do instead of scolding.

According to the report, the staff now thinks, "Wait a minute—count to ten—then find out what's going on!" But Lone does not do this. Why? Maybe because it is so obvious what is going on: Two children are running and shouting in the hallway. But according to Maja, something else is going on. Christina: "Do you think that it's okay that you were scolded?" Maja: *"No, because Gro was chasing me."* Lone even writes it in her own account: "Maja won't [go outside], *because she was being chased by Gro.*" Maja's stubborn refusal to go outside may stem from her sense of being treated unfairly. There may also be other reasons, but Maja does not reveal them, and Lone does not ask. Lone maintains her *power of definition.* This means that she alone decides which aspects of the events within the field of social relations enter into the description of what was going on. In other words: Lone determines what information and interpretations to include or exclude. Based on her definition of events, Lone decides for a sanction: Both children are sent outside. Maja not only questions the sanction, but also challenges Lone's right to impose it: "You can't make me do that!" Lone: "Here, in the kindergarten, I can make her do that—and . . . right now, I am ordering her to go." Subsequently, Maja is struggling with the issue, and three days later she seeks Lillian's confirmation that *she* (as the director) is indeed the boss in the kindergarten.

Lone finds it natural that children who continue to make noise in the hallway, despite repeated reprimands, are sent outside. And as Maja refuses, "Lone has had enough," according to Jan, who according to Malene had also just told the children to stop, "and she scolds Maja." Malene also hears Lone scold Maja, "In fact, she sounds angry."

Lone herself does not talk about scolding. She "tells" the children to stop. "I ask her repeatedly" [to go outside]. She does mention, however, that she was annoyed and "wanted to . . . simply grab her and put her outside."

It seems telling that the adult who does the scolding will tend to describe his or her statements in other terms than "scolding," even when observers agree that a scolding in fact is what is taking place. One of the key results of the development project was for the adults to realize that the initial difference in perceptions about the amount of scolding—where the children saw much more scolding than the adults did—was not due to differences in the *general* perceptions about what constitutes scolding, but rather due to the fact that *in the situation,* the scolding adult tended to characterize his or her utterances as something other than scolding. At the end of the development project the adults find that they mostly agree with the children as to when a series of utterances should be termed "a scolding."

There is a striking difference between Lone's and Malene's description of Maja's reactions. These are Malene descriptions of Maja's utterances: "with tears in her voice," "crying now," "the crying stops, her voice turns angry/firm." Lone says about Maja, "won't," "tells me that I can't make her do that," "struggles," but nothing about crying. Jan, too, writes in his journal, "Maja begins to cry and promises not to run in the hallway anymore." Malene notes exactly the same: "'I don't want to go outside . . . I am not running anymore' (crying)." Only toward the end of her reflection does Lone write that Maja was "very upset," and apparently she never heard Maja's promise of not running anymore. Instead of responding to the content, according to Malene she says, "Then what do you want me to say to you?" At this point it all turns sour for Maja, who had probably hoped that Lone would drop the matter and accept her promise of not running: "The crying stops, her voice turns angry/firm," Malene writes.

Thus, Maja lives up to Lone's perception of her: " . . . others tell me she can get really angry. I saw her as a stubborn girl, but she was really upset without shutting me out." When Lone does not hear Maja's submission despite the perceived injustice, "I am not running anymore," Maja's tearful stubbornness is replaced by angry and defiant stubbornness. She succeeds in making Lone go away.

Afterward, according to Malene, "Maja sticks her head into her locker and stays that way until Christina goes out there to interview her." Maja tells Christina that she is upset, feels that she has been treated unfairly, does not feel well—and that she is angry with Lone. Jan writes, "Afterward, Lone is looking a little beat. Now, 15 minutes later, Maja looks cheerful; she is having a good time and playing Memory."

How can Jan and Malene have such different perceptions of the situation? Maybe because Jan describes Maja after she has been interviewed by Christina, while Malene describes her before.

The Impact of AWA

If that is the case it demonstrates the impact of the AWA approach on the *mental welfare* of the children. The staff agrees that after a scolding the adult has to tell the child that he or she is no longer angry with the child. Lone did not do that, but Christina's questions saved the day. Maja has an opportunity to express her sadness, anger, and feelings of powerlessness, and she cheers up again.

Lone has an opportunity to learn that both Malene and Jan understand how she feels and what she wants to achieve, but that their accounts (and the accounts of the child witnesses) are also different from her own, which may help her reflection and professional growth. (The AWA texts are also discussed in a staff meeting.)

For the institution as a whole, the AWA and the interviews gradually make it easier to express different opinions about a case. The adults still make most of the decisions, but these decisions can be questioned now. The institution has not only lost its aura of absolute power, but has in fact taken active steps to relinquish this position by moving from a formal to a rational form of authority. Later, we shall explore this topic in more depth.

The case really does have more than one side. Is it a case of a "miscarriage of justice" or a stubborn child who needs a firm hand? Or is it much more complicated? The AWA approach brings contradictions and opposite notions to light, which disrupts the idyllic image of the institution as a venue for skilled and dedicated professionals to provide unselfish care for weak children who are poorly developed and in need of protection. The children are both weak and strong, the adults both unselfish and egocentric, both skillful and flawed.

Everything is written down. This means that the matter is taken seriously and made public. Uncomfortable and difficult issues are not swept under the carpet but put under a spotlight. One example of this: Toward the end of the development project, it had become commonplace for a scolding early childhood educator to ask a colleague to observe the scolding. Another example: The observations are discussed as part of the everyday routine, and both children and adults can listen in. Initially the incidents were only discussed in staff meetings. Thus, in combination with other methods, AWA contributes to the democratization process—democracy being seen as the obligation to contribute and the right to be heard, taken seriously, and respected.

But we are still talking about a democracy within the forced system of an institution where the children *must* spend their time and where the adults have the right to make the decisions. At the same time as the standards of democracy are being established, the institutional power is also reproduced. The children are asked for alternatives and opinions, but the basic assumption is usually that an intervention *is* going to take place in any case. Christina: "Would you have preferred if it had been another adult scolding you?" (With the implication " . . . since you did, of course, have to be scolded.") Maja: "No." (With the implication, "I should not have been scolded.") Jan: ". . . have to learn to listen."

Preschool facilities can go far in terms of democratization, which is demonstrated in the closing chapter of the book as we visit the project kindergarten, Vognmandsparken Kindergarten, a few years after the end of the development project. The AWA approach has been instrumental in this development.

CHAPTER 3

On Sanctions and Scolding

WHAT IS SCOLDING?

It's like hitting someone with your voice.
—Italian kindergartner, approximately age 5

Scolding is not an actual pedagogical term, like "stimulating" or "motivating." But it is very old, and familiar to everyone.

The word "scold" can be traced back to the Old Norse word *skellr*, which means a blow or a slap. *Skielde* or *skelle*, as it became in older modern Danish, meant to slap, hit, knock out of position or tell off. Thus, the word has referred to physical violence, loud noises, sudden alterations of a condition by outside forces as well as to the modern meaning of the word, *reprimand*.

Old Norse also had the term *refsa*, which is reflected in the modern Danish word *revse*. The term referred to corporal punishment, spanking, but also reprimands and reproach. Today it refers to parents' physical punishment of their children and is almost only used in reference to parent's legal right to use corporal punishment.

According to both *The Jutlandic Law* (from 1241) and *The Danish Law of King Christian V* (from 1683) a man had the right to "castigate [children and servants] with rod or wand if they trespass, but not with weapons." In *The Jutlandic Law* this was not a right, but an obligation, but both laws also contained legal protection ("not with a weapon"). In *The Danish Law of King Christian V* we find the first specific protective measure: It is no longer legal to hit a child so hard that the child's health is endangered. In 1866 the type and extent of the beatings are restricted. From 1920, a man is no longer allowed to hit his wife, and from 1921 this protection is extended to the servants. From 1937, masters are no longer allowed to hit their apprentices. In schools, however, teachers—outside of Copenhagen—retain the right to hit the children until 1967; in Norway, this right was abolished in 1936.

The first attack on parents' right to spank their children came in 1985, with the new wording in section 2 of the *Custody Act:* "Custody entails the obligation to protect the child from physical or mental violence and other abusive behavior." It was unclear, however, whether parents were only obliged to protect the child from violent behavior of others, but an act passed by Parliament 1997 (with a narrow margin against the parties of the right) made it illegal for parents to hit their children; the act specifies that the child "must be treated with respect for his or her person and may not be exposed to corporal punishment or any other abusive behavior."

Mental violence, which was mentioned in the *Custody Law* from 1985, is not mentioned here, but the comments accompanying the act state that mental violence is punishable by up to two years of prison under the penal code.

Neither the 1985 act nor its 1997 successor mentions scolding. "Mental violence," however, should probably be interpreted to include severe scolding. In practice, however, the 1997 act probably must be seen to exclude scolding from consideration even more clearly than the 1985 act.

Sweden abolished parents' right to inflict corporal punishment some years ago. Since then, the number of parents who report having punished their children physically within the twelve months prior to the survey has dropped considerably (1988: 51%; 1994: 11%; 2000: 8%) (Barn och misshandel, 2001).

In a representative Danish study from 1995, 46% replied that it might be necessary to punish two-to-four-year-olds physically if they played too rough (Sigsgaard & Varming, 1996). In a Gallup opinion poll, also from 1995, 42% said they were in favor of moderate corporal punishment. In a poll by Epinion in 2004, this number had dropped to 27% (Mikkelsen, 2004).

In Norway and Finland corporal punishment of children was banned in 1987 and 1983, respectively.

In 1985 the EU's Council of Ministers encouraged member countries to change their legislation on corporal punishment. To date, the right to corporal punishment has been abolished in Austria, Cyprus, and Italy and is being debated in many countries.

In 1987, the UK—as the last country in Europe—removed public school teachers' right to hit their students; in 1999 this was extended to teachers in private schools, but the private schools appealed the act to the European Court of Human Rights, claiming that parents should have the right to choose a school where the teachers spank the students. The matter, the Williamson Case, has not yet been heard by the courts, but is scheduled to decided by the House of Lords in December 2004.

In 2000, the British government was forced to impose restrictions on parents' rights to inflict corporal punishment on their children. The Human Rights Court turned down a ruling by a British court that acquitted a stepfather who had repeatedly hit his stepson with a bamboo cane. The European court found this punishment to be so severe that it constituted a breach of the boy's human rights and rebuked British legislators for not protecting children from this sort of treatment.

The United States still has no law to keep parents from hitting their children.

In 1991 Denmark ratified the UN's 1989 Convention on Children's Rights. Article 19 requires countries to "take all appropriate . . . measures to protect the child from all forms of physical or mental violence, injury or abuse . . . while in the care of the parent(s), legal guardian(s) or any other person who has the care of the child." In Danish legislation six years later, the term "mental violence" had been removed from the text.

Webster's International Dictionary defines the modern meaning of *scolding* as follows:

> *Intransitive verb*
> . . . to find fault usually noisily or rudely : utter harsh rebuke : chide sharply and severely . . .
> *Transitive verb*
> 1 : to force by scolding—used especially with out of
> 2 : to chide loudly or rudely : rebuke with severity : censure severely or angrily . . .
> *Synonym* . . . SCOLD, UPBRAID, RATE, BERATE, TONGUE-LASH, JAW, BAWL OUT, WIG, RAIL, REVILE, and VITUPERATE mean, in common, to reproach or censure angrily and more or less abusively. SCOLD suggests the censure of a disobedient child by a mother, or implies irritation or ill temper.
> —*Webster's Third New International Dictionary, Unabridged* (2002)

PHYSICAL AND MENTAL SANCTIONS

So over the centuries the original term, *skellr*, has separated out into more distinct, separate terms. As is the case in other areas, the verbal aspect has become more and more removed from the physical.

	Physical Disciplinary Measures	*Mental Disciplinary Measures*
Active	Spanking, grabbing the child's arm	Includes scolding
Passive	For example, withholding food and drink	For example, ignoring

Still, children who are spanked are usually scolded at the same time, but if the sanction of choice is scolding, it is only rarely accompanied by physical sanctions—although there are exceptions, like grabbing the child's arm or forcing the child to look the scolder in the eye.

SCOLDING—THE REPLACEMENT FOR BEATINGS?

It is not always easy to distinguish between physical spanking and scolding. The Spanish word *reñir* may mean both scolding and slapping. In English, one may refer to a scolding as "having your head ripped off," "getting a slap on the wrist," "being jumped on," or "being put through the grinder," for example. A tirade is a stream of words that may have the character of scolding. The stem of the word *tirade* means to pull, but also to shoot or to throw.

All of these metaphors have a physical referents. *A beating hits not only the body, but also the mind—and scolding hits not only the mind, but also the body.* Does the abolition of the right to corporal punishment mean that there is less punishment in today's society? That is a difficult question. One might argue the opposite, that spanking has been replaced by intensified mental and organizational controls in the form of exclusion; the establishment of special groups, classes, and schools; referrals to specialist treatment; and medication.

What is the relation between physical and verbal sanctions today? Outside the institutions there is a great deal of corporal punishment. In a Danish survey, 41%–44% of respondents felt that it might be necessary to spank young children when they persist in refusing to obey, playing rough, and so on (Sigsgaard & Varming, 1996). According to a Japanese survey, about half the parents spanked their children frequently or very frequently (Kato et al., 1998).

If we look at homes and institutions together, verbal sanctions clearly outweigh physical sanctions, partly because approximately half the children never experience physical sanctions at all. Some estimates suggest that for every child who experiences corporal punishment, there are about 100 who are exposed to "verbal violence" (Elgin, 1980).

Overall, there seem to be three distinct trends:

1. A gradual transfer of disciplining from home and community to school and preschool institutions. ["If an early childhood educator scolds a kindergartner, that is acceptable, like when a parent scolds his or her own child, but if the neighbor does it, the parents get very angry" (Pædagog, personal communication, 2000).]
2. A shift from punishment (verbal or physical) toward management and psychological control. (Otherwise healthy children are diagnosed—as "boundary-testing" for example—and are fully or partly removed from the class. There is an attempt to discipline the individual through the establishment of personal goals and development plans.)

3. A movement away from corporal punishment and—due to the strong increases in the extent and intensity of institutionalization—toward an increasing emphasis on verbal sanctions.

DIFFERENT FORMS OF MENTAL DISCIPLINARY MEASURES

One way to establish a more accurate understanding of the concept of scolding is to try to determine how to categorize the concept. Among the few researchers in the field, some have attempted such a categorization.

Botor (1987) studied 148 mothers' relationship with their 2- to 3-year-old children in Japan, the Philippines, and Thailand. She distinguished between three types of disciplinary measures: *interference* (typically in a conflict), *enforcement,* and *scolding.* Elgin (1980) introduced the category *verbal violence,* which includes scolding. Kato and colleagues (1998) distinguished between *loud shouting* and *verbal threats.* Other researchers describe *expulsion from the room, activity, or social group; time-out room; threats; being told to move to another seat either permanently or temporarily; a ban on speaking; removal of toys or materials; being sent home from an excursion or camp; being picked up in a rough or harsh manner; being addressed with irony or contempt; being ignored; being given overly difficult tasks; exposure to extraordinary surveillance; separation from a friend; withholding of consolation; suspension; expulsion from school or institution; public scolding; exposure to random or unjust punishment;* and *exposure to nonspecific criticism* (Honig, 1992; Johnson et al., 1992; Perris et al., 1980; Serbin et al., 1973; Sigsgaard & Varming, 1996). As recently as 2004, a mother complained that her 6-year-old daughter, who had just started school, had been repeatedly told to stand in the corner and now did not want to go to school anymore.

In addition, Termansen (1998) describes *exposing children,* for example by ridiculing them in front of the class.

Of these approximately 25 sanctions, more than half have a physical aspect. This is in accordance with previous research into institutionalization, which showed that disciplining primarily has a physical aim (Foucault, 1979).

From this pool of proposed categories one can devise a list of 15 different forms of mental disciplinary measures, six of which would have a dominant verbal element and fall under the category of verbal interventions, abuse, or violations (see Table 3.1).

The six verbally oriented forms are not mutually independent. Scolding can be an aspect of bullying and often includes general criticism. Scolding is often done through shouting but may also be done with repressed anger. What turns shouting into scolding? If a teacher shouts, "My, what great weather we're having today!" no child will perceive it as scolding.

Table 3.1 Categories of Mental Disciplinary Measures

Verbal interventions	Bullying
	General criticism
	Exposure (e.g. ridicule)
	Scolding
	Shouting
	Threats
Removal of autonomy	Force
	Interruption/intervention
	Being denied certain materials
Removal of attachment	Expulsion
	Isolation
	Being grabbed in an unkind manner
	Being ignored
	Being denied consolation
	Being denied love

The shouting has to be directed at the child and concern th child's acts or character, and it has to contain derogatory criticism and a negative emotional charge for the child to perceive it as scolding.

The child may be "exposed" through general criticism made in public, but not all general criticism constitutes scolding. Scolding may include threats, but threats do not necessarily take the form of scolding.

The last nine categories describe restrictions of the child's actions or relations. The interventions are not primarily verbal but often have a verbal element. The mother may threaten to withhold her love ("If you don't do as I tell you, you're not a nice girl!") and may follow up by speaking angrily to or ignoring the child.

Overall, all but three categories involve pushing the child away or keeping the child at a distance.

In institutions, scolding is one of the six disciplinary measures that are mainly mental (although they do have physical aspects) and mainly verbal.

SCOLDING AS A MENTAL DISCIPLINARY MEASURE AND AS A REACTION

Above, we discussed scolding as one among many types of disciplinary measures; that is, as an adult's chosen and deliberate action toward a child. Now we will look at scolding that is neither chosen nor deliberate.

An adult may scold a child out of sheer fright, as when a child suddenly darts into the road and narrowly misses being hit by a car. Instead of comforting the terrified child, the equally terrified parent scolds him or her. The parent's shock is released through scolding, which the child experiences as a second shock after the close encounter with the car. Usually, though, the child will understand that it is the parent's shock that leads to the scolding, so the scolding does not strike very deep. This form of scolding is not a disciplinary *action,* but a spontaneous *reaction.*

In a kindergarten close to a busy road, which the project team visited, the staff would scold the children preemptively in order to keep them from running into the road. In a school in Bosnia, the early childhood educators and teachers take the children into the hills and use scolding as a means of making them alert to the many concealed landmines. This form of scolding has the character of a collective mental disciplinary measure, which also does not strike very deep. Both forms of preemptive scolding are, by their nature, *public.* This is often the case with scolding directed at an individual child as well, because the action that leads to the sanction often takes place in groups and may involve several children and because the scolding typically follows immediately after the act. As demonstrated in the development project, some children find public scolding particularly unpleasant.

Scolding as a mental disciplinary measure or action is *intentional,* whereas scolding as a reaction is *responsive.*

GLOBAL VS. SPECIFIC SCOLDING

Some scolding is directed at specific acts or omissions: "How many times do I have to tell you to untie your shoes before you put them on. You should be able to get that, damn it!" We may distinguish between scolding that revolves around the behavior as such and scolding that revolves around the effect of this behavior on someone: "You know how much it scares me when you do things like that" (Juul, 1995).

But scolding may also concern the child's "global self" as a "global, painful and devastating experience where the child's self, not just its behavior, is painfully scrutinized and evaluated negatively" (Tangney, 1991). If this occurs frequently, it may have serious consequences for the child's personal development, as we shall see later.

UNJUST VS. DESERVED SCOLDING

"I don't really remember if I hit anyone, or if I did it by accident."
    —Malthe, age 4½

One of the worst experiences is being scolded unfairly: ". . . and I didn't even do it." The children involved in the development project experienced such scolding often at first, but more rarely toward the end of the project, as the adults had agreed to inquire about events before deciding to scold anyone. Unfair scolding causes a powerless rage in the child, which in turn may lead to even more scolding. To the adult, the child's angry reaction confirms that the scolding was justified. A negative cycle has begun.

If the child "did it" despite knowing that it was wrong—and didn't just "do it by accident"—he or she will usually accept the scolding as justified. Many children expect—and may even demand—to be scolded in that situation.

WHAT IS THE VERBAL CONTENT OF SCOLDING?

The mode of expression in scolding is very important to the child: "She said it in an angry sort of way, er, she doesn't look angry, but she scolds, but she doesn't get mad."

But what is the actual verbal content of scolding? That was the topic of a survey that asked college 300 students and 300 11- to 12-year-old schoolchildren in Japan to write down scolding episodes from their childhood (Endo, Yoshikawa, & Sannomiya, 1991). They were asked to reconstruct what was said. The material included 1,670 scolding utterances. The subsequent analysis led to 14 types of utterances:

Direct speech
- "Stop that!"
- "Do that!"

Indirect speech
- Specifying what the child is not to do
- Reminding the child that he or she has been told before
- Explaining the reason(s) why the child should not do something
- Talking about the punishment
- Creating a double bind: "If you don't want to do your homework, then don't do it!"
- Criticizing the child's personality
- Ignoring the child
- Asking/being reproachful: "Why won't you help?"
- Expressing discomfort
- Expressing dissatisfaction by cursing
- Describing the consequences of the child's action/omission
- Other

Scolding may be viewed as a collective term for many types of verbal sanctions and behavior-modifying interventions, usually carried out by adults toward children who are dependent on them. It is the mode of expression rather than the actual verbal content that characterizes a message as scolding.

A typical scolding process may be described as follows: The adult receives information, directly or indirectly, about a child's behavior, reacts emotionally, and incorporates this emotional response into his or her perception of the situation and the child. If the adult perceives and assesses the situation as undesirable and deserving of sanctions, he or she will deliver a message aimed at the child or the child's action(s), a message that normally has negative and critical content and takes on a form that has a negative emotional charge.

This creates a confrontation. The child interprets the message based on context, previous experience, his or her own state of mind, and the relationship between the verbal content and the expressive mode of the message. With power relations being the way they are, the child is unable to respond in kind, but does of course respond, as we shall see later.

Thus, the *unilateral* character of the communication is characteristic of scolding.

SCOLDING AND OTHER TYPES OF ADULT BEHAVIOR

Above, we described scolding as one among many types of mental disciplinary measures. It may also be seen as a special type of communicative teacher/early childhood educator behavior. Instead of asking, "What forms of discipline does the teacher or early childhood educator use?" we may ask, "How does the teacher/early childhood educator communicate with the children?" A British project (Allen & Casbergue, 1997) arrived at eight forms, seven of them verbal:

- Information giving
- Listening
- Direction giving
- Asking questions
- Giving answers
- Monitoring
- Scolding
- Praising

More detailed categorizations can be drawn up, and more physical forms, such as cuddling or touching, may be added. The categories are useful if one wants to get an idea of the most commonly used forms of communication in a place, based either on self-assessment or on colleagues observing and recording each other's communication patterns.

An Icelandic study showed that most teachers spent up to 25% of class time rewarding, scolding, or punishing (Sigurdardottir, 1997). If this could be avoided—and in some places it does play a very small role—it seems that the time required for basic education could by cut by several years! But, some might say, if it were avoided, one might lose the socialization gains that result from rewards, scolding, and punishment.

This points to a fundamental issue: Is scolding a regrettable evil or a desirable and indispensable instrument in the socialization of the coming generation?

This issue requires a distinction. In the Bosnian school mentioned earlier and in many Western kindergartens, scolding is considered a necessary means of teaching the children to be wary of landmines and highways. But this involves collective, public, preemptive scolding, not guilt and shame-provoking scolding, which we will examine more closely later.

The primary focus of this book is not on global scolding or scolding as a spontaneous reaction, but instead on teachers' or early childhood educators' use of scolding as a verbal, mental disciplinary measure aimed at the children who are placed in their care and who are, therefore, to some extent in their power. We address the scope and extent of this form of scolding, the perception of it, its effects in the short and long term, and potential alternatives.

REGULATIONS ON SCOLDING IN INSTITUTIONS

It is taken for granted today that teachers and early childhood educators have the right to scold children at will and as much as they want. But that has not always been the case.

In connection with the agrarian reforms in Denmark in the 18th century, progressive landowners began to set up schools for the farmers' children in the 1780s. L. Reventlow's 1784 book *Brahetrolleborgs Skolevæsens Instrux* (*Directive for the Educational System of Brahetrolleborg*) emphasized the importance of ensuring that young schoolchildren "always maintain their joyful spirit and that school should not be a burden on them." With that in mind, it was decided that ". . . the young children remain for the first year no more than one hour in school." The directive also stated: "Corporal punishment and coarsely worded reprimands should not be the schoolmaster's means of maintaining order among the children."

The national education directive of 1814 introduced the universal school, the school for all children. The teaching instruction that accompanied the directive stated:

> As parents entrust the teachers with their children, their most precious possession, they have cause to expect these wards to be treated well. For this and for other reasons, no teacher may ever, however justified he might think himself in

doing so, address any child in a derisive, mocking tone, with abusive language and indecent terms. Even less may he assume the right to inflict, immediately and on his own impulse, bodily harm on any child with blows or jabs.

As late as in the 1840s, at most three in four children went to school, and authorities had to convince parents that education was beneficial and necessary. The Copenhagen City Council made a dual decision:

1. All children had to attend school.
2. Parents were granted the right to visit and to lodge complaints.

Parents were allowed to visit the school whenever they wanted, and the teacher had to "assist them with good advice concerning their children's upbringing. When they visit the school, he should also greet them cordially and allow them to partake in the education, as long as this is not in any way disruptive." The parents also had the right to complain if they suspected that the teacher had transgressed "by using harsh and arbitrary behavior toward a child."

The increasing professionalization of the school led to the removal of this regulation in 1887, and most schools eventually introduced scheduled parent–teacher meetings to replace the spontaneous visits.

By then, the 1814 regulations to protect schoolchildren from blows or abusive language had been largely forgotten.

Exactly 100 years later, the relations between teachers and students in Copenhagen were defined by "regulations and disciplinary rules" that regulated the behavior of the students, not the teachers. These did not include restrictions on scolding. On the contrary, the teachers were granted the right to impose a number of sanctions, including "reprimands." A similar trend is evident in the 1986 "Executive order concerning the promotion of good behavior in school." 1986. Section 3 states: "The students should strive to carry out the assignments handed out to them by teachers. They should also follow the directions given them and in every way exhibit good behavior."

The picture has changed here. It is no longer the citizens' school, obliged to treat the citizens' children decently, as in 1814—during the absolute monarchy. (From 1660 until the first democratic constitution in 1849, the king held absolute power. The capital city of Copenhagen, however, enjoyed special privileges.) Now—under democratic rule—the school has become the property of the public authority, and the students owe it obedience and respect. If they do not show sufficient obedience and respect, they are guilty and must atone their guilt through punishment.

The dismantling of democracy in the schools at this point is probably not the result of conscious political decisions, but rather a reflection of the dynamics of institutionalization. Once an institution has become fully institutionalized, the hierarchy and power balance are laid out in an extensive set of regulations, and the institution in question has gained independence from the surrounding society: It is no longer acceptable for parents to simply show up whenever they feel like it; instead they are expected to take part in scheduled meetings.

It is no longer up to the parents to make demands on the school, but up to the school to make demands on the parents.

By 1970, there were new developments in Denmark, evidenced in *Den blå betænkning* (*The Blue Report*) from 1960–1961. *The Blue Report* was a major step away from the segregated school, where the children were divided into groups according to their abilities (which was often equal to a division along social lines), and toward the integrated, universal school. The emphasis was now on the students' active involvement and democratic participation, and the traditional curricula were changed to reflect a greater emphasis on in-depth work with selected topics. A similar trend was seen in Norway, where the *Primary School Law* of 1969 had a section with the headline "Order and discipline." With the change in the law in 1975, the corresponding section now had the headline "About the working environment and about students' rights and obligations." This reflects a shift away from punishment and spanking toward care and support.

The citizens' time-honored and rather informal right to observe classes and ask the teacher for advice at any time changed to representational democracy in the 1980s in the form of school boards supplemented with the already familiar and formalized parent-teacher meetings about the standing and progress of the individual student.

INSTITUTIONAL SCOLDING AND EVERYDAY SCOLDING

Some children think that if they did something really bad in the institution, they should be scolded by their parents, not by the early childhood educators. Why does scolding at home differ from scolding in the institution? One reason may be that kindergartners—in contrast to older children and teenagers in school—have not yet accepted the early childhood educator as an authority figure in their life. Another likely reason may be that scolding at home usually coincides with the act it refers to and is carried out by an adult who is directly involved with the child.

This link between action and sanction used to exist not only within the family, but also on a community level. If a child was caught shoplifting, the grocer would be able to tell the child immediately that stealing is wrong. If a child tore down the neighbor's laundry, the neighbor—and victim—would be able to let the child know instantly that that was unacceptable. But the grocer has closed shop, and the laundry is in the dryer. "Functional scolding" at the scene of the crime has been replaced by "formalized scolding." The victim of the "crime" is often not present. It is no longer the neighbors' laundry that gets dirty, but the early childhood educators' norms ("boundaries") that are violated. Over the past few centuries, we have gone more and more from concrete childrearing to abstract and moralistic childrearing.

This development has been complex. Children are certainly subject to less corporal punishment in today's institutions than they were in the schools and institutions of the past, but at the same time they are disciplined more—mainly because disciplining now takes place during 25,000 hours of a child's life, but also because the disciplining has many more faces today than it did in the past.

CHAPTER 4

How Much Scolding Actually Takes Place?

"I've been scolded like — 600 times." (Boy, 4½ years old)

"Do you think that this is a kindergarten where there is a lot of scolding?"
"Yeah, but then there are also other kindergartens where there's a lot of scolding. But Ahmed, you know, he can get into a lot of trouble."

(Boy, 6 years old)

"It's not every day I see someone getting scolded. It's not everyone I see that gets scolded." (Girl, 6 years old)

"Which one of the adults does the most scolding?"
"I'm not really sure, but mostly there's many that scold in one way or another." (Boy, 6 years old)

"If it's just in this kindergarten, then I guess I think it's almost just all of them, but only almost." (Girl, 6 years old)

There have been few studies to determine *how much* adults actually scold. Few studies register scolding episodes, and then only in a peripheral way. A few more — but still only a few — address what adults report concerning their sanctions on children.

In the project kindergarten, 40% of the children said in the individual interviews that they were scolded, another 40% that they were not scolded. Some children were not able to answer, and others simply shrugged.

- In the United States, a group of preschool teachers were observed for about 50 half-hour segments. Their actions toward the children were registered. Direct scolding accounted for about 1% of their actions; "negative requests and prohibition," however, accounted for 9%. It was difficult for the observers to distinguish between scolding and negative requests/prohibitions, and the teachers were clearly affected by the observers' presence. Besides, "scolding" was only a subcategory under "social emotional negative," and it appeared toward the end of the questionnaire. The project is small in scope (Honig & Lally, 1988).

- A study on disciplinary control in two Icelandic schools showed that "most teachers spent less than 25% of every lesson on direct disciplinary control." A distinction was made between rewards (mild/strong) and punishment (mild/strong). Punishment that could be characterized as scolding or closely related to scolding (raising one's voice, admonishing or threatening, ordering/shouting, grabbing the student, spanking, deriding or preaching) occurred 3.4 times per lesson in younger classes, 1.4 times per lesson in fourth through seventh grade, and 3.1 times per lesson in eighth through tenth grade. Thus, with five daily lessons, a given student in the younger age group would experience sanctions of the scolding type 17 times a day in addition to any scolding during the breaks (Sigurdardottir, 1997).

- In Scotland, 871 teachers were asked to report their sanctions on difficult students (Johnstone & Munn, 1992); 99% of the teachers had used scolding ("verbal rebukes" or "telling off") recently, 64% scolded often, and only 7% found scolding to be effective. The second most common form of punishment was isolation/movement of the students within the classroom, used recently by 78% of the teachers and frequently by 29%. Extra schoolwork had recently been used by 61%; 44% of the teachers had recently sent a child out of the classroom, while 7% did so frequently. Thus, scolding is by far the most common sanction. It is used by all teachers, two-thirds of whom used it frequently or rather frequently.

- In Denmark, a study looked at one group of children who were described as "boundary-testing" as well as a group of children described as "normal" (Kragh-Müller, 1997). The "challenging" children especially experienced severe scolding, as reflected in their statements:
  — "The adults in the kindergarten scold. They scold me a lot." (6-year-old, "boundary-testing")
  — "They'll scold you over just about anything. When you play Game Boy, and you're not standing up." (8-year-old)
  — "If I could change my mom and dad and my teacher, I would make them nicer so they didn't do any scolding." (7-year-old)
  — "When I have been scolded, they send me to bed or into my room." (5 -year-old)
  — "They don't scold me. I am used to doing what they want." (7-year-old)

- — "The worst thing is when the teacher scolds you; then you just don't want to be in the class at all." (7-year-old)
- — "I feel bad [about being scolded]. I get mad at them. I want to just walk away from this school and go outside and play war games." (8-year-old)

- In a survey in Japan (Kato et al., 1998), some 1,500 parents, 750 early childhood educators and 750 heads of educational institutions were asked about children's rights and about violence, including scolding. Almost all the early childhood educators and parents in the survey were women. About half the parents said they spanked their children frequently or fairly frequently, 83% frequently or fairly frequently yelled loudly at their children, and one-third verbally threatened their children frequently or fairly frequently. To the question, "Do you use words against a child that will hurt the child's pride?" 17% of the early childhood educators answered "frequently" or "sometimes," 72.5% answered "rarely," while 10.7% answered "never" (however, 35% had heard or seen "mental violence" being used against children frequently or sometimes).

  The survey also showed that there is a relationship between violence against children in the family (including verbal violence) and the following factors: the mother's emotional stability, conflicts between the parents about childrearing, the parents not playing with the child, and parents' lacking an inclination to deal with childrearing.

- In a Danish survey, the mothers of 5,300 3½-year-olds were asked how often they scolded their children: 81% said "weekly," 18% said "less frequently," and 1% said "never." In a parallel study of some 500 children from immigrant families (from third world countries) living in Denmark, 56% of the mothers said that they scolded their children "weekly," 34% said "less frequently," and 10% said "never" (Jeppesen & Nielsen, 2001).

- Early in the decade, UNICEF published a survey on the welfare of children in Europe and Central Asia according to the children themselves (*Young Voices*, 2001). A total of 15,200 children in 35 countries took part in the survey. Of the 400 Danish respondents, 17% said that they had witnessed or been exposed to corporal punishment, 75% had experienced severe scolding ("screaming"), and 27% did not feel that "the right to not be hurt or mistreated" was protected in Denmark.

  The children were also asked to name their main occasions of happiness and unhappiness. The main source of happiness was being with family and friends (67%). The main sources of unhappiness involved punishment (32%), having problems or quarrels at home (31%), and having difficulties at school (29%).

The strength of these surveys lies in their size, their weakness in the fact that most of them do not register scolding episodes per se, but rather the scolders' accounts of them. If we assume, however, that the scolders probably do not exaggerate the occurrence of scolding—since they are generally not proud of scolding—we may conclude that scolding is widespread among both parents and professionals.

There do seem to be exceptions, however. In a Danish-Mongolian school development project, the Danish advisers were to educate the Mongolian teachers, who had been used to following orders, about democracy in schools. It turned out that Mongolian teachers do not scold. "It is not only embarrassing, it is pointless," said one of the advisers. Instead, the teachers provide positive feedback (Respekt for læreren, 1997).

It remains to be seen whether the Mongolians will take up scolding, now that they have become democratic!

In summary, there is a great deal of scolding, both at home and in school. In school, the children in the younger classes may experience scolding during the lessons up to twenty times a day (Iceland). In Scotland, 99% of the nearly 900 teachers in one study reported having scolded recently. In a Danish survey, 75% of Danish children stated that they had experienced severe scolding. They also said that punishment is what makes them most unhappy.

There are signs that, all things being equal, large educational institutions have a greater incidence of scolding than smaller ones.

There is less scolding—or maybe even no scolding at all—in a number of non–Western educational institutions (including Mongolian schools and some schools in New Zealand), and immigrant mothers living in Denmark do less scolding than Danish mothers.

The amount of scolding varies considerably from one educational institution to the next. In the project kindergarten, 40% of the children experienced scolding. At the outset of the development project the adults did not feel that they did much scolding, but toward the end they came to agree with the children and now felt that they did a great deal of scolding.

Generally speaking, teachers and early childhood educators in preschool programs and schools do not tend to consider scolding a serious problem, perhaps because it is not actually viewed as punishment—and certainly not as violence.

There may be a tendency for a more systematic use of scolding in institutions and schools than in families, and, as we have seen, many children do feel that "there is more scolding in kindergarten."

ESSENTIAL CULTURAL PROCESSES

In the following pages, we will seek to explain why the clouds of scolding seem to gather over families and produce such a heavy downpour over some institutions and schools.

To shed light on this issue we will listen in on a brief exchange between two girls, both about 11 years old, who are talking in the sauna after a swim in the pool:

A: You can come to my birthday. As long as you don't cry. Why did you cry?

B: I was upset. It was that thing with my green bag. I always get scolded when something happens to my stuff.

A: But that's nothing to cry over. It's stupid having a little brother. It's much better to have a big brother. When he is out they treat me like an only child.

B: Sometimes I feel left out. Like they [the parents] don't see me at all.

A: As long as I tell mom and dad that they are nice. . . . Tonight we're having ice cream!

. . .

B: Do you remember the time you played with C and D, and I was playing alone? You wouldn't let me join, I played alone all day.

A: Yeah, but that was secret, we had a girls' club.

B: A what?

A: A girls' club.

B: Can't I come?

A: No.

B *(puzzled):* Why not?

A: Because we talk about special things.

B: But I would like that. Can't I come? (Pleading.)

A: No. Oh, gee! Look at the time. I've got to go. Come on.

The adult who later wrote down the conversation felt her heart breaking. Children can be so cruel! Why would they not include her? What would be the harm in that? It is so sad when someone is being left out.

B is scolded a great deal and also feels left out both at home and among her peers. Life is not fair!

That said, what is actually going on here? The children are exchanging notes on brothers and parents, on loneliness and manipulation.

They think and consider, and by sharing their thoughts they get a better knowledge of themselves, each other, and the world; they develop a firmer conceptual grasp of their world and develop their communicative skills, but they also make friends and enemies, discover what it takes to be accepted, and block out outsiders. In short, they are becoming members of society, "social" beings.

Such processes, in all their diversity, make up the *essential cultural processes*. Within the walls of the pool building, the participants are autonomous: They decide what to talk about, what to voice or leave unsaid, who is in, and who is out.

If this event had unfolded in an institution or a school, and if an early childhood educator or a teacher had overheard it, he or she would probably have intervened, saying something like "Don't be mean to B" or "Everyone gets invited to the birthday party." This interference might well have taken the form of scolding, or at least something A might have perceived as scolding. Such scolding is often aimed at making the children more socially aware, but by interfering with essential cultural processes, it may in fact hamper the children's ability to become full-fledged social beings.

In the project kindergarten, the staff is aware of this risk: "Last week, the boys were playing really rough and fighting. It looked pretty brutal— especially with this one guy who was at the bottom, but he was okay. . . . We are very aware that they have to be allowed to do these things. In other kindergartens they may break it up much sooner than we do, where we try to assess the situation: Is anyone actually getting hurt, or is there one kid who is always at the bottom of the pile?"

To take it a little further: Girls' clubs and roughhousing may in fact be crucial to our children's language development and literacy, their humanity, their entire education and personal development. Maybe you learn more in a girls' club than in class? Maybe girls' clubs are more important than after-school centers?

Maybe there will be room for girls' clubs in tomorrow's schools and preschool facilities—when institutionalization becomes so global that there is no room for them outside the system.

OTHER PERCEPTIONS

The System's Colonization of the Child's Life World

Others have addressed the conflict between life inside and outside of schools from a different perspective. Jürgen Habermas talks about *system* and *life world*, saying that the system will tend to *colonize* the life world (Habermas, 1987). The life world is the arena for what Habermas calls communicative action, while the system is the arena for instrumental-cognitive rational action. The civilization process itself causes a rationalization of our life world. As the girls, whose lives are increasingly institutionalized, have to resort to creating a girls' club within the setting of the after-school center, the early childhood educators may require that the club be open to everyone. The instrumental-cognitive rationality of the system is imposed at the cost of the communicative rationality of the life world. Habermas's proposed "solution" is to strike a balance between system and life world. The story above about roughhousing in the kindergarten may be interpreted as the system's (the early childhood educators') attempt to achieve such a balance.

The Systematic Reduction of Complexity

In Niklas Luhmann's (2000) theory about social systems, one of the basic tenets is that any system will constantly seek to *reduce complexity*. This ongoing attempt is in fact what defines it as a system. The system only deals with certain problems and only on the basis of certain, increasingly differentiated rules, while other problems and untraditional solutions are either excluded entirely or incorporated into the reduced complexity of the system. Preschools and kindergartens may seek to reduce complexity by declaring that everyone has to be invited to birthday parties. But this is also a reduction of the children's autonomy.

So the typical picture is for the staff of the institution to interfere with essential cultural processes (the life world), using scolding as one of the means. The purpose is often to protect children who are at risk. The overall effect, in Luhmann's perspective, is a reduction of complexity; in Habermas's perspective, it is a rationalization of communicative action to make it more instrumental-cognitive.

With this discussion of "essential cultural processes," I wish to point out that any attempt by the institution to replace the girls' autonomous processes of self-creation with institutionalized socialization is a far-reaching and radical intervention whose consequences we are still—only 200 years after the onset of the institutionalization of childhood—far from able to understand in full. The children's social network may simply fall apart if the essential cultural processes that help create networks are significantly disturbed, and such a breakdown might necessitate even more colonization, including heavy use of sanctions.

DEPENDENCE, RESISTANCE, AND SCOLDING

Back to the institution. The clashes between life inside and outside of school, between system and life world, or between the system and its elements can be fierce:

— What's stupid in the kindergarten?
— That's all that stuff when the adults are scolding and stuff.
— What do you do then?
— I grab them by the arm.
— The adults?
— Yep. Into the playground, out the window, then I close and lock both the doors, and I close the windows, too, also the ones by the hallway and in the kindergarten. There's a door where they can get in, but I just lock that damn door and lock the shed so they can't get in.
— So you can be left alone?
— From the adults. I lock them out in the playground.
— Then they get mad, don't they?
— No, not if I, no, they don't get mad at all, like, open the door, and stuff, open the door already!
— Then what do you say?
— I just hold the lock, right? I just lock it harder. Instead of unlocking it, I just lock it even more.
— If there is something in kindergarten that you think is really stupid?
— Then I just go and make a fort in a corner.
— Is that so you can hide if there is something you don't like?
— And if someone is after me, I just hurry and build a corner cabin to hide in. (Sigsgaard, 2001)

This 5-year-old boy, who is explaining what he imagines doing to the adults when they scold him, attends a warm and friendly kindergarten where he appears to be on good terms with the staff. But sometimes he has to bow to the superior power of the adults. In his powerless state, he fantasizes about power. The adults are to be punished the same way he feels punished by their scolding, and there is to be no mercy. They will be locked out the way he has been locked out (from civilian life); if they complain, he just locks the door even tighter.

"They just sat there screaming like mad beasts in the wardrobe, out of sheer powerlessness," one early childhood educator said around 1980 about some kindergartners. Back then, when the institutionalization of the younger children's lives was a relatively new phenomenon and not yet as complete as it was 20 years later when 92% attended daycare, many saw the children's screaming as a sign of resistance to the way institutionalization had restricted their options or as a sign of defeat. Now, 20 years later, the children's screaming is typically seen as a cry for more restrictions because the children are viewed as victims of laissez-faire parenting. This institutionalization of the staff's perception of the children serves to legitimize sanctions against the children's challenging behavior, including scolding. In this view, the children's screaming or disruptive behavior should be seen as a cry for help, a cry for firmer control.

The children's articulated *protest* against adult supervision and sanctions is seen as the opposite, an expressed *need* for control and supervision. Thus, the system has colonized the staff's perception of the children. The system has reduced its own complexity.

From this point of view, scolding is tantamount to giving the children what they need. On the other hand, if the children's screaming is seen as a sign of powerlessness and resistance, scolding is pointless because it only serves to increase these feelings.

DO WHAT I TELL YOU TO DO

The traditional view of socialization is that children should acquire the practices of the adult. This is achieved through imitation: *Do what I do!* Remnants of this approach still exist: Aspiring artists work alongside an established painter or actor and learn from seeing him or her in action. In one after-school center, the director described how the staff learns: "We *gawk* at each other!" But generally, such apprenticeship is a dying form. The math teacher does not in fact dig ditches or trade stocks, but he tells his students—who also don't dig or trade—to calculate how long an unknown group of ditch-diggers will take to dig a ditch, or how much a group of anonymous brokers make on transactions that have absolutely no bearing on the children's lives. The lessons become abstract (and perhaps a bit dull). "Do what I do" has been replaced by "Do what I tell you to do!" Rational authority and communicative action have been replaced by instrumental-cognitive rational actions that tend to become authoritarian: "Do what I tell you to do," not because it is necessary, but simply because I tell you. Necessity has given way to demands. Demands without necessity run the risk of causing dissatisfaction, protests, and maybe even resistance, which in turn lead to sanctions—for example, scolding.

So, institutionalization in itself leads to more scolding. To counter this, we need to devise and practice a pedagogical approach in the institutions that counters the inherent authoritarian tendencies of institutionalization.

AN OUTSIDE PERSPECTIVE ON INSTITUTIONALIZATION

No one describes the authoritarian character of Western institutionalization more mercilessly than early childhood educators and pedagogy students who have grown up in cultures that Westerners tend to see as rather authoritarian, having parent–child relations characterized by demands for obedience (but also a rather free everyday life).

A Romanian-born early childhood education student, who is also a mother of two children, offers this description of Western institutional culture:

- The children are scolded constantly: "Do that," "Stop that," "No, no, no!" The adults in the kindergarten use "must" all the time—it's scolding. They often speak in a stern and harsh tone of voice. This makes the child feel guilty and reduces the child's self-worth. The constant disapproval is humiliating.
- The adults interfere with the children's life and actions far too much—just the fact that the adults are always around is irritating (and the irritation then gives the adults a reason to scold).
- Scolding causes the same feeling that all restrictions create: You don't hear the words, but the tone of voice sticks in your mind.
- The tone of voice in scolding is like the tone of voice in "must," "No!" "Stop it!"
- Shared decision making can never be real when "You must!" permeates the relationship.

In Romania—as in most other countries around the world—institutionalization is far less advanced than it is in the Western industrialized world. Therefore, many foreign-born early childhood educators are surprised at the amount of scolding in Western institutions. Teachers and early childhood educators who grew up in the West have gradually and almost imperceptibly come to find it natural that a child cannot decide whom to invite to his or her birthday party, and that adults decide when the children can play outside and what they can do. Since this has come to seem natural, it is a small step to assume that this sort of cognitive-rational life is probably also good for the children. If the children resist, it is because there is something wrong with them, and they need to be treated (with therapy or medication) or forced—for example, through tighter restrictions and scolding.

An outside perspective makes it easier for mentally institutionalized early childhood educators to see the link between institutionalization and scolding. But the link may also become obvious if a locally born and raised early childhood educator views life in the institution through a scolding-sensitive lens:

- A group of boys were playing in the "pillow room"; when a boy left in a hurry he yanked the curtain slightly, and an early childhood educator burst out, in an automated response: "Don't do that! You don't yank the curtains at home, do you?"
- I was talking to some girls in the common room, and three or four other

girls in there began to climb from chair to chair. I didn't interfere, as I didn't see anything wrong with it, but I guess I was wrong, for next thing I heard the director yelling from across the building, "Stop that! We're not playing 'Lava Pit' right now."

- Mads and Morten were chatting. Morten, who was holding a big beach ball, had to go blow his nose, and he asked Mads to hold the ball. Right then, one of the adults came in and said, "Stop that, you two, there's no ball playing inside!"

- A couple of boys came running into the hallway from school. They called out "Hi!" to the early childhood educator who was in charge of the entrance that day. One boy had a paper airplane, which he threw into the common room after proudly announcing that he had made it himself. The early childhood educator said, "You know you're not supposed to throw airplanes in here, don't you?" Right then, another early childhood educator came out from the common room, saying, "Yes, and you know you're not even supposed to make them, so put it in your bag right away."

- Some boys were sitting at the table in the big common room playing a Lego game, but they soon began to build individual things from the bricks, and at some point one of the pieces fell to the floor. The director saw it and yelled, "That's it, that's not what the game is meant for." She gave them a string of explanations why they should not do that, and in the end she told them to pack it all up, and if they felt like building things some other time, they would have to take proper care of the Lego bricks.

- It was Friday, and when the kids come in after school a couple of girls asked me if they could play computer games in Room 3. I told them it was okay, but that they would have to turn the machines on themselves, as I have no idea how they work. They did that, but about 10 minutes later one of the other early childhood educators came into the room. Without even asking if they had permission, she simply asked them in a very angry way why they were playing when they knew that Friday is "game-free day," and told them to turn the computers off.

- Some kids were sitting on the sofa, playing a game. They were really into it and did not notice that another child wanted to get by. He tried to squeeze through without bothering them, but had to climb onto the sofa and get through that way. That worked fine until an early childhood educator saw it and ordered him down. As she put it, "You don't walk on the furniture at home, now do you?"

- There is a rule that if the children want to borrow something from the shed, they have to leave their bag as "collateral." A boy, who was on the way home, came in from the playground and asked for his bag. The early childhood educator asked, "Where is the tennis ball?" The boy apologized and said that he had not been able to find it. This was ignored, and the boy was sent out to look for it again. He repeated that he had already looked for it, and that he didn't know where it was. Then another early childhood educator butted in, "Well, at this rate, all our things will disappear, so either you go and find it now, or we have to send your parents a bill." (Intern in an after-school center, 2002)

IN SUMMARY, through a colonization of children's communicative acts in their mutually self-creating essential cultural processes, institutionalization in itself causes resistance, which is typically met with sanctions. These sanctions produce either submission or additional resistance, which in turn is met with additional sanctions.

The process does not run the same course in every institution or school. It can be affected by the choice of pedagogical approach, as the final chapters of the books will illustrate.

CHAPTER 5

What Makes Adults Scold—And Why?

> Undoubtedly, the success of discipline is due to the simplicity of its means: hierarchical observation, normalized judgment and their combination into a distinct method, examination.
> —Michel Foucault (quoted in Rasmussen & Smidt, 2000)

Most studies do not describe the behaviors targeted by scolding, probably due to a certain taboo surrounding the topic. Johnstone and Munn (1992), however, did include a list of teachers' reports of unacceptable student behavior in a Scottish school in a given week. The top 12 problem behaviors, in descending order of frequency, were:

- Talking out of turn: 98% (at least once a week)
- Hindering other students: 94%
- Calculated idleness or work avoidance: 90%
- Eating/chewing in class: 85%
- Not being punctual: 83%
- Making unnecessary noise: 80%
- Persistently infringing class rules: 72%
- Getting out of seat without permission: 71%
- Cheeky or impertinent remarks or responses: 71%
- General rowdiness, horseplay, or "mucking about": 67%
- Verbal abuse toward other students: 66%
- Physical aggression toward other students: 50%

The teachers said that scolding is the most important sanction by far—almost everyone had used it within the past two weeks—but they did not say what caused the scolding. It would be reasonable to assume, however, that the unacceptable student behaviors listed above would have been the key causes of scolding. Another large project that studied both positive and negative response found that positive response was mostly used in relation to academic achievements, while negative response was used most frequently in relation to social behavior (Merrett & Whelldall, 1992).

John Jacob Rambach, Rules on good behavior for children, 17th century

Avoid all uncouth and indecent gestures and behaviors in school, such as:
1. Extending your arms or entire body in laziness.
2. Gnawing on fruit or similar foodstuffs in school.
3. Putting your arms or elbows on your neighbor's shoulders, resting your head in your hand or leaning over the table and placing your head on your arms.
4. Putting your feet on the bench, scraping or kicking the floor or the base of the chair, crossing your legs or stretching them out when sitting or standing, spreading your legs wide open.
5. Scratching your head.
6. Drumming your fingers or picking at them.
7. Turning your head this way and that or getting up to other misbehavior with your head.
8. Sleeping in your seat.
9. Crawling around underneath tables and benches.
10. Turning your back on your teachers.
11. Changing your clothes in school.
12. Any other form of uncouth behavior.

(Quoted in Juncker, 1998))

Of the 12 cited types of behavior, four are physical, while three deal with speech. Two have to do with rule violations and punctuality, and two deal more directly with education ("hindering other students" and "idleness and work avoidance").

WHAT CAUSES THE ADULTS TO SCOLD IN VOGNMANDSPARKEN KINDERGARTEN?

Both children and staff were asked what makes the adults in this kindergarten scold. The children said:

- "I just knocked something over by accident. I don't remember what it was, but it was something that Lillian was really fond of, and that made her mad. Real mad." (Stine)
- "Some children dropped a bowl; that made me laugh. And then I was scolded." (Siw)
- " . . . because they do something they're not supposed to do." (Nadja and several others)
- " . . . because I teased someone." (Ane and several others)
- "Because sometimes maybe they've broken something." (Stine)
- "Because the children do stupid things, but I don't." (Laura) [Many other children mentioned "stupid things."]
- "If you are noisy." (Signa)
- "Because you're always doing something annoying." (Lea)

- "Because you've done something you're not supposed to." (Jesper)
- "If you run in the hallway." (Lars)
- "Because you do something that hurts." (Mikkel)
- "Because they think the children are stupid." (Markus)
- "If you've done something wrong, and you haven't done anything good." (Jon)
- "Because they feel sorry for the other kid." (Lau)
- "Well, you know, it's 'cause the kids, they do bad things. But most of the time I don't." (Johan)
- "It's because I think they're mad at me—because I did a dumb thing." (David)

The children hit each other, run, make noise, destroy things, and do bad things. Perhaps they do it intentionally, though sometimes they just do it by accident, which is a very different matter indeed. Briefly put, the children do "what they're not supposed to," or they do "stupid things." They express this by saying that "the others do," or "but I don't." But they can't always help it. Sometimes, one might even slip up and laugh when someone else does something bad.

When children do stupid things, the adults think the children are stupid, then the adults get angry, and then they scold—and maybe the children learn, before they grow up, not to do bad things.

In this kindergarten—as in the Scottish schools—physical acts are a common source of scolding. According to the children, scolding is not directed at verbal behavior, but often at behavior that may harm or bother others.

But what does the staff think? As mentioned in Chapter 2 about the development project, each kindergarten staff member was asked: "What do you think you do the most scolding over?" and "What sorts of things can make you really angry?"

The most frequently mentioned problem is noise and disruption: "running in the hallway and making noise," "I can get absolutely hysterical around lunchtime, from the noise of forks being banged into the table." Fighting is mentioned almost as frequently: "if they don't fight fair," "when a child hits another child," "they get to fight, but if someone 'gets killed,' that makes me mad."

Many mentioned teasing or bullying: "if it's cunning, and they ridicule someone deliberately," "when a group of children gang up on a child." Damaging things was not mentioned quite as often: "deliberately destroying the things we have here," "not treating our things well," "throwing toys around."

The word *deliberate(ly)* was used by four out of eight of the staff members in answer to the question, "What sorts of things can make you really angry?"

Four situations are mentioned as particularly likely to produce scolding: outings, tidying up, eating, and running in the hallway.

One person says, "Bad language can just make me furious."

More generally, Lillian, the director, says, "When my norms and standards are violated, well, I respond." This is a common guideline: Everyone reacts on the basis of his or her personal norms. This is difficult, especially for young or new staff members. Christina: "I have sometimes scolded a child over something that I personally thought was okay behavior, but something that might make Lillian mad. Like plucking leaves off a tree or licking the ice cream bowls." Lillian: "But should you do that? Can you ask that?" Lillian also says, "I am very much the one who sets the standards, for the children as well as the adults. That is one thing that this project has made very clear to me."

Everyone reacts on the basis of his or her personal standards, for that is the only way of keeping it real. There is great variation among the adults, but there is also a tendency for their standards to reflect Lillian's. However, there is also a common standard: One needs a good reason to say "no": "'I didn't feel like it' is not good enough" (Lillian). But what is a good reason, then? Lone: "Is it *my* good reason, is it *our* good reason, and are they the same?"

In a discussion concerning when an adult may feel free to say "no" to something that others accept, Malene asked her colleagues, "Would it be okay for me to say, 'I'm not sure, I think it's too dangerous, but if you ask another adult they might let you'?" And she added: "I say that to the kids sometimes." Gitte provided a graphic description of the dilemma: "Of course it's hard to know if there is a guideline, or if it's just a thousand trip wires put up all over the place."

The topics of scolding differ from person to person. In their report, the staff wrote:

> One person scolds the children when they bang their knives and forks into the plates before lunch, another person gets angry if they run in the hallway, and a third person gets angry when they break branches off the trees.
>
> This made it easier for us to understand why the children felt that there was a lot of scolding. (p. 31)

The staff agreed to maintain the principle of relying on one's personal assessment of the possible need for intervention. "But one has to be prepared to assume responsibility for the things one allows." This runs the risk, however, of making the children insecure, since they can never know what sorts of actions will lead to scolding.

WHAT CAUSES SCOLDING IN 11 DANISH PRESCHOOL FACILITIES?

Concerned that the project kindergarten might be atypical, we felt the need to develop a broader picture of "scoldable" offenses in kindergartens and preschools.

Many educational institutions have new interns come in several times a year as part of their studies. They stay there for 6 months, and they are trained observers. In brief, they are excellently suited for taking a qualified and reasonably open-minded look at the relations between children and adults. Therefore, some 100 students in the last year of their educational studies were offered an introduction to the Scolding Project, guidance, and a follow-up evaluation if they would write their intern report on scolding. Some chose to do this. Others focused on scolding without actually writing a report on it; a couple of them were attached to the research team. Everybody was asked to register the behaviors that led to scolding. This provided us with a list of the scolding episodes observed by these students during their internship. We gathered material from 11 preschool programs, including two nursery schools and three after-school centers. Scolding occurred in all these settings. However, one of the after-school centers was reported to have had very little scolding. The observers answered two questions:

- What are the children [in your institution] scolded over?
- What may cause scolding on the playground?

A total of 63 acts, omissions, or events that led to scolding were recorded. They are listed below in descending order of frequency.

> *Physical and mental violence (29):* Hitting, teasing, bullying, throwing things at each other, annoying the adults or the nice girls, killing animals, destroying plants
>
> *Rule violations (16):* Trying to climb the fence, climbing up the slide instead of using the steps, climbing on the tables, roller-skating on the ramp without wearing knee pads and a helmet, roller-skating indoors, going outside without permission, climbing onto the windowsill in order to jump down (all of these are interventions against physical activities), beginning to eat before one of the early childhood educators says, "Let's eat," children older than age 1 continuing to eat with their hands, unapproved games with water or dirt or rocks. Nonspecific descriptors were: not heeding orders, rule violations, breaking rules, and disobedience.

Disobedience (8): Continuing to do something after being told to stop, refusing to tidy up, squirming during lunch, pinching and teasing and continuing despite reprimands, not tidying up after being told to do so, not honoring agreements.

Disruption and unruliness (8): Noise, messiness, roughhousing.

Violation of property rights (2): Stealing, playing with other children's things.

Miscellaneous (3): "Wave games" before and during lunch (spitting, slamming the table, turning the plate upside down, banging the glass into the table), irresponsible behavior in the woodshop (with power drills, saws, and hammers), scolding due to parental omissions (wrong clothes, wrong food, being late).

There is more scolding on outings than on days spent in the institution itself. The amount depends on the type of outing, however. There is more scolding indoors than outdoors, and more scolding in winter than in summer. And often, there is more scolding in the afternoon: "I can feel a big difference in my tolerance level . . . I am clearly more tolerant and easygoing in the first part of the day."

Thus, the safest place for a child who does not want to be scolded is the playground in the summer—and in the first part of the day.

THE BODY, SOCIAL SELF-CREATION PROCESSES, AND SCOLDING

On page 63, we saw that at least a third of the recorded unacceptable student behavior in the schools is physical, and that preschool facilities also regulate physical or bodily activities heavily. This confirms what Foucault and Goffman have reported and what Norbert Elias has emphasized: that all institutions will regulate bodily activities and bodily secretions (primarily urinating).

We have noted tendencies to decrease the use of sanctions. Many places are democratizing child–adult relations. But the opposite also occurs: The school needs to increase its "productivity," which often leads to more discipline and a heavier use of sanctions, and preschool programs are increasingly expected to ensure learning and development, which leads to more intense institutionalization—more structured activities and tighter schedules.

And the more intense the institutionalization, the more regulated are the bodies. "They make lessons all the time," the schoolchildren complain, and during lessons "it is not allowed to tilt one's chair or wear . . . caps, and you can't speak without first raising your hand, and you can't talk to your neighbor either" (Sigsgaard, 1995).

In addition, there is the relationship between adulthood and childhood. On one level, they are approaching each other. Adults and children are communicating on more equal terms than before. Children are involved in problems from the adult world that they were previously kept in the dark about. On another level, perhaps, the two are sliding away from each other.

Perhaps this began hundreds of years ago when the Western world began to liberate itself from the mindset of tradition and religion—traditional rationality—and instead sought economic-material rationality. This soon enabled the West to surpass more traditional societies in economic growth (Weber, 1920/1992). But gradually economic rationality also came to supersede other rationalities, such as emotional rationality or value-based rationality. The captain of yore who would stay on his sinking vessel because his values and his sense of honor and duty obligated him to do so acted irrationally from an economic-material perspective. Today's postmodern captain also makes it into the media, but for other reasons—for example, for dumping waste oil into the ocean for the sake of economics and efficiency. To him, value-based rationality is hopelessly obsolete and meaningless.

Economic rationality and the relativistic view of values make it more and more difficult for parents and children to understand each other in our postmodern world. Childlike behavior, spontaneity, bodily sensuousness, emotions, and immediate and naive trust are excluded more and more from the practical lives of most parents. The strictly economic rationality, the aggressive decisiveness, the strategic perspective are what is required. Emotions, spontaneity, and naive trust can be costly. These conditions of adulthood in postmodern society are not just external; they get under our skin, so to speak, and reduce our ability to empathize with children. More scolding is just one of the consequences.

On another level, the distance between childlike and adult-friendly features is growing—for example, in the role of the institution as a workplace for adults, with rational decision making, productivity measures, strategic goals, policies, and scheduling. Preschool is turning into school. The children no longer "go out and play," they "work with Learning Through Play." But children are not geared for efficiency or productivity; they are not goal-oriented or interested in strategic schedules. It is therefore to be expected, as the project data also indicate, that regulatory interventions by the adults will target behaviors that are specifically childlike, incompatible with the requirements of the "schoolified" preschool. What is, then, the specifically childlike? It is perhaps most clearly evident in the younger children, who are not yet as heavily molded by the adult world, society, and institutions.

Previously there was only moderate interest in the social life of 1- to 2-year-olds, partly because it was assumed to be nonexistent, and partly because the role of adults in relation to these children was seen as mere child-minding, but in recent years a great deal of knowledge has emerged about the social life of toddlers (see Alvestad, 1999, and Løkken, 2002).

It turns out that children bond through play. They create *meaning* through the interactive creation of common themes: 2-year-olds will take turns jumping off a row of chairs while "singing" together. This is not a random act. On the contrary, the event falls into specific phases: First a common focus of awareness is created, then common intentions and common emotional states—intersubjectivity. The children experience *themselves* through the experience of a "we." They have embarked on the difficult process of becoming social beings. Thus, playing with other children, primarily other children of the same age, is the main arena of socialization for 1- to 2-year-olds. In particular, this takes place through the more "global" physical forms of play—tottering, tumbling, falling, and running.

This poses a problem, then, since the *social bodily activities* that younger children use to establish themselves within their world are exactly the activities that cause the greatest amount of scolding. All this jumping off chairs accompanied by loud shouting seems like a noisy chaos to many adults and may be almost unbearable in small and overcrowded rooms.

On the other hand, research demonstrates that it is exactly the bodies that educational institutions attempt to tame, discipline, or even silence— out of "necessity" and the very best intentions.

Disciplining the children's bodies—for example, through scolding— creates a negative cycle: It weakens the children's *intersubjective socialization processes*. This causes even more conflicts with other children and with adults, which causes additional scolding and, in turn, results in further weakening of the socialization processes.

The bodies are disciplined and tamed, but it is through their bodies that the children create themselves and become participants in life (instead of being mere consumers of it).

When forces in society feel that children are not learning enough, institutionalization is intensified. That means additional restrictions on their bodies. And that makes it harder for children to learn. We have to reach out in order to grasp the world, both physically and metaphorically. Without the body, we cannot grasp anything.

Social bodily activities are the essential arena for our processes of self-creation—and the most prominent target of scolding.

It should be added that the link between institutionalization and interventions against children's bodily activities is by no means automatic. It is influenced by the chosen pedagogical approach and is therefore open to modification. When Gitte was asked, some time into the development project, whether she was still annoyed with the children when they slammed their knives and forks into the table during lunch, she said no. "Why not?" The laconic answer: "We now use a tablecloth."

CONTROL AND RESISTANCE

In one relatively liberal kindergarten the children insisted that they had no say over anything. "We don't even get to decide where we want to be." When pressed, they had to admit that they were allowed to do many things that were normally not allowed; for example, they were allowed in the kitchen and in the staff room. "So where is it you are not allowed?" "You know, in the playground, there is a shed—we're not allowed to go in there, we can't even touch the lock!"

It was difficult to understand that children who had such unusual freedom in their kindergarten could feel this way. It was only when we noticed that the adults had used the phrase *to be allowed* an unusual number of times during an interview that we began to understand. The adults felt that the children had a great deal of latitude; they were allowed to do many things. The children felt that they were under tight control because they had to ask permission all the time. And even though their requests were rarely turned down, they never knew when they might be. Every instance of having to ask permission was a reminder of the basic power relations: The adults are in control.

Maybe that is how all institutionalized children feel—more or less. Might that explain the additional scolding that often takes place during outings?

During the development project, an adult had a peculiar experience after a day at the beach, as the group was getting ready to go home. Three girls had gone into the water:

> I tell them not to go out too far, as we are leaving soon and they'll need to put their clothes back on. I can tell they have no intention of listening to me. They go farther and farther into the water. . . . I feel powerless, as I stand there on the beach, fully dressed, knowing that they can do more or less as they please . . . and they do. I call them several times, yelling at them to get out *now*. I can tell that I am getting irritated, and I look up at Lillian and Berit who are farther up the beach. Lillian says something like, "What a nerve!" and I can tell that Berit is coming toward me to help. To me, that expresses some acceptance of the fact that I am angry with the kids. Then I simply

wade into the water, and Berit follows. We reach the girls and tell them that this is it, and it's time to get out, and that I think they're being really mean. I can tell that I am very angry with them, and I have this feeling inside me that they're not being reasonable by making this nice trip end with a bawling-out.

The early childhood educator adds that earlier in the day she had had a very positive experience with one of the girls.

Why would children who are otherwise happy with their very pleasant kindergarten do something like that?

Well, they cannot do it in the classroom, where it is easy for the adults to reach them. So if they are going to do it, it will have to be during an outing—and preferably at a time like this, when the adults are fully dressed and ready to go home, so that they cannot chase after them in the water.

But why do it at all? One answer might be that it is wonderful to be able to turn a deaf ear to the adults, who are in charge all day. Where the doors and walls of the institution might present a clear sense of "this far, but no farther," the beach seems to extend forever, open and inviting.

In a previous project, a boy was telling me about his mom and dad, whom he loved, he said, but they corrected him a great deal, so even though he liked them it was nice when they were not around. "Like running in an open space," he said (Kragh-Müller, 1997). Maybe that was how the three girls felt, but there was probably also some amount of rebellion mixed in—not against the early childhood educators themselves, but against their control.

If the early childhood educator had considered these aspects, she probably would not have been quite so angry with the girls, and she would not have blamed them for making such a "nice trip end with a bawling-out."

Children resist institutionalization. In the project institution, the degree of institutionalization is fairly mild; that is exactly why these girls even *dared* rebel so openly. In other, stricter educational institutions, the children may only dare to rebel in more anonymous and passive ways, such as suddenly suffering from temporary two-sided hearing loss when "collective messages" are delivered.

If the early childhood educator in the beach incident had understood the resistance and recognized it as healthy and necessary, she might have been able to retrieve the children with authority while expressing appreciative understanding for their desire to forget about buses and schedules and institutional logic. If—perhaps another day—she dares to throw caution and "must" to the wind and let the children see this, they might be delighted, as they are when the institution director sometimes shows up in the guise of the wicked witch Amalie who does all the things that are not allowed.

In summary, incidents of verbal or physical violence, rule violations, disobedience, disruption, and unruly behavior (in this order) cause scolding in all institutions.

The more institutionalized a place is, the more rule violations and omissions there will be to impose sanctions on. The "schoolification" of preschool and the demands for a stronger emphasis on subject-related learning and skills in school mean increased institutionalization and will, all things being equal, lead to more scolding.

The adults' perception of the relations among children, adults, and institution also influence the amount and type of scolding. If the adults perceive the children as highly institutionalized and controlled, their reactions will be interpreted as resistance. They will attempt to reduce the degree of control, and resistance will rarely be met with scolding. If they instead perceive the children as floating free in an inconsistent postmodern society characterized by value relativism, they will see them as challenging and disruptive and impose "firm boundaries and restraints," typically with scolding as a significant ingredient.

HOW DO THE ADULTS MOTIVATE THEIR SCOLDING?

One major difference between home and institution is that it is acceptable to be grumpy at home, while scolding is often less accepted. In institutions, it is the other way around. It is considered unprofessional to go around complaining about the children's behavior all the time, while it is usually considered acceptable or even necessary to scold someone. Thus, scolding is in fact considered an essential element in the job requirements of the early childhood education staff. In educational theory and practice, as in all other disciplines, it is considered essential to justify subdisciplines, activities, methods, and values. Without justification, early childhood education would fail to qualify as a professional discipline. The education student who is able to explain, on the final exam, what he or she wants to do and how, but not why or to what end, will fail. It is considered especially important to be able to justify interventions into the children's lives and their interactions with each other. Scolding is such an intervention. It often has the character of being a sanction and therefore represents an interference with the child's ability to actualize his or her intentions, volition, and desires.

We might therefore expect scolding to require particularly good justification. That is not what we see in the training of early childhood educators, however. Scolding is not usually a topic, and it never or extremely rarely figures as an exam topic. A study of training in the Danish colleges of education found no examples in which scolding was featured in courses or in the exams (Rasmussen & Smidt, 2001). Similarly, when early childhood educators put their plans or goals into writing, scolding is rarely included: In a large number of workplace journals kept by selected assistant early childhood educators, practically all aspects of their work were discussed—except for scolding, which was not even mentioned (Hind, 2001).

The same is true of pedagogical theoreticians and scientists. A list of literature about discipline with more than 1,000 titles (Slee, 1995) includes nothing about scolding, but many entries about hyperactivity, ADHD, and so forth.

Thus, scolding appears to be a tacitly accepted, self-explanatory, and natural part of educational practice, which is, however, absent from educational theory. Doesn't it bear the light of day? Or is it so obvious that it is invisible?

And what happens when scolding becomes the focal point in a development project, as it did in the project kindergarten? Then, surely, scolding will require justification?

In the project kindergarten, the adults were interviewed one-on-one about scolding. But not a single question focused on the reasons or justification for scolding. And when the consultant (the author of this book) reviewed the questions before the interviews took place, he did not propose any additional questions concerning the reasons for scolding.

So, on the one hand, everybody knows that scolding takes place in institutions; that is so obvious that no one even asks for reasons or justification. On the other hand, scolding is practically absent from the early childhood education curriculum and from educational textbooks.

Why is that? Let us examine some possible explanations.

Scolding Is a Part of the Culture

Some 70 years ago, the late Hartvig Frisch, a cultural historian and prominent member of the Social Democratic Party, offered an eloquent definition: *Culture is habits.* A people's culture, then, is the sum of its habits. Most habits have a bodily character. They are the things we usually do. Through our repeated actions, we turn into the people that we are, and it is through our actions that we reveal who we are.

The thing is, however, that we are usually blind to our habits. We eat sitting down, we sleep in beds, we hurry, and we scold our children. If anyone were to propose that we lie down to eat, sleep in a chair, walk slowly like a Somali or Turkish woman, or stop scolding our children, we would be puzzled, and we would have a very hard time living like that.

Most of the time we are blissfully unaware of the fact that what we consider commonplace and practically immutable appears curious and alien to others—like the Indian anthropologist who described with a sense of true astonishment how Danish parents will put even very young babies into a dark room and shut the door on the child at bedtime. If we hear about a feature of another culture that differs greatly from our own lifestyle and habits, we tend to reject it, point to the huge differences in living conditions—or simply overlook it.

Everybody knows how stern Japanese educators and parents are with schoolchildren, perhaps because we are able to grasp it within the concepts of our Western culture. But hardly anyone knows how liberal and loving Japanese childrearing often is, even though it has been described in book after book, study after study (see, e.g., Bettelheim, 1988). Why? Because it is a self-explanatory feature of Western culture to be relatively stern with young children: They must be in bed by a certain time, they must taste what is served for dinner, and they must have "boundaries" (Sigsgaard & Varming, 1996). Hence, we reject other cultures, other habits, even without knowing it. They simply do not filter through.

Scolding may be considered a habit, something that we simply do, without giving any thought to why, whether it actually works, or how it might work. In the previously mentioned study of 500 children with immigrant or refugee parents (see Chapter 4), 44% of the mothers stated that they rarely or never scolded their children. In the corresponding study of children with ethnically Danish parents, only 19% of the mothers stated that they rarely or never scolded their 3-year-olds. Similarly, 84% to 99% of the refugee/immigrant mothers stated that they rarely or never used corporal punishment, while the corresponding number for Danish mothers was 97% to 100%. The researchers' initial analysis focused exclusively on the limited difference with respect to corporal punishment, while the distinct difference concerning scolding was not mentioned. The Danish researchers did not notice this variation because scolding is a part of the culture and therefore does not stand out as much as corporal punishment, a practice that is widely condemned in Denmark today.

Similarly, Norwegian researchers condemned the corporal punishment of children in Latin America at the same time that they wrote uncritically about Norwegian "boundary-setting" (Sabillón, 1999). Appreciative relationships are the focus of a fair amount of attention in Sabillón's report, but scolding is not mentioned, despite the fact that it must have occurred naturally during the project. Thus, the researchers must have had quite a few scolding episodes in their viewfinder, but did not "see" them.

An additional Danish example: The report *Elever der forstyrrer undervisningen for sig selv og andre i folkeskolen [Students who disrupt classes for themselves and others in elementary school]* (1997) features the section "What characterizes the disruptive student's surroundings?" The second factor mentioned is *teachers/teaching/management*. Under this heading, the authors discuss the "teacher's personal style," "good pedagogical skills," and "dedication," and they state that "boring and uninspiring teachers invite disruptive behavior." But scolding is not mentioned even once. Are teachers who have substantial disciplinary problems characterized by a large or a small amount of scolding? What is the relationship between disruptive behavior and scolding?

The section "What does the school do when attempts to curb disruptive behavior do not work?" also does not mention scolding.

Consider the Romanian student, training as an early childhood educator in Denmark, who said (in Chapter 4), "The children in many Danish kindergartens are constantly scolded." Her statements on scolding are just as strong as the Norwegian researchers' statements on corporal punishment in Latin America, because she is an outsider to the culture that she is observing.

"Why do you look at the speck of sawdust in your brother's eye and pay no attention to the plank in our own eye?" asks the Bible.

Scolding is a part of the culture. Therefore it goes unnoticed or is trivialized by the people who live in that culture.

Scolding Is a Belief

What do progressive and conservative early childhood educators or teachers agree on? Nothing, as far as they know. The disputed issues are so many and so substantial that they seize all attention. The issues that the two groups do agree on therefore go unnoticed and are not discussed, but they are there:

> Educators at all levels agree, more or less on certain beliefs and values . . . These are primitives. They are taken as given and not questioned. They are not defined. Often, they are not mentioned. These agreements are the basis for what educators say and do, and normal professional discourse and practice is possible only because of them. (Cherryholmes, 1988)

What are the values or beliefs that are never questioned? That competencies and development are good? That children must learn? That childcare or education is best facilitated by gathering concentrations of specially trained adults in particular buildings where the children are placed after having been forced to leave their local environment? That lessons should last longer than breaks? That adults determine the standards and norms? That adults decide when the children should be allowed to go outside? That scarce resources, such as afternoon fruit or adult attention, must be divided evenly? That it is the adults who evaluate the children, not the other way around?

These may serve as useful examples of beliefs that go largely unquestioned. They are hard to define, as any writer is also a part of the "system" (cf. Luhmann, 2000) that rests on them.

Is scolding one of these beliefs? Well, maybe, since almost everyone admits to scolding—more or less frequently. We have seen previously that rules were introduced in the early 1800s to restrict the use of scolding and ensure the parents' right to complain if things got out of hand, and that these rules later practically disappeared. Does the disappearance of these rules reflect the establishment of scolding as an inescapable necessity as the school and, later, preschool facilities developed from being the citizens' institutions, required to treat the citizens' children well, to being the property of the public authority, to which the children owe obedience and respect? And how will it affect scolding if the public authority is one day forced to hand over the school/preschool service to the marketplace, while children and parents are reduced to being consumers? Will a great or a small amount of scolding be a selling point with the parents? Or is scolding going to be replaced with controls that operate through the child's own volition, not against it?

If scolding is a "belief," that would explain why it is not the subject of debate, definition, and exploration. Perhaps it is a part of a broader "belief": that children need to be reared. They have to be guided in terms of values and choices, and their actions are to be corrected or met with sanctions (including praise); otherwise, they will not "in time make decent human beings," the phrase used by a concerned Danish priest in his report to the bishop in the mid-1800s on the liberal approach to childrearing among the peasants (Sigsgaard, 1995).

Scolding Is Not Considered a Pedagogical Activity

There are a great many activities that are not included in early childhood education textbooks. For example, the textbooks typically do not cover such topics as:

- Bathroom breaks
- Smoking
- Mowing the lawn
- Making coffee
- Chatting to one's colleagues about what was on TV last night
- Table manners
- Maintaining a pleasant tone

These are not pedagogical activities. True pedagogical work is what is covered by the institution's "organization plan." And it is not considered appropriate to include coffee drinking, collegial chatting, and TV-watching in the organization plan.

Does scolding fall under this category of ever-present but never-mentioned phenomena? If it does, it cannot be because these phenomena are not important. Cultural changes in the approach to taking breaks, chatting, or scolding all have the potential to change an institution more deeply than many pedagogical activities.

But what these phenomena do have in common is that they require no justification. The staff will take breaks, chat, drink coffee, and require the children to display good table manners, without ever thinking that they need to explain why. Maybe scolding has a similar status: It is simply a part of everyday life. As we have seen, 80% of Danish mothers state that they scold their 3-year-olds at least once a week. Scolding, like taking breaks or coffee drinking, is brought into the institution where it becomes a part of the common sense system—"it's what *people do*, after all."

As the preschool programs are charged with providing more direct school preparation, and "learning" and "development" take priority over "childcare," early childhood education activities move into focus. And mowing the lawn, cleaning, addressing each other nicely, drinking coffee, and scolding move out of focus. "As long as the kids learn something," many would say.

And no justification will be required.

Scolding Is an Obvious Necessity in the Institutional Logic

What happens if too many living beings are crammed into an over-crowded place? They will peck at each other if they are chickens, bite each others' tails off if they are pigs, and harass and bully each other if they are children. To avoid this, one will have to shut the mouths of the chickens, the pigs, and the children (unless it is possible to provide more space—Danish children experience four times as much bullying as Swedish children, who have more space). This is achieved by regulating life within the institution: no shouting, no running in the hallway, and no teasing. Violations are punished with some form of scolding.

It is an aspect of institutional logic that children have to eat at the same time (to fit the kitchen staff's or early childhood educators' schedule), and that all the children must go outside at the same time (while the early childhood educators or teachers are on break). As a result, interesting work areas, like the kitchen, and great places for running, like the playground, are empty much of the day and overcrowded at other times.

It also means that the children are ordered around a great deal and that there are plenty of conflicts, which in turn lead to scolding.

Scolding is an inescapable consequence, so to speak. It is an aspect of the institutional logic. Justification is rarely an issue.

Scolding Does Not Bear the Light of Day

No one is proud of scolding. No one mentions in a job application that he or she is big on scolding. No institution or school newsletter tells the parents: Lately, we have not been getting much scolding in, but we plan to increase the amount in coming weeks. No obituary ever read: He will be long remembered as a stern scolder. No one thinks: I want to be a teacher/early childhood educator so that I can scold a lot.

On the contrary, when a group of young teachers in a course was asked to describe what had surprised them the most during their internships in schools, they mentioned the amount of time spent getting the class to settle down and be quiet. They had had to do a great deal of scolding, and this was an unpleasant surprise to them.

Early Childhood Education Work Is About the Good We Seek to Do, Not the Bad We Do

Organization plans and mission statements describe what we strive for, not what we seek to avoid. The effort is to "develop," "stimulate," "create," "encourage," "promote," and "praise." Not to stop, inhibit, break up, and punish. The same goes for staff meetings, where early childhood educators discuss how to promote the children's language development but rarely debate the ways in which institutionalization inhibits language development. A new issue in recent years is how to support children's development of friendships, but there is little focus on the way that institutionalization tends to damage the conditions for friendships by splitting the children up, interrupting their activities, and organizing their relationships.

The textbooks used in early childhood education training usually do not provide references for such keywords as *interruption, punishment,* and *scolding.* Hence, they also do not provide any justification for the necessity of scolding.

There appears to have been a change in recent years with the great emphasis on "boundary-setting." The vague and abstract character of this phrase confirms, however, that any discussion of the early childhood educators' (sometimes necessary) violation of children's rights and autonomy and their (often unavoidable) interference with children's wishes and desires is off limits. By rephrasing the unmentionable in the abstract and, in fact, incomprehensible concept of "boundaries," we turn it into a pedagogical-psychological term, a perceived "need" of the children. The teacher or early childhood educator who may appear to be punishing, stopping, interrupting, or scolding a child is now seen to be doing the opposite: He or she is meeting one of the child's vital needs, providing something, and ensuring the basis for the child to grow and develop.

But the teacher/early childhood educator is never safe. Every now and then, the young child from *The Emperor's New Clothes* pops up, as recently graduated Tine relates:

> A kid (almost 3 years old) in the nursery has bothered another child (who has just turned 2) several times. Each time, the other child said "No!" and she has now begun to cry. I have tried to make the 3-year-old stop, but she continues to tease and bother the crying child.
>
> Eventually, I get angry; I pick up the 3-year-old and take her away from the crying child. I sit her down on a stool at the other end of the room and squat down in front of her. I raise my voice and tell her very firmly (I am scolding!) that I want her to stop bothering the other child, and that she has to stop when the other child says "No!" I also tell her that the fact that the other child is crying is a sign that she definitely doesn't like it, and that I want her to stop. I emphasize with the closing statement, "I will get angry with you!"
>
> As I am almost done with scolding her, another girl (she has turned 3 and is waiting for an opening in the kindergarten) comes over and begins to hit me. I tell her to stop and ask her why she is doing it. She says that she is angry with me. I tell her that she can be angry with me later, and that right now she has to step away, as I am talking to the other child. The girl replies, "No, you're not. You're just scolding and being stupid!"
>
> As she says this, I realize that she is actually right, and I cool down pretty fast. I tell the girls, and this time I try to do it without scolding, that I don't want them to hit me, and that they have to listen to what the crying girl is saying. They walk away and continue to play.

The older, independent 3-year-old helps Tine name the unnameable and make the invisible visible. Tine realizes that she is bullying the "bully." She is not "socializing" the child, she is not "rearing" it, and she is not "setting boundaries." She is simply scolding. Once she sees this clearly, she is able to think rationally and decides that she has to achieve her goal without scolding.

Our educational goals usually describe only the good we strive for, not the bad we do (and sometimes *have to do*). Consequently, the "bad" is not mentioned and not justified. Consequently, our pedagogical work lacks self-criticism. A strong 3-year-old may be able to reveal what is going on—but only if the early childhood educator is able to hear her clearly.

IN SUMMARY, if we ask how adults justify their scolding, the answer is: They usually do not. There are many reasons for this. Above, I mentioned six possible reasons. These six factors interact with each other and with other factors to create a situation in which most adults find it unavoidable or natural to scold children, especially when many children are together in one space.

WHY DO ADULTS SCOLD CHILDREN?

After this analysis of the reasons why professional adults, who are used to justifying their actions, do not justify scolding, we will now look at early childhood educators' and teachers' motives for scolding.

Reaction, Imitation, Action

The gap between the many who scold and the few who believe that it actually works suggests that scolding is not always an educationally well-considered action, but rather a spontaneous, emotional reaction. This view is supported by the kindergarten staff's replies to the question, "What is scolding to you?" The responses included words like *angry, upset, irritated, annoyed,* and *shouting.*

A hypothesis about frustration and aggression was stated in 1939: When a person is frustrated, he or she responds with aggression (Dollard et al., 1950). Adults are often frustrated when they are around children. "What I really wanted to do was simply grab her and put her outside," wrote one early childhood educator after a conflict (see the section "A Conflict—All the Way Around," in Chapter 2). "I can tell that I am just getting so damn irritated," said another early childhood educator to a child who was ignoring her.

So, adults scold or display other forms of aggression when they are frustrated.

But some adults never or hardly ever scold, even when they are bothered, offended, or frustrated. Why is that? One young early childhood educator, who took part in the development project, said:

We have been reading about these things, so of course we see that it's not reasonable. The problem is that I, for one, grew up in a system where I was scolded by people who had the same childrearing role that I am about to assume. The question is whether I am going to revert to that. Whether I am going to forget some of the things that we have learned here. I hope not. But whether some mechanisms are automatically going to take over, because that is my background, that is what I have experienced.

According to this early childhood educator, the fact that adults themselves were scolded may be a reason for them to go on scolding. As an 8-year-old once said, when he was asked in a radio interview what childrearing was: "That's when someone has been spanked, and then they go on to spank their own kids." On the other hand, if an adult was not scolded much as a child, he or she may turn into an early childhood educator or teacher who is less likely to scold, as there is no early pattern to revert to.

Finally, an early childhood educator or a group of early childhood educators may choose to use scolding as a pedagogical instrument, as in the example mentioned above (p. 44) where the staff in a kindergarten that usually did not use scolding used it specifically to keep the children from running into a busy road. This is an example of a kindergarten staff with a childrearing philosophy that includes sanctions.

So, scolding may be a psychological reaction, a culturally conditioned pattern, and/or a pedagogical instrument: reaction, imitation, and action.

The dynamic interaction between these three has a significant impact on the amount of scolding in an institution. We may assume that the institution will have a great deal of scolding, for example, if the following conditions apply:

- The institution has as its common philosophy that adults should express their emotions honestly to the children, including anger.
- Many staff members have experienced a great deal of scolding as children.
- Their childrearing philosophy emphasizes restrictions, sanctions, and "boundaries."

The director of a highly rule-oriented kindergarten, where particularly the older boys received a great deal of scolding, points to another aspect that may increase scolding:

The boys had "inherited" a culture from the previous group of older boys, with a pecking order where the strong dominated the weak—

the "tyranny of the pillow room." A similar pecking order was in place among the staff. The staff members had low self-esteem and had a tendency to focus on their weaker points rather than their successes.

At Home

Since childhood, most parents have been in an emotional trap, waiting only for a chance to discharge their unconscious, pent-up anger. They can find no other door out of this trap than their own children, for only those children may, under the guise of childrearing and with impunity, be beaten, scolded, and humiliated just as the parents once were. (Miller, 1991)

The parents are angry because of the aggression that their own parents directed at them when they were young, when they were unable to scold or strike back. But now that they have children of their own, it is risk-free for them to express this anger. That is how tough this psychiatrist's analysis is.

A Danish politician who is active in the debate on childrearing and education writes:

The necessary evil in measured doses is an instrument in any childrearing. "Setting boundaries" means serving up evil in a measured dose. If the children stray outside these boundaries, they feel the "evil." This may take the form of a normal request for the child to behave properly, but if that does not work, one has to invoke increasing degrees of evil. This may include raised eyebrows, scolding, or sending the child to his or her room (exclusion from the group) . . . if there is no evil, no consequence, everything will fall apart. (Moos, 1995)

From where do parents get the evil that they are required to serve up to their children, according to Helga Moos? Perhaps from their pent-up anger over the evil that their parents once served up to them. The mechanism is described clearly in the project kindergarten by Malene, who scolded Jesper for bullying a younger child, Martha: "I know that this is about me and my standards, but I hate it when people don't treat each other properly and with respect, I just can't take it, it hurts my soul. I recognize the feeling of being the underdog, unable to defend myself."

Malene was treated with "measured doses of evil," so now she is tough on Jesper because he is harassing Martha—probably because he was treated with "evil" by someone else. Jesper says, "Some of them [the early childhood educators] are mad, but the maddest one, that's me, because everybody's always teasing me." Jesper does not have to wait to release his anger until he has children of his own. He can take it out on the other kindergartners. The drawback is that they may fight back, tease him, or call down the wrath of the adults on him. His own children will not be able to do this when the time comes. In other words, the current situation is different from the situation in Alice Miller's Switzerland in the 1980s. Children raised with Moos's evil may either be bullied by others, like Jesper, or become school or kindergarten bullies themselves.

As mentioned above (p. 68), Denmark has four times as much bullying as Sweden does, and Danish parents are far more likely than Swedish parents to say that it may be necessary to hit a child. These are facts. But we do not know whether these two facts are interrelated. Are children more likely to be bullied or to become bullies if they have been punished often? We do not know, but we cannot rule either out. As illustrated by Alice Miller's statement above, such a connection would certainly be conceivable and understandable.

It should be pointed out here that a great many children are treated with dignity and respect by their parents. One young early childhood educator says, "When I was a kid, my mother always talked to me as if I understood what she understood, just in a different way." No "necessary evil" here! One might assume that families of this type breed less anger and, thus, less latent violence.

The previous discussion has shown how scolding and other forms of violence may cause anger, which is released either outside the home or on the next generation. We have also seen an example of contemporary argumentation for the necessity and desirability of the use of power, including scolding, in childrearing.

This leaves us with the question of whether today's children actually invite scolding or physical violence through their behavior. Well, yes, they probably do sometimes, but not "on purpose." In recent years, there has been so much talk about the competent child that we may tend to forget how helpless younger children are. Often they are unable to achieve what they believe to be in their own best interest. It is out of their reach. Therefore, they have to try to gain power over other people, primarily their parents, and use them as instruments to achieve what they want. And young children do sometimes manage to make their parents bend over backward for them—but only sometimes. For suddenly the parents stand firm and demonstrate—by simply expelling the child—that they are ultimately in charge. The child is taken away from home and placed in an institution until it suits the parents to pick the child up again. Once the child is back home the fight goes on—until the next "removal." The parents' daily victory represents a permanent threat to the child: When will I lose my parents? What if they don't like me anymore? Will they not come and get me? Children seek protection from this threat by shielding themselves: You are not the boss of me! I decide—when and what to eat, the order of events, blue dress or green dress, and so on. When the child is around 3 or 4, the battle lets up slightly. By now, the child feels secure in the knowledge that he or she will be picked up again, and is also in a better position to achieve some of the things that he or she believes to be in his or her best interest.

Some families are relatively unmarked by all this. Perhaps the family atmosphere feels very warm and safe, and perhaps the parents and preschool manage to turn the daily "drop-off" into an awaited and desired "arrival." But in principle this reflects a modern condition: The parents, the child's protectors, turn the child over to others on a daily basis, and the child is forced into an institution. This is bound to cause anxiety, power struggles—and scolding—in many families while the children are young.

This condition reflects a basic change in our society: 40 years ago, families worked about 50 hours a week outside the home; today this has risen to 95–100 hours, including commuting time. Mom is less available than she used to be—dad has remained relatively inaccessible for the past 150 years. Both at home and in the institution, the child has to vie for attention, sometimes using means that the parents find somewhat unpleasant. Time has become so scarce that parents do not always manage to play with their children. And family life is so limited that the children may not acquire essential social skills.

The Japanese study, which was discussed in Chapter 4, can perhaps be better understood against this background: In this questionnaire survey, which included 1,500 parents of children in preschool programs, researchers were trying to determine, among other things, the relationship between physical and mental violence against children. It turned out that the amount of violence increased if the mother was emotionally unstable or if the parents disagreed about childrearing methods. There was also a relationship between violence on the one hand and a lack of playing with the child—or a lack of desire to spend time with the child—on the other (Kato et al., 1998).

Previous studies have shown that Danish parents do a great deal of scolding. Few parents never scold. The current section has identified several sources of scolding:

1. "Social legacy": The child's stored-up anger about being punished/scolded may cause the child to scold once he or she becomes a parent (or a teacher or early childhood educator).
2. The parents' belief that sanctions are a necessary part of childrearing.
3. Power struggles that spring from the insecure position of modern-day children in combination with the helplessness that is characteristic of early childhood.

4. The parents' combined work and commute time, which has almost doubled over the past 40 years, makes family time a scarce resource; this may lead to stress.
5. Disagreement between parents over childrearing and a lack of involvement with the child.

In the Institution

"Scolding may be a psychological reaction, a culturally conditioned pattern, and/or a pedagogical instrument." That was our conclusion a short while ago. Let us take these considerations a little further: Scolding is not taught at educational colleges or debated at early childhood conferences. As already mentioned, it does not feature in organization plans, mission statements, or newsletters. The exceptions are few and far between, as in 1986 when a special issue of the Norwegian periodical *Debattserien for Barnehagefolk [Debate Series for Kindergarten Staff]* suddenly featured a number of articles on *kjefting* (scolding). The headline of the special issue posed the question: "Why is scolding so widespread in early childhood education?" The introduction read:

> Critical voices have stated that adults take too passive a stance towards children's play. The only active part of the body is often the mouth. Doesn't it seem excessively prone to opening and closing constantly? What does this mouth communicate? Kind, friendly, and constructive words—or negative, derogatory, and moralizing admonitions reminding the children how stupid they are? (Taiet & Allgot, 1986)

The authors then go on to offer five explanations of why early childhood educators are always scolding:

1. We scold because we think that is the way for children to change and become nice.
2. We scold because we need a release mechanism for our own frustration.
3. We scold because we are worn out.
4. We scold because we have no alternatives.
5. A good mix of 1–4.

"Because we are worn out . . ." This explanation also features in our data material. One early childhood educator in the project kindergarten said, "The amount of scolding depends on the number of people who are at work." Let us take this to a societal level: Throughout the 1990s the number of staff hours per child was cut and cut and cut. And, all things being equal, every time 1,000 man-hours are cut, the amount of scolding will go up. "The less time you have to listen to the child, the more necessary it is to pressure the child into doing something he or she does not want to do" (Kragh-Müller, 1997). A recent study showed that more than 30% of children suffer a hearing loss before they reach school age. Twenty years ago, the incidence was only a fourth as high (Gissel et al., 2000). It is much more difficult to measure the increase in scolding caused by cramming more children into a smaller space, and almost impossible to measure the damage done. Here may lie yet another reason for the silence on scolding.

Taiet and Allgot proceed by asking the question: Why do we allow ourselves to scold? They provide seven suggestions:

1. Children have low status, enjoy little respect in society, and are small and defenseless.
2. Scolding is an acknowledged method in childrearing, deemed acceptable, for example, when a mom is shopping with a child in the shopping cart or a dad wants peace and quiet around the house.
3. Adults wish to assert themselves—and believe that they do this by scolding and behaving in an authoritarian way.
4. There is a low level of professional training among kindergarten staff. As a result, negative attitudes toward children and the way they learn are allowed to flourish.
5. There is a lack of professional discussions and evaluation of work.
6. There is a tendency to slide into a passive laissez-faire role— scolding after things have gone wrong.
7. There is a lack of goals and purpose in early childhood education work.

This debate and the sharpness of the tone were unique in Norway. Fourteen years later, however, according to the authors, nothing more had happened. The debate quickly turned to acknowledged topics in early childhood education. The matter was dead.

Why? One key reason may be that the topic is touchy and unpleasant, but then, there are other unpleasant topics. Sexual abuse, for example. These topics are discussed at length, initiatives are launched, cases go to trial, and new employees' criminal records are checked prior to recruitment.

Naturally, the consequences of sexual abuse are very serious indeed, and they are easier to recognize and perceive than the ill effects of severe

and systematic scolding. But what about the discussion about Individual Education Plans (IEPs) in kindergartens? Should the children acquire
more academic skills before they start school? There are no studies to document that this will help them do better in school. Nevertheless, the topic
has been debated for years, while the scolding debate does not even get off
the ground. Why? Perhaps because there is an unspoken understanding
between parents and early childhood educators that scolding is a necessary occurrence both at home and in the institution or school. It exists, and
it is necessary. So why discuss it?

Sometimes we may see controversial and unusual statements, like the
following:

> One reason discipline is such a problem in many schools is that students are
> bored by course content which is so divorced from their real world that it
> seems not worth their efforts. (McNeil, 1988)

This statement addresses disciplinary problems and suggests that they
may be caused by curriculum planning, and that is bad enough. But there
is precious little discussion about the sanctions that early childhood educators and teachers use to counter the problems that they themselves have
created.

Of course, it may be difficult to recognize problems of one's own
creation. It seems telling that the following statement came from a very
young early childhood educator: "If people are used to living in chaos,
they won't need to scold the children for running in the hallways."

Slightly older early childhood educators and teachers lead well-ordered
lives. For them, "take it easy," "calm down now," "easy does it," "regular-
ity," and "cozy and relaxed" describe important concepts, which they try
to impose on the children (and young people), who are more into "let's
go," "full speed ahead," and "awesome." "The adults' chairs were great
for wheeling around," one young early childhood educator recalled from
his own experience, but ". . . in every institution I've ever been in as an
intern, the children have been banned from using the staff's chairs."

The gap between the children's norms and the early childhood educators' norms is considerable, and it expands with increasing age and culture differences.

Compared with the way that children play with each other in the
park or in the backyard, life in the institution is characterized by a great
number of rules that restrict their activities. The children often protest the
rules, and the protests frequently take forms that lead to admonitions or
scolding. Thus, in addition to the norm gap there is a power conflict between the early childhood educators and the children.

Scolding as an Educational/Psychological Instrument

"We scold because we think that is the way for children to change and become nice." That was Allgot and Taiet's first thesis. Later, we will see that scolding does not automatically make all children nice and compliant. In fact, scolding may have quite the opposite effect. So why do early childhood educators and parents believe that children will change for the better when scolded? Would it be far-fetched to claim that they learned this as part of their training—in psychology class, no less?

From the 1950s and on, child psychology has given the educational world a better understanding of children—their unique characteristics and general human nature. The flip side to this, however, was some psychologists' rather mechanical view of the child: If the stimuli were scientifically optimized, the desired outcome could be easily accomplished (the Stimulus–Response model). Everyone probably remembers Pavlov's dogs and Skinner's experiments with mice and rats. If a bell is rung at feeding time, eventually the sound of the bell alone will be enough to cause the dogs to salivate. If an action is followed by a negative sanction, the action impulse is expected to be extinguished or dampened. If children are scolded they will stay away from the forbidden fruit, just as electrical shock would make a lab rat shun the otherwise attractive food bowl. Children were seen as objects that respond to the teacher's stimuli. Only the most irreverent troublemakers would think to turn things on their head in the annual school play and present the teacher as the object responding to the students' stimuli. This school of psychology was in accordance with the "wisdom" of traditional childrearing, where the child is the object of the adult's childrearing efforts. Thus, behavioral science confirmed and legitimized the prevailing childrearing philosophy. That is why it is Skinner and Pavlov who are remembered from the older psychology courses, not Charlotte Bühler, Erich Fromm, and Sergei Rubinstein.

Whether it was in fact strictly ethical to use psychotechnical methods on children in this manner was not subject to much consideration. Children's rights were rarely a topic in the training of early childhood educators and teachers. Much more common were such topics as "reward and punishment," "praise and criticism," and "conflicts" (where the early childhood educator's right to intervene and, preferably, "resolve" the conflict was taken for granted). At the same time, few would have thought that doctors had the right to scold their patients or that nursing home staff had the right to scold the elderly residents. Children were not viewed on a par with other human beings. Children were not "other human beings." This is evident from the way adults would refer to children: "the little rascals," "the little darlings," and so on. If the elderly residents in a nursing home were to be referred to as "old-timers" or "the dear old creatures," the patronizing ring of such labels would be jarring to anyone.

In educational/psychological terms it was also possible to describe a child as aggressive, without anyone considering that they themselves would not have liked being described that way when they were angry. If a child is perceived as "aggressive," the early childhood educator's attention turns to the child, and scolding may seem a natural response; if a child is described as "angry," it seems obvious to try to understand the anger and the source of it: "What are you angry about?" The attention instead turns to the child's relationships.

Let us conclude this chapter with a summary: Scolding takes place in practically all institutions. The more heavily regulated and scheduled life in the institution is, the more scolding there is. Spontaneous bodily expressions or activities are an especially frequent target of scolding.

What do we know now about adults' reasons for scolding? Whereas early childhood educators are normally able to provide justification for most of their other actions, they do not normally provide any justification for scolding. We have pointed to six possible reasons for this: (1) Scolding is a part of the culture. (2) Scolding is a belief. (3) Scolding is not considered a pedagogical activity. (4) Scolding is an obvious necessity in the institutional logic. (5) Scolding does not bear the light of day. (6) Early childhood education work is about the good we seek to do, not the bad we do.

So, scolding takes place for several reasons:

- Because the adults themselves were spanked or scolded as children
- Because adults believe that scolding makes children change
- Because children have low status, are often unable to defend themselves, and are not respected
- Because adults suffer from stress
- Because parents, teachers, and early childhood educators have a shared consensus that they are allowed, perhaps even required, to scold
- Because children and adults spend too little time together
- Because behaviorism supports the authoritarian aspects of traditional pedagogical approaches
- Because there is a norm gap between children and adults

Additional factors within the family come into play:

- The insecure position of modern-day children in combination with the helplessness of early childhood leads to power struggles with the parents.
- Parents may disagree about their relationship with the child or be inadequately involved in the child's life.

Additional factors within the institution also are a factor:

- The children are under stress due to too much institutionalization, too many activities, too little room, too much noise, and too much boredom.
- Alternatives have yet to be developed.

CHAPTER 6

Which Children Are Scolded the Most?

They that have power to hurt and will do none . . .
They rightly do inherit heaven's grace.

—William Shakespeare, Sonnet 94

We have demonstrated that scolding is an intensely common form of sanction. We have not in this project, nor in previous projects for that matter, found a single child who has never been scolded, either at home or in the institution or school.

The danger in a type of sanction being so widespread is that it may appear "normal." The fact that it is normal in terms of quantity—just as it is normal for temperatures to be low in winter—fosters the perception that it is also "normal" in the sense that it is appropriate and acceptable. A teacher or early childhood educator who hits a child will be let go. But teachers and early childhood educators can go on scolding until retirement, at no cost, as *this is what we do, after all.* The "normal" character of scolding is probably part of the explanation for the otherwise astonishing scarcity of scolding studies.

One may take solace from the knowledge that most children, as far as we know, do not suffer any lasting damage from occasional scolding. But what if some children are scolded much more than others? Well, that would mean a very different situation, as we will see.

For now, we will simply review the question of whether some children receive more systematic scolding than others, and we will examine what characterizes these children.

WHAT DO THE CHILDREN SAY?

In a conversation in *Hvad er et godt seksårsliv? [What is a good life for children?]* (Sigsgaard, 1993b), Anna said spontaneously: "I know who gets scolded the most in the kindergarten!" Mette: "I do, too!" When asked, "Well, who?" the girls answered almost in unison, "Jesper, Line, and Tommy."

Mette: "Mostly Jesper, then Line, and then Tommy." Later Mette said, "Morten also gets scolded quite a bit." Anna: "Yes, and Claes." Of the 40 children in the kindergarten, these five names came up without hesitation as the ones who "get the most scolding."

This result corresponds with information from other children in other institutions. Typically, some 10%–20% of the children will receive a great deal of scolding, according to their peers.

What can we point to as characteristic of these 10%–20%?

SCOLDING AND AT-RISK CHILDREN

The 10%–20% figure corresponds more or less to the number of children characterized as "at-risk children" in other studies, children who are at risk of "slipping out of the group, thus losing their opportunity for personal development" (Jørgensen et al., 1995). It is clear that it is not the children with the best social backgrounds or from the best families who are scolded the most, but that does not necessarily mean that it is the children from social-risk groups who are. But is there a connection?

Let us take a brief look at the concept of "neglected children." What are the typical symptoms of neglect? Let us draw up a list:

- No ability to feel joy
- Involuntary discharge of urine or feces
- Temper tantrums
- Low self-esteem
- Withdrawal
- Seclusion
- Suspicion
- Compulsory or obsessive behavior
- Adult behavior
- Concentration problems
- Learning difficulties
- Uncritical in contact with others (clingy, submissive) (Halse, 1998)

It is easy to imagine that children who have temper tantrums will be scolded more than calm and even-tempered children, that children who have trouble concentrating are scolded more often than children who are able to focus, that suspicious children who are wary of adults are scolded more than trusting children, that withdrawn children meet with more disapproval than open children, and that children with learning difficulties—perhaps unable to learn proper table manners—are scolded more than "easy" children.

These conclusions may seem obvious in the light of everyday experiences. But do they correspond with early childhood educators' professional experiences?

In order to examine this, the Scolding Project interviewed some early childhood education students who were close to graduation, as well as some recent graduates. One of the questions was whether it was possible to identify types of children that particularly attract scolding.

One of the early childhood educators told us about a boy named Nikolaj. Wherever he showed up in the institution adults and children alike would burst out, "Get out, Nikolaj!" Surprisingly, it turned out that everybody in the group knew a "Nikolaj." They all agreed: "Every institution has a kid to whom everybody says 'Get out!' as soon as they see him or her indoors."

But who is this "Nikolaj"? And who are the other children that adults tend to avoid, reject, and scold?

The group was able to define at least three types of children who are often scolded. We shall now take a closer look at these three types and try to describe them.

The Contact-Seeking Child

Judith is almost 3. She is a cheerful girl who often contacts both children and adults. Especially in her contact with the adults in the preschool she may seem somewhat clingy. She "devours" the adult with her eyes and pushes away all other children who try to get close to her and the adult. She climbs around on the adult and grabs one's face with her hands, so that you are constantly forced to look at her and talk to her. When the adult has fun with the children, her smile and laugh do not seem sincere. Instead, they seem false and very tense (her jaw looks like it is about to cramp up at any moment). On a few occasions I have seen natural smiles from her, and that is almost like a personality change—that's great to see!

The Overly Active Child

Kim is 6 and very physically active. He often gets scolded and feels unfairly treated in these situations. He "takes up a lot of space" in the kindergarten because he is often running around, shouting or screaming. His play reflects his great need for physical activity. He often play-fights, climbs trees, races his bike around the playground, and so on. Other children are often bothered by his rowdy behavior. Therefore, Kim's shouting and screaming are often accompanied by a nearby crying child. The adults often yell at Kim, often preemptively in order to try to avoid the next incident.

The Whiny Child

> Mikkel is 2. He whines and whimpers many times a day. If he is
> having his diaper changed, it's "Nooo, I don't want to!" over and
> over again. At naptime, he will lie in bed, kicking his legs into the
> wall. When the early childhood educator tells him to be quiet, he
> responds with whining and complaining: "Nooo, I don't want to."
> This can go on for a long time. The early childhood educator's re-
> sponse will gradually intensify—from "But when you're being noisy
> the other kids can't sleep" (in an angry whisper) to a curt, definitive,
> and pent-up "Well, but you have to!!" The early childhood educa-
> tor says, "My response becomes so intense because it goes on for so
> long, and it takes up so much of our time."

Elsewhere I describe why children who typically assume an aggressive
defense position attract so many sanctions. But let us dig a little deeper
here. An early childhood educator in a remedial school said,

> The children that we deal with here are kids who have really been
> scolded a lot. They are locked into a stance where they challenge
> our authority as adults in an aggressive and provoking way, but also
> more defensively—behind our backs. They are all children whose
> families are having difficulties, in one way or another, and the chil-
> dren act as messengers in a way, telling us, "Hey . . . something is
> really seriously amiss here . . . and I need help." And I just get so
> damn angry and really kind of appalled when I listen to the chil-
> dren's stories and discover, time and again, that no one responded
> sooner—I mean, looked into the children's behavior and tried to find
> out what it means. They have just been busy scolding little Bo in-
> stead of helping him with his problems.

Let us recap: Kindergartners have no problem picking out the 10%–
20% of the children who are scolded the most. When queried, early childhood educators and students in the field are all aware that every institution has at least one "Nikolaj" that everybody shuns. They are also able
to describe three types of children who are typically scolded: the active,
rowdy child; the whiny child; and the highly contact-seeking child. The
descriptions of these children correspond more or less with Halse's description of neglected children (e.g., temper tantrums, no ability to experience joy, low self-esteem, clinginess).

There does seem to be a connection. The behavior of hyperactive, whiny, or clingy children may signal an insecure relationship with the parents, characterized by anxiety, cool distance, or perhaps corporal punishment. In relationships such as these, scolding is probably a daily ingredient.

It seems that the children who are scolded the most at home also receive the largest doses in the institutions.

It is a commonly held view that preschool facilities and schools ought to compensate for the shortages or weaknesses that may be present in the children's family background. It appears that the opposite may in fact often be the case: that the institution exacerbates the disadvantaged children's problems, obviously unintentionally. We may well have a situation in which the children who enjoy support and security at home receive the same in the institution and thus live in environments that are doubly positive, while children who have a hard time at home may wind up having a hard time in institutions and schools as well; and thus live out their childhood in doubly negative environments.

The most severely disadvantaged of these children may eventually end up in rehabilitation schools, where they are finally free from some of the scolding.

SCOLDING MAY BE LINKED WITH CULTURAL DIFFERENCES

No one wants this *polarization* in institutions and schools. Let us examine why it occurs anyway. Part of the explanation, as already mentioned, is the behavior pattern of these children. Whether they are whiny, clingy, or overly active, they are a burden to the staff, who may feel that they are ignoring the other children in order to deal with these children.

But there is also a sociocultural explanation. Some of the children who are scolded more than others come from socially disadvantaged families with norms, communication patterns, hierarchies, ideals, and attitudes that differ from those that most early childhood educators and teachers are familiar with from their personal background.

Scolding often results when the early childhood educator or teacher does not recognize or understand a child's actions. The moral condemnation that occurs when something seems meaningless and, at the same time, provoking is expressed directly through scolding and indirectly through facial expressions, body language, tone of voice, and other nonverbal expressions—signals that these children in particular are often experts in reading. This locks the children into a set of strongly negative expectations. An educator in a multi-age facility in Denmark provided this example of scolding arising from a lack of understanding:

> One thing that will really get me angry and make me scold, you know, with recriminations and everything—is when the older girls are mean to each other, especially when they gang up on one girl, that really sets me off. I guess it's probably 'cause my girls at home never did that. I never allowed it, and I don't see why that would be necessary . . . but that's a long story, I guess, and it also relates to my own childhood.

Her closing statement refers to the fact that she grew up in an environment without such cattiness.

Thus, the initial answer as to which children are scolded the most is that it is the children who receive the least care and love at home. A second answer is that children from socially disadvantaged families are scolded more than other children.

YOUNGER VS. OLDER CHILDREN

The third answer is that older children appear to be scolded less than younger children. This corresponds with results from other studies where adults in Western countries believe that one has to be stricter with younger children than with older ones. Indeed, scolding does have a stronger effect on younger children.

One might expect older children to be scolded more than younger children because their age and development might make them seem more accountable for their actions. However, it appears that the intensity of scolding decreases with increases in the children's age. An intern says, "Here, the oldest children are kindergartners, so they have no great need for reprimands."

A U.S. survey (Honig, 1994) reported that children as young as 6 months of age are scolded. In various public places, 75 situations were recorded where children between 6 months and 3 years of age were either frightened or stressed and reacted by crying. Almost all the children were then picked up by their caregiver, but some in an unkind manner. Some children were scolded, and others were slapped. Overall, the study showed that adults are more likely to scold their young children than comfort them when the children are frightened and begin to cry.

An early childhood educator in a multi-age facility said,

> I have sometimes scolded the young kids, and that is obviously not very pedagogical, it has a very strong effect on them . . . their eyes get all big and round, and they get sort of quiet-before-the-storm, and then comes the reaction, then they cry uncontrollably, you know, the kind of crying where it is almost impossible to comfort

them. And it is not quite clear whether they cry from fear or shock, or whether it comes from that feeling of "you can't treat me like that." A sort of protest.

Once they reach school age, younger children appear to be scolded more than older children. The previously mentioned Icelandic study (Sigurdardottir, 1997) showed that the teachers meted out punishment (admonitions, threats, spanking, mocking, grabbing the student) 3.4 times per lesson in first through third grade, but only 1.4 times per lesson in fourth through seventh grade.

Schools, preschool facilities, and after-school centers probably also have the effect that Foucault has demonstrated for prisons, that is, making the children gradually adapt to the desired behavior. Hence, the 5- to 6-year-olds are not scolded much in kindergarten, where they are the oldest, but more so in schools, where they are the youngest and therefore have yet to "learn the ropes."

In addition, newcomers run into more trouble than "veterans" because they do not know the others yet and have not yet formed relationships with them.

So we can add some nuance to the third answer by saying that younger children are scolded more than older children, especially in school, and that newcomers are scolded more than veterans—except for very recent newcomers:

> *Two 5-year-olds were relaxing at the dining table in one child's home:*
> **A:** If you sat like this in my kindergarten, you'd get scolded.
> **B:** In mine too.
> **A:** When you're new, you don't get scolded.
> **B:** No—you should only stay until the early days were over.
> **A:** Then you should quit.
> **B:** Yeah, and then you could start over and be a newcomer somewhere else.

GIRLS VS. BOYS

We have seen that early childhood educators and teachers may have difficulty understanding children with a social background that differs from their own. But whom else does the professional adult not understand?

Boys are often said to have a hard time in institutions because the institutions are dominated by feminine values that may prevail over the boys' behaviors, communication patterns, and needs.

At first, the Danish after-school center Baduljen focused on the quiet girls who were subdued by the loud and rambunctious boys. A girls-only computer day was introduced. But then the staff discovered that it was hard being a boy. Then the boys got their own playhouse where they could be together on their own terms without always having to be the way that "the women prefer them . . . quiet, sensible, able to remember 20 messages in a row, not running in the hallway, not talking too loudly . . ." For the first two weeks, the house was extremely noisy, but gradually the boys' house became "both calm and cozy." At times, the boys would even use a tablecloth and candles.

Both boys and girls enjoyed being apart, but they often invited the other sex over. After a year, boys and girls actually spent more time together than ever before. And the female early childhood educators developed a much more open and generous attitude toward the boys—accepting more noise, for example.

Most people would probably expect boys to be scolded more than girls. And that would be a well-founded guess. An English study of 4 teachers and 87 students (Etaugh & Harlow, 1973) looked at the way in which male and female teachers behaved toward younger schoolchildren. The study showed that both men and women were more likely to scold boys than girls. There was also a difference as to who would praise whom: The women were more likely to praise the boys, who nevertheless liked the male teachers more, while the girls preferred the women.

However, the study showed that there was no real difference in the girls' and the boys' behavior in the classroom. They were equally attentive, equally bad or good at remembering to raise their hand before speaking, equally good at reading, and so forth.

Thus, the study demonstrated both that boys are scolded more and that there does not appear to be any connection between scolding and classroom behavior. Does the explanation for these findings lie in the teachers' internal perceptions of the girls as more delicate and the boys as more resilient? Or of the girls as well behaved and the boys as being in need of correction? Or of the girls as well adjusted and the boys as difficult/troublesome/demanding?

In a Danish kindergarten the director saw that the older boys were scolded a great deal. She describes how the boys existed in a culture created by the female early childhood educators where the setting and the rules were so tight that "any initiative towards free expression led to scolding . . . the playground was well equipped with swings, sand boxes, stationary equipment, and bicycles, but there were no possibilities for testing your strength, constructing, digging holes, lighting fires etc."

On this background the director felt that the boys had a "pent-up surplus of energy that was released in . . . very unfortunate ways, which led to scolding." The adults in the kindergarten therefore started a project aiming at giving boys the space and the possibilities they needed.

At the end of the project the staff concluded, among other things, "As scolding turned to dialogue, the boys began to see us as valid partners, and we gained more insight into their universe and, thus, more understanding for their actions. This caused us to change both the rules and the physical setup of the playground."

Thus, a lack of understanding of the children's actions means more scolding—or, conversely: Insight into motives and intentions reduces the amount of scolding.

SUMMARY

It appears that 10%–20% of the children are clearly scolded more than the other children. In some institutions the number is 10% or less, in some—as we shall see later—even zero (institutions and schools without any scolding at all). In other institutions the number is closer to 20% or maybe even higher. If we take a closer look at the children who are scolded the most, they typically fall into one or more of these categories:

- Younger children
- Newcomers
- Boys—especially those who are physically very active
- Children who belong to sociocultural groups different from those of the staff
- Children with troubled family backgrounds, who are therefore typically also scolded a great deal at home.

We should bear in mind that the extent of institutionalization means that a great deal of scolding in the institutions typically means a very great deal of scolding indeed.

On this background it may not be hard to understand why some children show such great dedication and progress in acquiring the skill of shutting their ears.

CHAPTER 7

Children's Perceptions of Scolding

We have seen that some children are scolded a great deal, while others are scolded only a little. Still, the great similarity in the way that children perceive scolding makes it meaningful to talk about the children as one group. Living in a setting where scolding takes place is, after all, a shared condition for them. We will now examine how children perceive scolding.

WHAT DO CHILDREN THINK IS THE REASON THAT ADULTS SCOLD?

In the project kindergarten we asked the children, "What do you think is the reason that adults scold?"

The most common answer was that adults scold because the children are stupid. Some say, "Because the children have done something stupid."

One girl says, "Because they can hear the children crying, and then they come over and scold them."

Another girl says, "It's because they have to when you've done something you're not supposed to. It's up to the adults whether they want to scold or not."

One boy replies, "Because we have to learn it for when we are adults, the things we're not supposed to do."

Many children have probably adopted such explanations for scolding from the adults. Henning says it clearly when asked why he thinks adults scold: "I had this explained to me once, I think it's so that you can learn that you're not supposed to do that again." Jonas finds it scary to be scolded, "but not as scary as a nightmare," and he adds, "I have heard from many adults here that they don't like scolding, but they have to when the children do something they're not supposed to." Knowing that the adults do not find the sanction desirable either may soften the impact of the scolding a little for Jonas. On the other hand, it might also make Jonas feel guilty: If only we weren't so bad as to force the adults to act against us in a way that they dislike.

The dominant view seems to be that adults scold because of the way the children are. First comes the children's unwanted behavior, next comes the consequential scolding. The problem lies with the children, not with the adults. This is emphasized by a 6-year-old who was asked what would happen if the children were not scolded: "Well, then they go on fighting, 'cause they will go on fighting until they're scolded." Not all children, however, see the link between disobedience and scolding as inescapable. Note the added "it's up to the adults whether they want to scold or not." The adults might choose something else, as the subsequent discussion makes clear.

Even at this early stage, some children are forming their view of childrearing, which may determine the way they raise their own children later on. One 6-year-old girl, who wants to be a teacher, says that she will probably be nice to the children, "but also a little mad when they tease each other." When the interviewer asks if they need to be scolded then, she says with conviction, "Yes, they do, always!" One mother talks about her work as an early childhood educator and mentions scolding. Her 5-year-old son, Mikkel, says, "They scold in my kindergarten too." Mom: "Well, that's because there are some things that the adults don't want you to do." Mikkel thinks this over: "No, it's so that we can learn to scold in case we become early childhood educators when we grow up."

Some children have a slightly different view. They do not say "because the children are stupid" but "because the adults think that the children are stupid." This is very different, as one may imagine adults who are "able to think pretty well in their head . . . how children should be treated" (Sigsgaard, 1993b). In this view, the scolding is due not to the children's behavior but to the way the adults perceive the children. One child in another institution sees scolding as a direct expression of the scolder's dislike for the child who is scolded:

> Kassandra, who is 4, once said to her mother in a puzzled voice that her favorite early childhood educator appeared to like Kevin.
> *Mother:* Why do you think so?
> *Kassandra:* Well, 'cause she doesn't scold him.

Other children find it self-explanatory that adults with power will use that power against the children. One child's answer to the question of why adults scold: "Because they are the strongest." According to her, they use their power because they have it, not because of what the children do. If the children had been the strongest—according to this view—they might well have been scolding the adults. Toward the end of the development project, there were several situations in which the children scolded adults, perhaps because of a slight shift in the balance of power between children and adults—in the children's favor—as a result of the dialogue and criticism employed in the development work.

Above, Kassandra said that when an adult scolds a child it might be because the adult does not like the child. Only a few children in the project institution pointed to this link between scolding and dislike. Perhaps that is a result of the development work?

In the views mentioned until now, the adults are in opposition to the children. They scold the children in order to change the children's behavior here and now—or perhaps simply because they do not like them.

Other children see scolding as future-oriented, as childrearing with a view to making the children adapt to society's norms during childhood so that once they reach adulthood they will know what to do and what to steer clear of: "We have to learn it for when we are adults, the things we're not supposed to do."

No child questions the adults' right to scold.

KINDERGARTNERS' REACTION TO SCOLDING

In Chapter 2, we quoted kindergartners' reply to the question, "How do you feel when you have been scolded?" Some of the answers were, "not very good," "I cry," "I hurt inside."

Other answers were, "I feel like everyone is looking at me, it is embarrassing," "A little bad—because there's been too much shouting," and "Then I won't do it again."

Amalie said, "I would rather have a pounding heart, even if I almost die." Julie: "A little good and a little bad inside the brain." Daniel: "I was glad I didn't cry." One girl: "I get sad on the inside and on the outside."

Daniel also said, "I wish they wouldn't do it . . . that's how I feel." One morning a 6- or 7-year-old girl said to her mother after a scolding, "It's time we had some children's language around here!" Maybe she is voicing a common perception among children, that scolding is a strange and alien thing to a child, not a natural part of their life outside of school. In that sense they may consider scolding somewhat uncivilized. Maybe this is what they express when they say that they want the adults to "say it in a normal way" instead of scolding. Saying it in a normal way typically means to speak in the manner that is the most common and most commonly recognized in a given culture.

The Eyes

The children in the project kindergarten were asked, "Could you try to explain how you can tell when an adult is angry?"

The children were able to provide a very accurate description of the way a scolder looks: "slightly angry mouth and a furrowed brow . . . and then she'll stare right down at the one who did something," "almost as mad as a polar bear, only smaller." The interviewer: "A polar bear, not a brown bear?" "Yeah, that's what I mean."

The strongest impact, however, comes from the eyes: "looks you, like, deep into the eyes, really, really deep!"

The answers were discussed in a group consisting of early childhood educators and early childhood education students attached to the project. Some of the statements from the discussion:

> I'm a little surprised with the way the kids noticed the body language. That it was the eyes and the face. I would have imagined that it would be this tall, scary adult towering over a small child who is sitting on the floor. But those are not the descriptions I see in the interview. It is the eyes that are dangerous, simply.

> It's almost a little scary the way they notice these things. You expect things like "puffing himself up" or "broad shoulders" or "flexing her muscles," but instead they notice the things that are subconscious to us. They see things that we don't expect them to notice. I was a little shocked when I read it. And I thought, well, I'll be damned, the things they notice. It's almost like they notice the throbbing vein in your forehead. I mean, looking into someone's eyes, that's pretty "up close and personal." You can see some really personal things that way.

What is the point of working with body language, crouching down, lowering one's voice, and so on if the child is able to see directly into the adult's soul, where the anger or the disapproval may lurk? How can one address those aspects?

Or does the children's focus on the eyes signify that the staff in the project institution has already come so far with the body language of power that the eyes are just about the only scary thing left?

"Look into my eyes when I speak to you," the adult says, perhaps with an implicit understanding that scolding interrupts the contact with the child, a contact that will have to be reestablished through a prescribed eye contact.

The Ears

While most children feel sadness or pain when scolded, a few say, "Scolding—you can shut your ears to that." The children who say that are not the ones who are never scolded, but rather the ones who are scolded frequently. One may see the shutting of ears as a defense mechanism. It is harder with the eyes, even though some children like to have a friend nearby to look at; that makes it more bearable, since one does not have to look at the scolder. Apparently it is slightly easier with the ears, but maybe this defense comes at a cost: Is it possible to shut one's ears without shutting oneself off completely? Several children mention that they try to shut themselves off, but they are too young, so they are not yet able to do so. Anton says, "Sometimes you don't cry, but then the tears are still coming down because you're upset." He is 6 and well on the way to being able to shut himself off, although he is not quite there yet.

PRESCHOOL CHILDREN'S REACTIONS TO SCOLDING

It was not possible to interview the youngest children. Instead, some preschools recorded episodes for later analysis. The recording was done by a group of early childhood education students who were close to graduation as well as early childhood educators attached to the research project with experience and training in observation and registration. Let us look at some of these episodes:

> The children have been put into their cribs to sleep, but three girls keep standing up and shouting at each other. I have tucked them in several times and told them that they must not wake up the others. Eventually, my patience runs out, and I scold them, telling them *very* loudly and firmly, "That's enough, now!" The girls give a start. I lay them down, tucking the covers in tight around them.
> Now they are all lying there, staring at me with big eyes and pinched lips. I stay with them until they sleep, thinking that I might have woken up the other kids with my shouting.

Perhaps the girls are not tired or do not want to stop playing. This means that they are not prepared to *do the same as the others*, which is often required in institutions, due either to the high ratio of children to adults or to a choice by the early childhood educator.

> Some 2-year-olds have abandoned their toys, which are spread out on the floor, and are now playing with something else. An early childhood educator instructs the children to pick up the "old" toys, and most of them comply. One boy, however, refuses her request. The more she scolds him, saying, "It's not right for the others to have

to pick up after you — get to it already," the more he refuses. Her voice gets more and more firm, and she is clearly getting more and more upset. Eventually she takes the boy's hand, places it over a toy, and picks it up "with him." When it is over, she says to him: "There you see, that wasn't so bad, now, was it!" The boy throws himself on the floor, crying and shouting, clearly feeling violated.

The early childhood educator is acting out a basic norm: You pick up after yourself. The child is too young to understand, and to him the forced activity seems meaningless.

It is shortly before lunchtime, and the children are playing. From the doll corner comes a shriek followed by a wail. The adult runs into the room towards the crying child, who holds her index finger out for the adult to see and points to the child next to her. The adult has no doubt that the teeth marks in the finger were made — as so many times before — by the indicated child. She picks up the child so that the child's face is level with her own, and says in a loud and angry voice, "How many times do I have to tell you not to bite?" The child, who is only 15 months old and is often scolded, starts to cry. The children have all stopped playing, awaiting what happens next.

As so often before, the biting — violent — child is exposed to the verbal violence of the early childhood educator, and once again in vain.
    Another observation:

We are sitting at the dinner table, and two children have finished, while the rest are still eating. One of the two starts spitting at the table while he laughs. An adult says, "Hey, wait a minute, that's gross. Stop that!" The child — a 2-year-old — continues, and now the other child joins in. They both find it amusing and look at the adult while they laugh. The first boy is told to stop. In response, he spits in the face of the adult sitting next to him. He is then pulled out of his chair and very firmly put on the floor. From then on, the adults ignore him — shut their eyes and ears to him.

This child is the one who is scolded the most in the group, and he has already learned to "shut his ears." In this situation, the adults combine active mental violence (scolding) with passive mental violence (excluding and ignoring the child).

Immediately after lunch, the adults are cleaning up while the children are playing. At the back of the room, a boy has climbed onto the seat of a chair about one foot off the floor. An adult cries out, very loudly, *"Nooo!"* and rushes across the room to pick the boy up off the chair. As she puts him down, she says, "Don't do that, you'll fall and hurt yourself." The boy turns his face away from her. As she talks she is looking at the other adults and signaling "whew!" with her eyes. The boy begins to cry. She responds by saying, "Well, it's just no good, now, is it!"

Children may have good reasons to climb chairs. Often that makes it possible to look out the window. As the adult yelled *"Nooo!"* from across the room, almost all the children focused their attention on her. They froze for a moment, and all playing ceased until the "chair climber" was back on the floor. Most of the children gave a start when the adult shouted. It seemed that several of the children felt that they had been targeted, at least until it became clear who the sinner was.

Preschool children are not able to tell us whether we are right in thinking that they feel targeted when other children are scolded, but an exchange between Gitte and 5-year-old Mads might suggest that this is the case. Mads has been scolded by Lillian and is later interviewed by Gitte:

> *Gitte:* So, did anyone else see you being scolded?
> *Mads*: Yes . . . they all watched, and I did not like that.
> *Gitte:* How do you think the others felt about you being scolded?
> *Mads:* Not very good, because they're thinking, "maybe it's me."

This reply implies that Mads has felt targeted himself when others were scolded. And if a 5-year-old can feel that way, maybe a preschool child can as well. That may explain the start they all gave when the "chair climber" was scolded.

Reaction Patterns

We may distinguish between two types of actions that cause sanctions:

1. The children are doing something that they appear to know they are not supposed to do. During the act they peer at the adults, presumably to see if they are being watched.
2. The children *accidentally* do something that is not allowed.

In the case of conscious rule breaking, even the very young children do not seem surprised to be scolded, but they may get slightly angry with the scolding adult. However, when children are scolded for acts that they did not know were forbidden, they look and act completely nonplussed. They act very puzzled and look at the adult with big eyes. Then they react with crying and want to be picked up and cuddled. Others just stand there, lost, crying without seeking contact.

The latter may have been scolded many times already and know that scolding involves adult rejection. The ones who cry uncontrollably and wish to be cuddled by the scolder react spontaneously and uncomprehendingly at the verbal rejection; they reach for the scolder and try to reestablish the bond that was broken. The scolder may sometimes interpret this as the child seeking to be comforted.

Many do not believe that a recently punished (scolded) child should be comforted; that appears self-contradictory to them. Some disapprove when a colleague comforts a scolded child. One might imagine that once the child learns that the rejection is an intentional part of the punishment, they will give up their attempts at reestablishing the bond with the adult. This may take the form of the child trying to "shut his or her ears," so that *what began as an exclusion by the adult may end up with the child excluding the adult.* But this process will usually take years.

OLDER VS. YOUNGER CHILDREN

Perhaps it is this exclusion process that is reflected in an 8-year-old boy's reply to the question of how he feels after being scolded: "I don't get upset or nothing. I feel fine." Or when a 10-year-old says, "I don't really care; I listen, but I just sort of blow it off."

A 9-year-old girl, however, said, "Then I think, well, okay, I shouldn't have done that." And an 11-year-old boy: "Sometimes I don't blame them."

The popular after-school center where this little survey was carried out offers many activities, few rules, and plenty of space. But even under these benevolent conditions, some children still shut themselves off when they are scolded. When the 10-year-old was asked to describe scolding, he replied, "It's when the adults tell you what's allowed, and what's not allowed in a very mean way. In a Flemming sort of way—in a mean way." (Flemming is a staff member.) When asked whether scolding works, both the children who shut themselves off had a brief reply: "No!"

Other children—often the children who are rarely scolded—simply see scolding as a sort of course correction. They listen. It gets through to them, but it does not get them down. They are more likely to think that scolding works. One says, "A little, sometimes. It does not work if it's the kind of kids that don't listen." Another child says, "Sometimes it does, sometimes it doesn't."

Apart from these groups, there are still many of the older children who simply get sad when they are scolded: "Not very good. I get kind of sad." A second-grader says, "You feel like you're less than nothing, and that you're no good at anything."

When the older children explain why adults scold, many of them use the phrase "doing something wrong." As we have seen, kindergartners do not use this phrase. They talk about doing "something stupid" or "something we're not allowed to do." Young children simply see the adults exercising their power (it is a matter of allowed or not allowed), while some older children see the adults more as the keepers of justice (a matter of right or wrong). This corresponds to findings in previous studies: A moral sense develops only after early childhood. An adult may preach long and hard to young children to explain that they were scolded because they did something bad and wrong, but the younger children tend to think that adults simply scold because they have the strength and the power.

Older children understand the adult terms of right and wrong—at least if they acknowledge the particular adult as an authority figure. But even so, they have their doubts as to the efficacy of scolding. Some state clearly that stern and scolding adults are harmful:

A Norwegian 13-year-old came home one day, very upset: "Now it's become impossible to learn!" The class had a new teacher who had very high standards and ran a very tight ship. The children were used to having a say, being allowed to work outside the classroom if they wanted to, doing their assignments in a personal way, and so on.

SCOLDING AT HOME

This book focuses on institutions, but since the children themselves bring up comparisons between home and institution, this factor has to be considered as well. Two 6-year-olds say that scolding also happens at home, but . . .

Interviewer: Where do you get scolded the most, at home or in the kindergarten?
Both students, in unison: In the kindergarten
First student: In kindergarten you're almost always scolded; that doesn't happen so much at home.

In another kindergarten three 6-year-olds were asked to mention some important differences between kindergarten and home. First, the girls mentioned the many people and the many rooms as key differences; then they were asked:

> *Teacher:* Are there other differences?
> *Anders:* Yes!
> *Teacher:* What, Anders?
> *Anders:* Err, they scold you more in kindergarten.
> *Mette:* Yes, I agree!
> *Teacher:* Why is that?
> *Mette:* Mmm . . . I don't know.
> *After a moment of shared and puzzled consideration:*
> *Anna:* We only make drawings the whole time.
> (Sigsgaard, 1993b)

This shared perception among the oldest children in two seemingly liberal and open-minded kindergartens was mentioned as part of the reason that one of the kindergartens chose to focus on scolding in the development project described previously. Apparently the children also felt that the parents were more "entitled" to scold them than the staff. This was reflected in some children's statements that if they had done something pretty bad, the staff should not scold them, but tell the parents and leave it up to them to decide whether to scold or not.

It is impossible to say how common this view is, but 6-year-old Mathias clearly feels differently: "I prefer getting scolded by the adults in the kindergarten, I don't know why." Previously, Mathias had said that he does not get scolded very often, either at home or in the kindergarten.

Five-year-old Mikkel, however, says, "I prefer getting scolded by my dad—he doesn't do it for very long." "Does your mom?" "Oh, yes . . . she talks a lot, but the worst thing is when it's both of them at once."

Only children especially may feel very lonely if both their key persons turn against them.

Sometimes, dad's scolding can be really painful. A 5-year-old girl says, "Sometimes, when my dad scolds me, I go into my room and lie down on my bed; then I climb under the blanket and take some deep breaths."

Former Danish prime minister Jens Otto Krag wrote in his journal during Easter 1967 about his daughter Søsser:

> Last night we watched TV. She was eating bread and butter and wanted to wipe her hand, first on my pants, then on a yellow pillow. I ordered her into the bathroom. She went out there, astonished. And returned seconds later— wailing. "Don't talk to me like that." I promised—foolishly. And like all foolish promises—sincerely meant. (Quoted in Lidegaard, 2002)

Perhaps severe scolding must be handled by a parent or another person close to the child, even if the close bond makes it more painful; the pain, however severe, is less severe than if it is inflicted by someone who is not as close. Is that how we should understand this complex statement from a 6-year-old boy?

> *Child:* . . . sometimes when it's someone else who scolds you, someone you think is nice, then you're hardly ever . . . then it may be painful. Then you've got, then you've got to not get so upset. That time when Laila scolded me. I, I *(stutters eagerly)* just thought it was fun when she scolded me. I didn't care.
>
> *Adult:* Because you knew that she liked you?
>
> *Child:* Yes, I knew it, because she didn't scold the way the others do.

If a beloved mother or father scolds, then it may be painful, but it is still easier to bear than when "others" do it, for mom and dad do not scold the same way that the others do.

This interpretation corresponds with the experiences in the project kindergarten: It is a delicate matter to scold a child with whom one does not have a close relationship.

But the relationship between parents and child is not always just close and loving, as this statement expresses: "People have kids so that they can have someone to scold." (Stated matter-of-factly by an 8-year-old boy who is in foster care.)

CHILDREN'S REACTIONS TO SCOLDING— CRITICISM AND RESISTANCE

> *Mother (to her 8-year-old daughter):* What should grown-ups be like?
>
> *Daughter:* Well, they certainly shouldn't be mean, for then the kids get mean, too, and then there's just even more scolding. (Observation in Roskilde, 1999).

Adults often scold children in order to make them nice, make them adhere to norms and rules, and be considerate and "good." The 8-year-old above states as obvious that they will in fact achieve the opposite.

In a TV documentary on competition dancing, we saw the coach boss around two 11-year-olds—one was his son—who ended up as world champions in Latin dancing and waltzing. The 11-year-old boy, Sonny, said, "When he scolds me, I get upset and nervous, and then I do even worse, and then he scolds me even more" (*Ingen slinger i valsen,* 1998).

These two children see scolding not as a single episode but as a dynamic action that leads to a reaction. Either you get "mean" like the scolder, or you get upset and nervous. In either case, the reaction causes renewed reactions, which means more scolding. So not only does scolding not work, according to most children, in the view of many children, it exacerbates the very aspects it set out to improve.

But how do the statements from these older children correspond to younger children's reactions to scolding? Here, we cannot look at the children's statements but have to read their actual reactions. The most common reaction to scolding among preschool children is to wrestle free from the adult and begin to cry, loudly and angrily. This may be seen as an attempt to shut the adult up, since children have been observed to start crying when they think they are about to be scolded and stop abruptly when they discover that they are not. This preemptive crying may be an anticipation of the pain related to scolding, or it may be an attempt to ward off the scolding. Other forms of resistance include a physical movement away from the scolder: Some children try to look away during the scolding, run off, hide or seek protection from another adult. At times, the pedagogical approach will anticipate and limit these defense mechanisms: One may require the scolded child to look into one's eyes; restrict the child's freedom of movement within the institution, so that there are few places to run to; or ask other adults not to comfort a scolded child. This makes it necessary for the child to attempt more sophisticated forms of resistance, such as the ruse of distraction—staring intently at something and asking, "Lookit. What's that?"

How do the children react once the danger has blown over and the scolding has perhaps hit someone else? Most children mainly look relieved that they were not targeted this time around. Generally, the atmosphere becomes somewhat oppressive, and most children try to make themselves invisible by lowering their voices and generally keeping a low profile. Some may try to comfort the child who was scolded.

Let us turn to the older children once more:

> On a sunny day in May, two boys, around 10 years old, were standing on a bike path, talking. Suddenly, one of them said, "I'm not looking forward to tonight . . . my mom is angry. I don't know what's gonna happen to me." (Observation in Skovlunde, May 2000)

Just like the little child in the nursery school, this 10-year-old is at the mercy of adults. But where the younger children may seek to avoid scolding by, for example, seeking the help of another adult, this 10-year-old has no escape. He is at his mother's mercy, he is alone with her, and he has to go back to her. Young children may try to avoid evoking a scolding. Not this 10-year-old. For it has nothing to do with him. It is simply there, and he knows from experience that his mother will take it out on him. "I don't know what's gonna happen to me" is an unusually vulnerable statement for a boy. It almost sounded like a cry for help, but there was no to help to be found. The mother's bad mood cast a dark shadow even on the time he spent with his friend.

One of the big strengths of the institution is that the children are not dependent on a single adult (perhaps with the class teacher as one exception). The institution may emphasize the children's freedom of movement and their right to become attached to adults of their own choice. This may make it a safe haven for children with an overly strong negative dependency at home.

WHAT DOES SCOLDING TEACH?

Adults often think that children learn from being scolded by parents, early childhood educators, or teachers. This is somewhat at odds with the children's point of view:

> — Sometimes, when you're being scolded and stuff by the older ones, right, like the ones that are not adults, then you can learn from it in your head.
> — What can you learn?
> — Like, it makes it easier to understand if you're scolded by your sister or someone like that.

Mette, who is 6, would like to stay in kindergarten until she is 8 or 9:

> — Then you wouldn't have to start learning math and English and all that until you were 9?
> — Well, yes, or you could learn it from the others . . . maybe they would have friends who went to school, and they would learn it from them, and then they could teach us.

Six-year-olds who are asked about learning do not even consider the possibility of learning from adults. To them, it is natural to learn from older children. Perhaps that is because the power balance has such a strong impact on child–adult relations.

It is hard to learn from adults when they scold. This is reflected in a story from the project kindergarten:

> Susan, Ania, and Morten have put one of the chickens into a basin filled with water. Two adults, Jan and Gitte, are "taking turns explaining to the children that chickens have to be treated properly." The children are upset and want to leave, but are told to stay. Jan says that it makes him very angry to see the chickens treated like this.
> Gitte says, "We talk a lot. I tell them that we adults have told them

that the three of them are only supposed to be outside when there's an adult with them. They don't want that. Well, then they have to remember how it works. Susan says she's not sure if she can remember. I tell her that she's going to have to. She has to imagine that she always has an adult running around after her, lifting her up, and putting her into a tub of cold water. I ask her if she would like that. She doesn't know. I ask her if we should try. No, we should not. And eventually she agrees to be nice to the chickens.

"A little later, all three of them come running, and Morten is crying again. They are upset because they were scolded, they say. I tell them I didn't scold them to make them unhappy, but to make sure that the chickens are okay, and that I am not angry anymore. Morten cries and says a lot of stuff about all sorts of bad things that are going to befall me and the others, and the kindergarten is going to burn, and axes and large rocks, etc. I tell Morten that I think he is very angry, but that I am not mad at him anymore. Morten: 'But you know what, Gitte, when I get home, I'm never going back to kindergarten again.'

"Susan leans against me. We talk about the chickens over and over again. I ask Susan what it would take for her to feel better. She wants to go on being angry. Why? Because she thinks it's mean of us that we won't let them catch the chickens. It was really hard scolding them, even though I think it was all very calm, no raised voices. I don't think that they understand that what they're doing is verging on cruelty, they are not able to put themselves in the animals' place, they don't understand that it hurts."

The adults are angry, so they scold and explain. The children do not get it. They may have just been playing with the chickens, the same way they do with their dog or their toys at home, but they are unable to defend or explain their actions, so they feel a powerless rage—despite the fact that Gitte and Jan avoid raising their voices, eventually explain that they are no longer angry, and ask what it would take for the children to feel better.

How would a big sister have scolded? Would she also have insisted on making the children try to empathize with the chicken? Her scolding would certainly not have come from a position of power; as a big sister, she does not have a position of power. Perhaps it is the power aspect, here in particular the adults' power of definition, that makes the children desperate and angry. The adults are defining the event as mean, verging on cruelty. There is no room for the children's point of view.

The adults' condemnation creates an inferno of guilt, anger, despair, and defeat that makes it impossible for the children to learn what the adults want them to learn.

"The adult has captured an innocent guy, but he doesn't care who did it . . . as long as he gets to scold someone." — Boy, 12 years old

Would the adults have reacted differently if they had remembered that until recently neither children nor adults understood that it might be wrong to inflict pain on an animal? In many cultures around the world, that is still the case.

IF THE CHILDREN DO NOT LEARN WHAT THE ADULTS WANT THEM TO LEARN FROM SCOLDING, WHAT DO THEY LEARN?

Let us take a look at another story:

Mads and Jon are cycling in the playground; they run into a flowerpot, and the pot breaks. They laugh and run away. Four adults see the incident from inside. "That's too much!" says one, "Let's go get them." "Let's wait and see if they don't decide to come clean," says another.

A little later, Frank, an early childhood educator who did not witness the incident, walks in with Ali, while he scolds him for breaking the pot.

Mads and Jon are called in. They maintain that Ali broke the pot. The adult: "No, that's not true. I saw you do it, and you just laughed." Jon: "I wasn't laughing. I was trying to brake, but Mads pushed me."

The adult says that it is "really low" to say that Ali did it, and later adds, "You have to pick up the broken pieces and replace the pot." Mads: "How are we supposed to do that?"

Jon is now accompanied out to where Ali is standing and told to apologize. Later he is supposed to talk to Frank, who unfairly scolded

Ali, but he says nothing. When he is asked whether he did, he says, "I
didn't do it. Mads did."

Jon and Mads are sent out to pick up the pieces and told to take
them home in a bag. They are told to bring a new pot for the kindergarten.

A little later, the two boys are talking:

Mads: "We're gonna have to pick up it. We have to buy a new one,
I'm buying a new one, and so are you, Jon."

Mads: "Jon, did you tell them you did it?"

Jon: "Mads, I told them the truth, I think we ought to, isn't that so,
Mads?"

When Mads' dad picks him up a little later, Mads breaks down crying.

The staff's position seems to be:

1. You are not allowed to damage or break the kindergarten's property.
2. If you do it anyway, you have to feel remorse and regret.
3. You have to confess, not lie and put the blame on others.
4. When confronted with the victim, you have to apologize for
   what you did.
5. You have to pay for the damage.

This pattern corresponds more or less with the views of most people.
Whether it leads to the desired results when used with young children, and
what the costs may be, is not very well described in pedagogical theory. This
seems to be a non-theorized practice field, which is not really addressed in
pedagogical training and therefore left to "conventional wisdom."

The boys' reactions suggest that the approach is inadequate. The boys
are not sorry for what they did; they are laughing. They do not confess,
but blame someone else. They are very reluctant to apologize and do not
really see how they might replace what they broke. (After the development project, the staff had a very different view; see p. 149).

A story from a different culture points to the possibility of very different reactions. Two Argentine early childhood education students were
interviewed shortly before their return to Argentina. They liked Denmark,
but one thing puzzled them: "The Danes talk so much about whose fault
something is." "Don't Argentines?" "No, but I guess it's because we are a
developing country. We have so much to do. We don't have the time." Is it
a waste of time to look for the culprits and make them confess and repent?
Might the energy be used in a more constructive way?

I clearly remember the shame and the blushing when, at 13, I was
caught as a co-conspirator in placing thumb tacks on an otherwise beloved

English teacher's chair. I have never since placed hidden thumb tacks on teachers' chairs, but is that because I was caught and scolded—or maybe in spite of it? My relationship with the English teacher was ruined, and I never became fond of English lessons again, for now she had seen the dark recesses of my soul. I had failed. What sounded like so much fun in the books was embarrassing and sad in real life. What if we had not been caught? I would have enjoyed two more years of English.

What if Mads and Jon had not been caught—would their moral development have been arrested?

The American scholar Urie Bronfenbrenner demonstrates in his book on the ecology of human development (Bronfenbrenner, 1979) that children become selfish from attending institutions—at least in competitive societies. Does scolding perhaps foster selfishness? Well, maybe. Mads and Jon are trying to protect themselves by blaming Ali and each other.

By scolding we hope to make the children more considerate and socially minded. Perhaps we achieve the opposite: The children act inconsiderately and without a social conscience.

CHILDREN'S ALTERNATIVES TO SCOLDING

Kindergartners

The children in the project kindergarten were asked individually, "What do you think the adults should do instead of scolding?" Henning answered, "They shouldn't scold. If they had to say something, they should say it softly and gently, not all harsh."

No children disagreed with Henning. Other alternatives were mentioned too, however. As mentioned in Chapter 2, the most common answer is that the adults should "just say it in a normal way."

What does this "just" imply? That adults should intervene less, stick to simply saying things in a straightforward way? Act more simply, straightforwardly, normally?

Some children do think it may be necessary to scold other children, but not themselves:

Child: I think the adults should just stop scolding.
Adult: If Anders hit you hard, should we then scold him or not scold him?
Child: Scold him!
Adult: If you hit Anders hard, should we scold you or not scold you?
Child: You should not scold me.

On the one hand, the children learn that scolding is necessary; on the other hand, they see scolding as so unpleasant that anyone would want to avoid it.

> *Anders:* Well, they should just say "stop." But if they didn't scold it would all just be a mess, if they just said "stop," nothing would happen, really. It works, but scolding is nasty.
> *Jonas:* Somehow I don't think that adults can avoid scolding—they can't simply smile, after all.

Most children, however, would like to see scolding abolished. Not everyone accepts the premise of an alternative, "do instead." This implies that sanctions are a necessary element in the institution.

> *Lasse:* They just shouldn't do it.
> *Tanja:* Leave go.

Simon also does not accept the necessity of sanctions: "They could tell you that you can't do it, instead of scolding. Then you'd learn it better, and you wouldn't get so upset."
Frederik and Jonas prefer other sanctions to scolding:

> *Frederik:* Send them outside.
> *Jonas:* I would do the same as Frederik.
> *Adult:* Just send them into the playground?
> *Jonas:* Yes, well, of course with their outdoor clothes on.

Barbara replies with a utopia, "Then they should just think that the children were nice."
Like many other children, Barbara seems to take scolding as a sign that the adults think the children are stupid, despite the fact that the adults actually try hard to tell the children that it is their actions, not the children themselves, that are the target of the scolding.
Amalie says, "They could be nice to you and tell you that that it probably couldn't be helped."
So, the adults are not supposed to abstain from intervention, but should instead support the child, look to the future and avoid making the child feel guilty.
Some children seem to view scolding as a function of the way life is organized in the kindergarten and of the pedagogical approach:

> *Natasja:* Maybe they could just play with the kids.
> *Sofie:* I think they should always let the children eat in the playrooms and let the children decide for themselves.

Liv: Maybe they could help them, the kids. Tie shoelaces or zip up the
snowsuit. . . . Teach them some things that they had learned.

Children want adults who are fun and playful—the most direct opposite
of scolding adults. According to Emil: "They could be happy, they could
also be nice."

Cathrine says that the children feel offended when they are scolded.
When asked what the adults should do instead of scolding she says, "The
adults might apologize—'cause the kids don't understand why they're always being scolded."

And Stine's suggestion would probably reduce scolding considerably:
"Instead, they should ask the children if they wanted to be scolded."

Amin sees scolding as an interruption of play. He says, "I think the
adults should just tell us not to do it again. And then they could just leave,
and we could go on playing."

Malthe also sees the adults as a disturbing factor: "I think there should
be fewer adults."

Finally, Jesper's radical solution: "I think they should just get another
job rather than scolding."

This upset Malthe, who was sitting in on Jesper's interview (with
Jesper's permission): "Nooo—would you want the adults to quit because
they scolded, then there wouldn't be any left."

Jesper: "Well, that might be nice sometimes, then the kids could decide."

As is evident from these quotes, kindergartners are fully capable of
making valuable contributions through interviews. They propose a number of alternatives to scolding. They are able to describe what sort of adults
they would like, envision utopias, and articulate specific criticism.

A large majority would like to see scolding abolished and think that
it could be eliminated or replaced with something else. Most think that
the adults should "say it in a normal way." Some think that changes in the
pedagogical approach, in the adults' view of the children, or in the number of adults would reduce the amount of scolding. Three, with regret,
find scolding indispensable.

These children attend the project kindergarten, where the staff put
scolding on the general agenda in order to improve child–adult relations.
The children's replies might suggest that their institution is characterized by
a great deal of scolding and by severe scolding. Other data in fact indicate
that the child–adult relations in the place are good and that the pedagogical
approach involves many features that aim to reduce the amount and severity of conflicts and, thus, the amount of scolding. It is therefore probably fair
to say that even the friendliest and most open institution has many sanctions, and that the children in such an institution gain the courage and understanding necessary to criticize conditions and imagine improvements.

The children's replies showed that the debate about relations and scolding has reached them, too, and that they may take part as qualified contributors. Their points of view are more radical than the adults' views, and their alternatives clearer. They are, after all, the ones who know "how the shoe fits." The pedagogical development that took place in the project institution during and after the project would not have been as far-reaching and as consistent without the children's input. Indeed, one of the key results of the project was the staff's newfound awareness that continued development is only possible if the children's opinions and suggestions continue to be expressed and taken seriously.

Children in After-School Centers

Let us now compare the kindergartners' statements with some older children's replies to a different question: "What is good scolding?"

> "Would you please stop that before it goes wrong, for your own safety—like if you put something on the power drill." (8-year-old)
> "Won't you please stop teasing the younger kids . . . or say it in a nice way." (11-year-old)
> "Good scolding is when it is said calmly." (10-year-old)
> "Calmly: 'Don't do that, won't you please apologize, what you did there was not so good.'" (9-year-old)
> "Just tell them not to do it again. It is better to say it calmly." (8-year-old)

Here the children were not asked to come up with alternatives, but to describe "good scolding." Three children use the word *calmly*. Three examples mention *please*. Good scolding: An appeal is made, but not a command; the adult is polite ("please"), and not patronizing; he or she speaks in a calm and friendly manner, not in a loud and angry way. In summary, good scolding equals nonscolding.

HOW MAY WE UNDERSTAND THE CHILDREN'S EXPERIENCES AND REACTIONS?

The Copenhagen children from the after-school center who were involved in this study agree with the kindergartners from the project kindergarten.

In the project kindergarten the staff had long debates about what the children had said. During one of these discussions Lillian said, "When I think about it ["saying it in a normal way"] it is because I see that Christina is able to say it in a normal way. And the thing about it being too harsh,

I have said that, too, I'm thinking: Can the kids actually take this, is it violence or abuse, does my face look like that . . . it's true, there's no doubt they know I am serious, but am I too explicit, can we overdo it?" Christina: "Too explicit?" Lillian: "Yes, too explicit." Christina: "Yes, I think that's a possibility."

There is a stark contrast between the children's experience of scolding as very intense—dangerous eyes, sad inside—and what they want instead—softly, nicely, gently, calmly. The children are not looking for small changes or minor adjustments, they are hoping for a new culture: They want to see a culture of control and sanctions as regulation mechanisms replaced by a culture that is based more on dialogue and guidance.

Similar contrasts are found in other types of institutions, such as schools or nursing homes. The residents in nursing homes want to be treated with respect and kindness—just like the preschoolers.

> A kindergartner told her friend, who went to another kindergarten, that she did not like the way the children were treated. Her friend simply said, "In my kindergarten, we're not treated at all."

Perhaps this expresses what nursing home residents and institutionalized children are really looking for: to be spoken with, not to; to be seen as active participants, not treated. In some institutions, children and residents have become participants and have stopped being consumers or individuals in forced placement. But if the hierarchy, divisions, and sanctions that characterize relations between staff and "detainees" are dissolved or pushed into the background, will the institutions cease to be institutions? At this point, suffice it to say that if we see hierarchy, dichotomy, and sanctions as essential pillars in the construction of the institution, their diminishing importance would mean the beginning of the *de-institutionalization of our institutions*. An institution that no longer or only rarely imposes sanctions, where the residents can come and go as they wish, and where life is no longer structured according to fixed schedules by the staff is no longer an institution in the dominant sense of the word.

But so far, the project kindergarten has remained an institution. Many children perceive scolding as unavoidable, like the red traffic light, something that is simply there. Scolding is almost a law of nature. It is the way of the world. Hardly any children think to question scolding.

Once they are asked for alternatives, however, the floodgates open, and the children come up with plenty of alternatives to scolding.

The inherent pain in the children's perception of scolding as both unavoidable and unbearable is suddenly lifted when the scolders begin to ask the children about their perception of scolding and ideas for alterna-

tives. This makes it possible to voice the unbearable and question the unavoidable. The development in the project kindergarten really got off the
ground when the staff began to ask the children about scolding. From that
day on, the legitimacy of the sanctions—and, thus, the traditional institutionalization—was under scrutiny.

That is the day that the floodgates opened. "Say it in a normal way
instead," was what most children wanted. So far, we have interpreted this
to mean in a normal voice and without the facial expressions and body
language that the children see as typical aspects of scolding. But it may
also be interpreted as a request for the adults to tell them what they want
in an open and straightforward way. Do the children feel that scolding is
a closed form of communication, that scolding has a hidden content between the lines? That instead of saying what they want from the children,
the adults are saying what they do not want—and that, instead of saying
things straight, they speak through the distorting filter of anger?

I have mentioned the opening of the floodgates twice now. But can
we say more about who or what it is that closes the floodgates? Perhaps
the majority of children never or rarely do anything to make the adults
scold. A girl who thought there was a large amount of scolding in her institution was asked if this was because the children did things they were
not supposed to. She answered, "No, because of course you don't want to
get scolded." Many children do what the adults want them to—initially
in order to avoid being scolded, later because they internalize the adults'
wishes and make them their own. But some children do not take this path.
Some give up trying to establish close bonds with adults and shut themselves off. Others may harbor rebellious thoughts and hopes, like a girl
who said, after having scolded an adult, "It's not like it used to be, damn
it—the old adults, they would listen to me. I hardly ever ask for help. And
then when I do, he says no!"

Another girl had also scolded an adult. "What happened then?"
"Then I was scolded even more."

These girls, and other children like them, stage small-scale rebellions
and harbor latent rebellious impulses, which do not, however, become
consciously noticed until scolding is put on the agenda.

A student in the project group said:

To me, they're almost like children living under a dictatorship.
They're fenced in. You know the fence is there, and it is not an issue
for debate. But still, you dream of freedom. That is sort of how I see
these children; they don't openly question these things; they just
don't do the things that are not allowed, and that way they avoid
being scolded. But still, they are keenly aware of how it affects them

and how they would prefer to live. I see it almost as an underground movement. . . . There is definitely no real room for personality and privacy, if you can put it that way. If you have to please everybody all the time, every day—that is complete self-annihilation. What a thought, who could live like that!

As already mentioned, the children's criticism is generally so radical that it points to a complete shift in culture based on a de-institutionalization as it affects three of the main pillars of institutionalization: dichotomy, hierarchy, and sanctions. In this view, a partial adjustment in the form of making scolding more civilized, as in the development project and the public focus on scolding, is bound to set off a process that will eventually lead to a genuine culture change unless it is stopped.

But the picture is not unambiguous. Let us take a closer look at one of these ambiguities. In Chapter 2, which described the development project, we wrote that some children prefer being scolded by an adult who is also "stern." When asked, "Whom do you prefer to be scolded by?" Liv answered, "Lillian—but she can also be stern and have a temper." And Dennis said, "You, Malene. You're better at it. Because you lose your temper."

Why is that?

Cold scolding contains only a rejection. Emotional scolding, however, has another side to it as well: It includes both rejection and involvement. When the scolder is furious, he or she may be seen as overwhelming; and if the relationship is weak, this may be frightening. But if the child has a good personal relationship with the scolder, the scolding may also be seen as an affirmation of the relationship.

Tough scolding may also be seen more as a punishment and "payment," and less as moralizing reproach. Punishment can be cleansing and liberating—if you "did it," that is, and if you developed a sense of guilt. The guilty person needs atonement and purification.

The worst scenario is when the scolder speaks softly, but looks angry. Recurring and substantial disagreement between expression and words makes the statement impossible to decode. The expression pushes the child away, but the words may be friendly and encouraging. That may make some children prefer someone who is openly stern!

A stern scolder may also be less demanding. If the child simply shows signs of being upset, the case may well be closed, while less stern scolders sometimes also want children to understand why they are being scolded, and perhaps why they should feel sorry for the other child (or the chicken). As we have seen, this may pose difficulties for younger children.

The child's attention, volition, and desire are focused on the present and the immediate future. The adult often directs his or her attention toward the past—especially in connection with scolding—and, for example, the child's reasons for acting in this way or that. The child rarely—and much more rarely than adults—has any conscious knowledge of his or her reasons for acting in a certain way. The child acts on the basis of impulses and urges, desires, wishes, and volition. Exploring exactly what happened, and why, is a difficult, meaningless, and irrational process for a child—who lacks the adult's ability to rationalize after the event.

Remember what Malthe said in a previous chapter: "I don't really remember if I hit anyone, or if I did it by accident."

CHAPTER 8

How Does Scolding Affect Children?

> Ill-founded praise makes [one] haughty, proud and awakens a love of self, just as strong reproach will make [one] despondent, frightened, unwilling, and often even more simpleminded and less astute, but the greatest praise should simply be: that is good. —*Brahetrolleborgs Skolevæsens Instrux*
> *(Directive for the Educational System of Brahetrolleborg)*

This quote talks about the ill effects of strong reproach. Since reproach is an element in scolding, we may see this as the earliest example of any writing in Danish educational history about the negative effects of scolding. It would take many years before the thread was continued.

Why this delay? The school does not like to see itself as an institution characterized by punishment and sanctions. It is far more "trendy" to talk about democracy, interpersonal interactions, a reorganization of the learning environment, close bonds with the local community, and so on.

Preschool facilities are also reluctant to talk about control and punishment; autonomy and creativity are more popular topics for discussion. But a critical approach and a daily awareness of sanctions and control are prerequisites to autonomy and creativity.

Criticism needs to have a basis, a point of departure: a vision and, if possible, memories of a life outside the institution. For that purpose, we include here an excerpt from Romanian-born early childhood educator Ana-Magdalena Pertea's critical observations of modern institutionalized life compared with her memories of her own childhood in the 1970s. The observations and reflections were written down for the purposes of the Scolding Project:

> A little boy sits quietly in a corner of the playroom. An early childhood educator asks him, "Are you bored?" The boy does not reply and shyly casts his eyes down. In his closed hand he hides his treasure: a small colored bead. He is the only one who knows about it. "What have you got there?" asks the adult. "A bead! Oh, it's beautiful. It is a little dangerous if you put it in your mouth, you know. It is better if you don't play with it. I'll keep it for you, okay?"
>
> The boy does not reply. He looks at his open, sweaty palm.

"Mia, what are you doing here?" an adult asks the little girl, who is standing still, leaning against a tree, her mouth wide open, her eyes half shut in the strong sunlight.

"I'm playing," she says, without hesitation.

"That's good," says the adult with a smile, and walks away.

Mia had decided for herself that she did not want to go to kindergarten. She just played on her own, walked up and down the stairs: first one step at the time; later in summer, two; and later she tried giant leaps—three steps at a time!

Sometimes she liked to watch a soft caterpillar on a fresh, deep-green leaf and touch the bug's delicate, transparent coat, which covered the black and green mosaic on its back.

She would also spin like a top, turning her skirt into a floating circle. This sometimes made her so dizzy that she fell down on the grass. While she lay there, resting, she would gaze at the fleet of whipped cream clouds and their mysterious transformations in the sky—a suspended ocean.

She loved to feel, with her eyes closed, the heat of the sun on her body, just like a lizard after a long, cold winter.

When she was at grandma's she would climb up to visit the cat in the attic. It had kittens, and she helped them find their way to their mom. She would watch them for hours.

Before she went to bed she watched the shadows play on the wall and dreamt, with her eyes wide open, about all the wonders on the earth: about trees, birds, and about the sky . . . about herself.

> Be bored,
> Little princess.
> Take the blue glass marble in your hand
> And see the blue world inside.
> Be bored,
> Little rascal,
> Splash in the water a million times
> Until
> You are grown.
> Be bored, my child.
> Be bored
> Like me
> When I was little.

With these intensely sensual memories, Ana-Magdalena Pertea is not rejecting the institution. She chose to be an early childhood educator. But by daring to hold on to her memories and articulating them, she clarifies the conflicts inherent in institutionalization. Her memories may be her critical guide in her effort as an early childhood educator in an institution. Placing a child into a kindergarten or a school—even the freest one—is a huge intervention, which may have negative effects. If staff and parents would only realize this instead of holding institutionalization up as an unambiguous benefit for the child, the preschool and school years might become a positive experience for the child.

In any conversation with a child, the word *decide* will come up, usually many times. This reflects the fact that placement in an institution is always a dramatic interference with the child's autonomy. Let us therefore take a closer look at the concept of power.

POWER

According to British sociologist Anthony Giddens, power is the ability to make a difference in the world, to change the state of things (Giddens & Held, 1982). Mia was exercising power when she helped the kittens. She had the desire as well as the ability to help them, and she chose to do it. Power in this sense makes a person a subject and an agent in his or her own life. Power is always restricted, not least by other people's power. Mia is able to do many things, but not everything she wants. She is little, has to come home for dinner, and so on.

The institutionalization of a child typically constitutes a dramatic restriction of the child's power. The child's status as subject and agent in his or her own life is diminished.

Children may have great deal of *dominance* in an institution. They take up room; they run, shout, and cry. But the adults decide where the children are allowed to do their running and their shouting. The power inequity inherent in the institutional logic leads to protests, resistance, resignation, or adjustment in the children. The protests and resistance are met with the exercise of power: force, manipulation, and other forms of social control, with scolding, as previously demonstrated, being the most common. Thus, traditional scolding is typically a response to children's exercise of power or their reactions to the way that institutionalization restricts their power. Scolding causes new reactions, which in turn spark more scolding and other forms of social control.

This is all totally logical and predictable. The interesting question, therefore, is not why there is so much scolding in one institution or another, but why there are institutions with very little scolding or with a different form of scolding. Earlier in this book we offered some partial explanations for the siginificant changes that took place in the project kindergarten during and after the development project. Perhaps the key explanation—to stick with the terminology of power—is that the distribution of power in traditional scolding, where the scolder has almost total power and the child is stripped of power completely, has shifted: The scolded child is no longer restrained, forced to look the scolder in the eyes, and robbed of his or her possibility to explain. Power also involves the ability to define reality, to create meaning and understanding through action, to express one's views, and to be heard.

Before we move on, we will look at two scolding episodes. The first shows a normal "small-scale" scolding, which nevertheless involves a restriction of the child's meaningful act, creation of self and world, and exercise of power. The intervention does lead to a heartfelt protest. But, after all, the early childhood educator has to protect the other children. Such small-scale incidents, like this one between an early childhood educator and a child, take place on a daily basis in most institutions:

> *Adult:* Michael, don't throw wood off the ship, it's dangerous, you might hit someone on the ground.
> *Michael:* But I have to, otherwise I can't get rid of it!
> *Adult:* Take it down gently, then.
> *(Michael walks over and drops another piece of wood).*
> *Adult (in an angry tone of voice):* Michael, I just told you not to throw wood off the ship!
> *Michael:* Nooo!! I want to!

And the next episode, recorded by Lone, the early childhood educator involved in it:

> Some children are sitting with Lone, drawing. Amin comes in and doodles on Malthe's drawing. Malthe gets upset. Lone says it is mean of Amin and tells him to find an eraser so that he can erase the doodles. He refuses. A little later he wants to do a jigsaw puzzle together with Lone, but he also teases her. Malthe also begins to tease Lone, who tells him to stop. Amin says, "You can't make me, you turd!" Henning adds, "Mega-face!" Lone asks if she should start saying nasty words to them, too. Amin says, "I don't care, you dick!" Malthe starts in, "Lone is in love with dick, Lone is in love with dick." Liv laughs. While a colleague of Lone's is present they stop. Afterward Amin continues. Lone is insecure, but says to Amin that the two of them had better have a talk in the staff room. "I don't want to, you turd shit!" Another colleague overhears the latter exchange and tells Amin to behave. Amin is about to cry. So is Lone. Malthe asks Lone if she would help him erase the doodles. Liv asks if Lone wants a book that she has drawn.

Later Amin says that he is scolded often at home. During the talk he slouches and looks sad.

The story illustrates that the language in a kindergarten can be quite rough and may easily cause scolding. Both stories also illustrate that surveillance, control, and adult regulation are present in most institutional contexts.

The adults could probably have chosen a more constructive approach. The fact remains, however, that it is difficult for children to steer clear of adult intervention and scolding, and that it is similarly difficult for the adults to avoid "strong reproach."

How does it affect Michael, Amin, and other children if they are frequently stopped, reproached, or scolded?

Do Michael's "Nooo!" and Amin's tears perhaps express their sense of powerlessness?

In good institutions, like the project kindergarten, the adults typically develop a common understanding of guidelines for life within the institution, but what the adults perceive as a flexible expression of these guidelines may well seem to be random and arbitrary abuse to the children, determined by whether the particular adult is "nice" or "strict," and whether he or she is in a foul mood on a given day or miffed at one particular child. To use Gitte's expression, some children may feel that a thousand trip wires are set up all over the place. Not knowing where they are, one is practically bound to trip.

SCOLDING AND LIFE FORCES

What is it that makes us human? Is it our ability to intervene and alter the conditions of our existence? Thinking and self-reflection? The ability to form bonds with others in communities? Volition?

If these capacities are indeed required to make us human, it is crucial to examine how frequent and severe scolding may affect these life forces, as we might call them.

The Ability to Act

Let us turn once more to the little nursery school boy who completes the cumbersome climb onto a chair, just to hear the early childhood educator's loud "Nooo!" as she rushes across the room and picks him up from the chair while she reproaches him: "Don't do that!" The boy turns his face away from her and cries.

He is proud at having climbed so high—under his own steam—and expects appreciation or at least understanding. Instead, he is met with "strong reproach"; his crying may express a sense of powerlessness, made worse by the fact that he is physically lifted up, losing his footing without know-ing what is about to happen to him. He is at someone else's mercy, with no recourse but to turn his face away. There is no room for his thoughts and ex-pressions. On the contrary, scolding typically silences the scolded person's opinions, intentions, and thoughts. If an institutionalized child experiences many interventions of this nature, he or she may come to think that there is no point in taking an initiative or acting to achieve change.

And if one does not think it possible to affect anything or anyone, one will eventually stop trying and instead let others decide what happens.

Integrity and Volition—"I Am Me"

Let us for a moment go back into the home sphere: The teenager's room is a mess. There are reproaches, maybe scolding, repeated requests for a cleanup. "I'll do it later." "It doesn't make any difference." "But it's my room, after all." "I like my mess." All to no avail. The reproach contin-ues, maybe for years. The teenager may say, "It's like torture in my head!" and may take the reproach and scolding as attacks on his or her personal expression. The messy room is a reflection of the messy, pubescent brain. The parents set the standards throughout the house—except for the teen-ager's room. If they seek to impose their standards here as well, the teen may feel threatened in his or her "intimate space."

Erving Goffman, who has studied institutionalization, uses the term *intimate space* to refer to "an inner mental world, an inner identity and will, and an inner place which one may retreat to" (Sørensen, 1991).

The teenager's room represents his or her intimate space. If the teen's arrangements here come under attack, it may seem like an at-tack on his or her intimate space. If the parents have a strong position of power and are able to enforce their demands, the attack will seem particularly severe, which by no means precludes the parents' seeing their reproach as necessary disciplinary measures or boundaries—"for your own good."

Similarly with the preschool child who is scolded, picked up, loses his footing, and can only resort to averting his gaze. The child's gaze is the door to his intimate space; controlling this door means controlling the intimate space. Hence, when the staff in the project kindergarten decided, as part of the development project, that they would never again ask a child to look them in the eyes, they chose to weaken their position of power—relinquish part of it—and loosen their control of the children's intimate space. And a loosening of mind-control may be even more essential than a loosening of external means of control.

The parents' enforcement of their own standards concerning order in the teenager's room and the early childhood educator's intervention with the "chair climber" are also violations of the young person's/child's expressed *volition*, and volition may be the strongest life force of all. It is also the most neglected, which is reflected in the fact that the professional term for the development of volition—*conative development*—is largely unknown (Sigsgaard, 2001).

A comparative study of mother–child relations in three Asian countries states, "What may be seen as negative behavior is simply the children's pursuit of independence" (Botor, 1987).

If a child's expressed will and control over his or her intimate space is frequently under attack, both at home and in the institution or school, the child's integrity—his or her sense that "I am me, separate from you"—will be at risk.

Self-Esteem

The child's sense of worth is strengthened when others see the child as an equal in human terms, treat the child warmly in the institution, and respect the child's expressions and opinions.

Self-esteem suffers if the child is seen as a pre-adult in need of development, treated as a number in the crowd or a "unit" within an organization, if the child's personal rights are not respected, and if the child is unilaterally the *object* of assessment, diagnosis, and sanctions. Assessment may take the form of grades, but it is also a major part of daily life in the preschool institution. In connection with scolding, the adults may judge events that they have only limited knowledge of on the basis of morals that the involved children do not always share. Since the adults hold the power of definition, they perceive themselves as just and the children as unjust, and they see themselves as logical, rational, and sensible in contrast to the children.

If the validity of children's words, actions, and intentions is frequently rejected, these children may end up losing their self-esteem, their sense of validity. This loss of self-validity will also often make them appear, in the words of *Brahetrolleborgs Skolevæsens Instrux* from 1784, "even more simpleminded and less astute."

Jeanette, the deputy director of the kindergarten Glæden (*The Joy*) (discussed in more detail in Chapter 11), says this about the link between scolding and self-esteem:

> It is only because they have been demoted that children can be addressed in the way that adults traditionally use with kindergartners. . . . No one speaks that way to other people.
>
> In choosing *self-esteem, confidence,* and *independence* as our guiding principles, we actually become unable to scold. If the guiding principle in the relationship is to be self-esteem, in principle one cannot scold, since that will

always undermine self-esteem, because in our definition scolding is something that comes from up here, you cannot scold like this (same level), right,
so therefore their self-esteem is threatened if we scold them.

Few early childhood educators share Jeanette's radical point of view. On
the other hand, no one will deny that there is a connection between scolding and self-esteem, and certainly no one would claim that scolding helps
to bolster self-esteem. It does therefore seem reasonable to assume that
scolding may threaten a child's self-esteem.

A number of studies bear this out. Some show that children's development of self-esteem is highly dependent on the parents' respect, approval, and involvement (Coopersmith, 1967). Senior researcher Mogens
Nygaard Christoffersen (2002) at The Danish National Institute of Social
Research says about the effects of physical violence against children that
violent behavior in troublesome youths "may be seen as a consequence of
humiliating or degrading treatment from parents, siblings, schoolmates
and significant others." The child's integrity is attacked on a fundamental
level if the transgressors are the child's parents or others in a key position
for the development of the child's identity and personality.

Scolding and the Society-Building Individual

People constantly create and develop mutual relations. Societies are
systems of relations, so to speak. Like self-esteem, actions for change, and
volition, people's bonding with others represents a fundamental life force.
Interfering with the creation of relations can therefore be a serious matter,
not least if it is related to scolding, as these observations by a kindergarten
intern make clear:

> Sofie admires Mette and wants to sit with her when we work and
> eat. She likes to show the other children the things that Mette has
> made; she may, for example, hold up a drawing and say, "Look what
> Mette has made!" Mette sometimes wonders about this.
>
> When we eat, Sofie often wants to eat the same thing as Mette.
> Generally, it seems that she likes to be able to demonstrate to the
> other children that she and Mette have a bond.
>
> The early childhood educators find this disturbing, and they
> scold Sofie when she contacts Mette in situations where they find the
> contact irrelevant. I find it hard to scold Sofie, as I think that she is
> trying to form a friendship.
>
> At the same time, Sofie has low self-esteem, and that does not
> improve from too much negative contact. But I have at times been

asked to hold Sofie back in her contacts to Mette. How will this affect Sofie's faith in the early childhood educators?

Mette and Sofie often choose to play together when the adults are not telling them what to do.

Here, the adults interfere not only with Sofie and Mette's developing attachment, but also with Sofie's actions, her expression of volition, and her self-esteem.

This type of conflict is not rare. Children seek unequal relations, even if adults seem to think they ought to play only on equal footing. Mette does not mind playing with Sofie despite Sofie's low self-esteem. Maybe right now she needs to feel strong and caring. The socially weaker Sofie may not get too many chances like this during her long institutional life. What, then, is the consequence of the adult's intervention and scolding? Will Sofie maintain the will and courage to try again, or will she stop trying?

Giddens (1992) says, "A strong position of power is often tantamount to the right to violate and take over the private space of the party with less power." In relation to the adults, both Sofie and Mette have weak positions of power. It is hard for them to defend their relationship. Or is it? Even deep inside the adult-run institutions, one finds pockets where the adult control loosens its grip: "Mette and Sofie often choose to play together when the adults are not telling them what to do." This remark concludes the observation.

Couldn't it be that an institution that fosters good relations is a place where there are many such pockets of time and space where the children can unfold their society-building powers?

The previous section was based on the assumption that the fundamental life forces include the ability to change the conditions of one's existence, thinking and self-reflection, volition, and bonding with others in communities. We have shown that they may be damaged in institutions—and families, of course—without any ill intent, and that scolding plays a part in this.

In the following section we will examine these damaging effects more closely.

PSYCHOLOGICAL EFFECTS OF SCOLDING

The primary psychological damages involved are humiliation, guilt, shame, anxiety, rigidity of behavior (psychological reactance), and stress. We will also look at the effect that scolding has on personality features and on the children who are not scolded.

Humiliation

Philosopher K. E. Løgstrup has coined the phrase "the zone of the inviolability," which is related to Goffman's "intimate space." This term describes a zone that every person has and where others have no admission. This zone is usually respected in the normal social life of adults. If on occasion it is violated, this violation is perceived as unpleasant. The violation may be physical, as when another person steps too close. It may also be psychological, as when someone probes into matters that one wishes to keep to oneself.

Løgstrup points out that while adults normally intuitively respect each other's zone of inviolability, that is not the case in relations between children and adults. For example, an adult is fully entitled to reject the reasons that a child offers for his or her actions in a given situation and instead assign motives of a more dubious nature. In relation to other adults, one may have one's doubts about the reasons stated, but one does not question them in public.

A certain reaction suggests that many children experience scolding as a violation of the zone of inviolability: They do not mind talking about scolding, but whenever possible they reply in the third person. The topic appears too unpleasant for them, perhaps also because scolding represents a violation of their integrity.

Initially the children also often deny having been scolded or they underestimate the extent: The others are scolded more. This may also reflect a reluctance to identify with the representation of them that is implied in the scolding. Their self-image is disturbed, perhaps even violated. Hence, they distance themselves from the scolding and may even block it out.

As part of the Scolding Project, early childhood educators who scolded very little—or maybe not at all—were interviewed. Several of them had grown up with parents, early childhood educators, or teachers who also did not scold. One of them (Birgitte) said:

> Scolding and humiliation were always a big deal to my mom. Now it is the grandchildren that cannot be scolded. The main thing about being scolded is humiliation. My mother can't handle that—but sometimes I do scold my own kids. They can be such a pain in the neck that I just can't help it. But I wouldn't dream of scolding anyone else's children.

Guilt and Shame

The research into scolding—extremely limited in scope, and none of it from Scandinavia—focuses on the concepts of *guilt* and *shame*. Let us therefore first draw a distinction between them. *Guilt* may be described as a sense of heavy responsibility, caused by questionable (reprehensible) acts, and *shame* as a strong sense of pain, caused by something that is inappropriate, deeply embarrassing, and almost dishonorable about oneself. One may feel shame about one's looks, one's base instincts, one's sinfulness.

Previously, parents and teachers would often consciously try to make children feel shame: "Shame on you!" "What will the others think?" And children learned to blush, feel ashamed, and be shy. Proneness to shame has to do with "global, painful and devastating experiences in which the self, not just behavior, is painfully scrutinized and negatively evaluated" (Tangney, 1991).

Why would adults go to such great lengths to instill this feeling of shame? They might have at least two reasons:

- In order to make the child adjust to the norms. If you were exactly like everybody else, then there would be nothing to point fingers at, to be ashamed about (but how could one be like all the other, nice people, with this multitude of incontrollable urges and forbidden thoughts inside?). The instilling of shame was a powerful tool for enforcing conformity.
- In order to make the child confess, apologize, repent, ask for forgiveness, feel sinful—even reject him- or herself (consider the bishop's shaming of Alexander in Ingmar Bergman's film *Fanny and Alexander*).

And there is an additional, third reason: Most adults have themselves been taught to feel ashamed.

Shame and guilt are often closely interwoven. When the teacher does not let anyone leave the classroom until the culprit has been found, and no one confesses, it may be because of the notion that by assuming the guilt, one also assumes the shame. Having to pay for a broken flowerpot is one thing, but exposing oneself to public derision may just be too much to bear. Shame can be worse than guilt. Maybe that is why most of the children in the project kindergarten did not like being scolded in front of other children.

But even if shame and guilt are hard to separate, Tangney (1991) still finds it possible to distinguish between two "moral affective styles," where one (guilt-proneness) emphasizes guilt and responsibility, while the other (shame-proneness) emphasizes shame and remorse.

We have suggested how children may be taught to feel shame. But guilt is instilled as well. When a child failed in an endeavor, the adults might say, "Why on earth did you have to climb that ladder in the first place?" or "I told you not to . . ." In other words: If you only had stayed on the ground, if you only had listened, you would not have failed. Ergo, "It's your own fault. You made your bed, now you must lie in it. My hands are clean. Don't tell me I didn't warn you."

A 4-year-old girl once sat with clenched, white-knuckled hands, saying, "It's my own fault, it's my own fault . . ." Over and over again.

The cause? Maybe too much reproach, too many explanations, too many cases of "but don't you see . . ." for one little girl.

Maybe even scolding.

In comparison, consider the preschool early childhood educator who saw two little boys fighting over a shovel in the sandbox and did not ask who had done it, did not tell them it was wrong to fight, and did not scold, but simply asked, casually, what might be done to fix the problem. The boys thought long and hard. "We could go to the swings," said one. "Yes," said the other. And so they went to the swings.

> If students are to learn how to control their own behavior, they need to have the opportunity to
> - make decisions on how to behave
> - carry these decisions through.

This is David Johnson and colleagues' (1992) conclusion regarding an experiment in which schoolchildren spent 30 minutes a day for 30 days practicing the successful mediation/resolution of their own and other students' conflicts. Maybe this sort of practice in self-regulation needs to be a feature already in preschools in order to make a real difference.

But how heavy is this burden of guilt and shame? Let us first consider a story, told by an intern in a Copenhagen preschool, of a very different character from the shovel story:

> A girl comes up to the early childhood educator and tells her that Maja has urinated on the floor. The early childhood educator runs into the playroom, and sees that Maja has peed all over the floor. She begins to scold her and tells her in a loud voice that she must go to the bathroom if she has to pee.
> She does not ask Maja any questions.

Why did Maja urinate on the floor? Is she afraid, angry, sad, anxious—or does she have problems with her bladder control? Does she do the same at home? Does anyone else on the staff have any knowledge about Maja's problem? We do not know.

Maja is young. She will soon forget this little scolding-guilt-shame incident. Or at least, that is the perception of many adults, who see scolding as trivial. Big deal—they were scolded when they were kids.

But what if Maja has a hard time winning the approval and perhaps the friendship of another child? Won't a public focus on her urination problem cause her difficulties?

We do not know, but a few studies have addressed the consequences of shame. An interview survey (Dutton et al., 1995) of 144 North American males with a history of recurrent domestic violence found three potential sources of "shame-proneness":

- Public humiliation by the parents
- Random punishment
- Parental treatment that affected the whole self

The study used the Swedish EMBU test (Perris et al., 1980). [EMBU stands for Egna Minnen Beträffande Uppfostran (*own memories concerning upbringing*).] The 140 men were presented with a number of statements—for example, "As a child, I received corporal punishment or scolding in the presence of others"—which they had to mark as true or false. As mentioned, the study found that guilt and shame appear to play a major role in the transmission of abusiveness from one generation to the next, and that public scolding is one of the three main sources of shame-proneness.

This result matches more thoroughly investigated relations between the corporal punishment of children and these children's tendency to use corporal punishment on their own children later on.

Scolding is mentioned first in the study about the violent men because "memories about being shamed seem more important than memories of corporal punishment in the formation of the violator's personality" (Dutton et al., 1995, p. 128). This does not mean that we can conclude that severe scolding (shaming) is worse than corporal punishment for ordinary children, but there does not seem to be any reason to think that shaming is less damaging to the formation of identity and personality than corporal punishment.

An interesting finding in the project kindergarten confirms this link between scolding and corporal punishment. Some time after the conclusion of the project, Lillian said that current scolding was much less reproachful and less focused on creating guilt. On the same occasion, Lillian mentioned that the children now "rarely use the invitation 'So, slap me.'" Jan said that he was now inclined to believe that scolding is always a mistake. Six months earlier, it was Jan who had written in his journal about the children who had put the chicken into the tub of cold water: "Then I told them I thought they were mean and nasty when they did things like that."

So, once the scolding became less moralistic and guilt-laden, the children stopped saying "So, slap me."

When the children say "So, slap me," do they mean "If I am really so stupid and mean and nasty, then cut to the chase, why don't you just slap me?" or "Since you're already hurting me with your words, why don't you slap me for real?" or "So, I'm guilty. Punish me, why don't you?!" or "Slap me, get it over with, so we can be friends again"?

This subtle change—that the children have almost stopped saying "So, slap me"—signals the beginning of a shift in pedagogical thinking. Knee-jerk scolding is turning into an equally automatic reaction of insight and understanding. Insight and help with achieving change have replaced judgment and punishment. And guilt and shame have diminished.

The Impact of Scolding on Social Relations

A child who is exposed to physical violence risks developing into a person with low self-esteem, which may make it difficult to develop close relations with other people. This is borne out by a study on child abuse. The researchers worked with a group of children, some of whom had been exposed to abuse. They studied the way the children functioned in their natural surroundings, without knowing which of the children had been abused. The study found that the abused children clearly had a lower status in the peer group. They were more frequently involved in fights, and others perceived them as stupid, uncooperative, or aggressive (Salzinger et al., 1993). Unfortunately, verbal violence has not been studied to the same extent, but one might fear that it has similar consequences.

In another study, Joubert (1992) set out to examine the relationship between narcissism and psychological reactance in young people and their parents' parenting style.

High psychological reactance means that a person is quick to feel offended, easily feels his or her freedom threatened, is high-strung, has negative expectations of others, is hotheaded, is prone to "fly off the handle," has "a short fuse," and often gets into fights.

Hong and Page (1989) asked 169 students to describe their parents' behavior on the basis of The Narcissistic Personal Inventory and The Hong Psychological Reactance Scale. The finding was an unambiguous link between scolding and reactance. In their replies, the more reactant students described parents who scolded more and with a stronger than average tendency to use "verbal abuse." These parents also praised their children less than other parents. Others have found links between the chronic anger of children and youth and the experience of coldness and rejection from the parents (Dutton et al., 1995).

The findings by Joubert and others point to some important assumptions:

- Many of the children who are exposed to a great deal of scolding as well as verbal abuse and who receive little positive feedback will develop a high degree of psychological reactance.
- This reactance does not develop overnight, in adolescence, but gradually over time.
- Already as young children some or many of the scolded and abused children must have begun to display reactant behavior.
- They will be acting out, violent, and unpredictable, and will therefore typically be scolded often in preschool settings and in school.
- For the same reasons, they will typically have a hard time establishing and maintaining friendships.
- Since the ability for self-regulation (for example, conflict resolution)—which evolves on the basis of real-life experiences shared with others, primarily in friendships—will be underdeveloped in many of these children, they will typically incur more scolding with time.
- The increasing amount of scolding and the lack of positive feedback, which seems inexplicable and unfair to them, will gradually cause them to assume an almost permanent defensive stance. The psychological reactance is developing. They may slide into frozen loneliness.

The tendency for children who are scolded at home to also be scolded in the institution was borne out in general terms by an American study, where parents' and early childhood educators' relations with children were divided into three categories: secure, avoidant, and ambivalent. Children with a secure relationship to their parents were found to receive more positive attention and less reproach in the institution than other groups. Early childhood educators had the smallest degree of involvement with the children whose parents were distant and avoidant (Howes & Hamilton, 1992).

Other studies have reported similar findings. Three researchers set out to examine the relationship between the parents' disciplinary strategies and children's relations with other children (Hart et al., 1993). In one study they looked at young children's behavior on the playground. They found that children who have difficulty getting along with other children (low peer competence) often have parents who are either authoritarian or laissez-faire.

Other studies (Hart et al., 1993) distinguish between two childrearing strategies, one they term *inductive* and the other *power-oriented*. Induction means going from the individual incident or example to the general: Parents talk with their children, logical conclusions are drawn, and the children's ideas receive attention. In the power-oriented strategy, the parents want immediate behavior changes: They use punishment and scolding and rob the child of possibilities to express him- or herself, or they reward the child for certain behaviors.

This study found a relation between the inductive strategy and the ability to engage in *cooperative self-regulation* (pro-social behavior). It also found a relation between the power-oriented strategy and subversive, destructive behavior, and between power-oriented childrearing and evasive, withdrawing behavior.

What if Maja's subversive, destructive behavior in urinating on the institution floor was related to a power-oriented disciplining strategy at home, so that all she found in the institution was more of the same?

Rigid Behavior—Emerging Reactance

Above, we stated seven assumptions based on Joubert's study of the relation between narcissism/psychological reactance and parenting style. These assumptions had to do with the emergence and development of psychological reactance. Let us now look at a few stories that outline the early stages of a pattern of reactance, which may later become completely entrenched.

After the incident with the chickens that were immersed in cold water, the children were told not to go into the playground without an adult. They did it all the same. Jan felt that Siri was too young to understand that the chickens are living beings. Malene said, "I think that Siri is unable to hear or take in the words, because she is afraid. This is clearly a difficult situation for her, and I see her as a bit of a complicated girl who finds scolding much too painful. So she uses all her energy to keep everything dangerous at bay. That is why she does not hear us or understand; she is too busy defending herself."

A child who takes scolding particularly hard or who is often scolded runs a major risk of feeling like a scapegoat and may eventually stiffen into a certain behavior pattern, which may in turn lead to even more scolding.

Tine has just finished kindergarten when she is interviewed:

Adult: Are you scolded when you are in the kindergarten?
Child: Yes.
Adult: A lot or a little?
Child: A lot.
Adult: Now, if you had to be scolded, Tine, and you could choose who should do it, who would you pick?
Child: Gitte.
Adult: Do you know why you would pick her?
Child: Yes.
Adult: Why?
Child: Because she is the angriest.
Adult: You would pick the one who is the angriest?
Child: It's fun.
Adult: How do you feel when you've been scolded?
Child: I don't know.
Adult: You're not exactly happy, are you?
Child: I don't know.
Adult: What if the adults had to stop scolding, what do you think they should do instead?
Child: Leave the children alone.
Adult: Yes, but, what if we say, for example . . . Do you remember when Muhamed threw that rock at Lisbeth's car?
Child: No.
Adult: But if one of the children threw sand in your face, and an adult saw them do it, what should the adult do?
Child: Get out of there.
Adult: Just walk away? What would you do then?
Child: Beat them up.
Adult: What if they were bigger than you?
Child: I would walk away.
Adult: When Malene asked what the adults should do, you said, "Leave the children alone." Then I thought, if there were a kindergarten where they left the children alone, would that be a better kindergarten?
Child: I think so.
Adult: Do you think such a kindergarten exists?
Child: No.

Tine is a big girl—6 years old. She is rebellious, like all 6-year-olds before her have been in this kindergarten, which does allow the space for that (Sigsgaard, 1993b). She is also scolded quite a bit and thinks that the adults should just get out and leave the children alone, but she has no real hope that they will.

Maybe Tine has stiffened in her attitude toward the adult or insti-tutionalized world as a result of repeated scolding at home and in the institution.

Children who are locked in a power struggle with adults, and who see that the adults aim to control them, even though—and perhaps especially when—the children offer resistance, will be hard to reach for an adult. The resistance risks stiffening into a pattern that might eventually come to define these children's personalities. Resistance will often be passive. The children may eventually stop making decisions for themselves, because they consider it pointless, but they do protest and may respond fiercely if others want to tell them what to do (Paul, 1991).

It is easy to imagine the problems they may experience later, as adults.

As we move towards the end of this section, let us consider a small study that raises certain ethical issues (Pfiffner & O'Leary, 1989). In the study, 40 children aged 18 to 31 months were exposed to two kinds of scolding:

- Immediate, short, and firm
- Delayed, long, and gentle

If the children were scolded immediately after their offense, and if the response was resolute and brief, there were fewer transgressions but more negative affect.

So, if children are scolded in a way that really gets through to them, and if it happens promptly, then it works. They will not offend again. But they also get angry, furious, or despondent—and they cry.

The studies suggest that this "negative affect" may build up in the mind, much like heavy metals build up in a person's body. And suddenly, a person may have become allergic to nickel. Or scolding.

> A woman tells us that when she was 7 or 8, she had a dachshund; the dog was her dearest companion. When they played, the dog would be Robin to her Batman. One day, the dog ate a small corner of the carpet, and the girl's mother scolded the dog and hit it. "My relationship to my mother was never the same again," says this now 60-year-old woman.

A single outburst of disciplinary violence had altered the nature of the most crucial social relation for this girl when she was only 7 or 8. How is this possible?

Fear and Anxiety

Hitting and scolding the dog, a defenseless animal, the girl's best friend, was like an attack on the girl herself. A mother is supposed to protect her child. Without the parents' protection, the child is lost. The parents protect their child because they love him or her as their child. A child who loses the parents' love must fear losing their protection as well.

The girl knew that the dog was not chewing on the carpet because it was evil or bad, looking for trouble or doing it on purpose, but simply because it was a dog. Because it was what it was, it lost the mother's love and protection.

The girl might not have been conscious of this, but a distance may have opened up between her and her mother. The trust, which had probably been jeopardized at times, and which was therefore fragile, had been compromised. The girl was afraid of being herself around her mother; she would have to play her part and be the daughter that her mother wanted, so that she would not be abandoned.

A study of 2- to 3-year-olds in Japan, Thailand, and the Philippines investigated the children's greatest fears: farm animals, imaginary creatures, dark places, and punishment. When the children were frightened, they would typically cling to their mom or dad (Botor, 1987). If we add all this up, we get the following:

Scolding and punishment frighten children. Their natural tendency when scared is to cling to their mother, but she is the one doing the scolding, and in doing so she is pushing the child away from her. This causes additional anxiety, and the child is frustrated—unable to act on his or her natural impulses. The people who are supposed to shield the child from anxiety and comfort the child are instead the source of an anxiety from which the child can find no shelter. This means that repeated and/or severe scolding may damage the child's fundamental trust (think of a child instinctively shielding his or her face with an arm).

So, severe scolding may be perceived as a threat of the loss of love, and it may push the child away at a time when the child's impulse would be to cling to the parent. Nevertheless, many children in the development project say that if they have to be scolded severely, they prefer to have their parents carry out the "sentence." Why is that?

The answer may be that a well-developed parent–child relationship implies a basic trust that is not permanently shaken by even a rather severe scolding: "Mom/dad is furious with what I did, but I know that they love me."

In an institution things are often, but not always, different. The basic nature of the institution is indifference; if one child is not there, someone else will be. The adults are replaced or are not "at work." Where the indifference is greatest, scolding may be especially serious because it is a simultaneous expression of emotional distance and rejection. But many places manage to combat the institutional indifference and make the children feel important and loved. All children may not feel equally loved, and not equally by all the adults, but still. . . . One of the findings in the development project was that children prefer being scolded by an adult with whom they have a close personal relationship—probably because the children know that this close relationship is not shaken, even by severe scolding, and because the children themselves will hold fast to the relationship and not be forced by doubts and ambivalence to distance themselves from the adults, as the girl with the dog did with her mother.

IN THIS SECTION we have focused on the anxiety caused by a number of threatening childhood situations that have hampered or prevented the formation of fundamental trust. Frequent incidents of this nature in a family will produce a form of behavior that tends to cause the child to be scolded a great deal in the institution as well; but there are institutions that are able to instill some of the trust that the child has not been able to develop at home.

The anxiety that springs from a lack of fundamental trust may be exacerbated by guilt-based anxiety caused by an overly guilt-oriented upbringing, and underneath these two culturally induced—or, at least, culturally intensified—forms of anxiety lies the ontological anxiety: the existential angst that springs from the human condition of being a living person who is fated one day to die and lose everything.

Scolding and Personality Features

In the previous section on the impact of scolding on social relations, we introduced the concept of reactance to describe a person who is always watchful and ready to "strike back." And before that, we talked about a pattern of resistance.

Let us now take a closer look at the impact that scolding may have on a child's personality.

Previously, we described how two boys knocked over a flowerpot, laughed, and ran away. They tried to lie their way out of the whole business and fingered an already somewhat weak boy.

They are caught, "found guilty," and punished: After being scolded, they must apologize and replace the flowerpot. The hope is that they will learn not to behave like that. But what if it is the other way around? The boys were not born yesterday. They have been in trouble before. They may believe that when one gets in trouble, one is judged and punished. They probably also know that this only happens if one is caught. So, the point has to be not to get caught. And many perpetrators are not caught. The kids run off, pretend nothing happened, and cover up their tracks. But this time it is harder. The flowerpot is big, and it shatters with a great crash. They are afraid of the anger of the adults. So, they have to lie, and even go as far as to put the blame on someone else.

The two may have long since learned to lie outside the kindergarten; nevertheless, the pattern of response in the kindergarten in itself is enough to produce the actual offenses: the shirking of responsibility, the lie, and the false accusation.

So, when asked what one learns in kindergarten or school, it may be fair to say that one learns to shirk responsibility, lie, and put the blame on others. Will any reader be able to honestly say they have never done that? Some have done it many times, and in that case it may eventually become a pattern, so that one's first impulse, even as an adult, is always to pretend that nothing happened if one has made a mistake.

Perhaps the most important outcome of the development project is that the children in the project kindergarten may now breathe more freely and no longer have to lie and run away from responsibility. That sort of behavior will still occur. Children have a life outside the kindergarten, after all, and they do not change their behavior overnight. But the trend is clear: the less scolding, the fewer transgressions.

> Nina was bad. She had been told so many times by so many different people—family, neighbors, schoolmates. It was a fact that she had long since accepted. Whether she had been born bad, or whether she had been good once, before she turned bad, was not evident from the verdict.
>
> In her exercise book she wrote on page after page: "Nina is bad." She did not write: "I am bad." For she did not know the nature of her badness. She did not know when or why she was bad, until she was told. "Now you're being bad, Nina. Bad again." Her face would turn red, and she would mumble a confused apology. Eventually she stopped apologizing. For even her apologies were considered bad. (Thorup, 2001)

The Child Bystanders

The concept of "child bystanders" arose during the project and was used to describe the other children who were almost always present during scolding. These children saw and heard what went on and were asked to describe the events in All the Way Around processes. But how did the scolding actually affect them?

At a time when Rebekka had just left the kindergarten and entered first grade, she said that she could not remember whether she was scolded in kindergarten or whether any of the adults scolded her more than others did. Later, when asked if children often do things they're not supposed to, Rebekka replied, "No, because they don't want to be scolded." A 4-year-old boy was asked whether he was often scolded. He answered, "No, 'cause I do what the adults say." Both children clearly express that scolding works. They experience it, they wish to avoid it, and they know how to avoid it. But why is it so unpleasant that Rebekka is unable to recall it the day after she left kindergarten?

When corporal punishment was abolished, *classroom management* became a new discipline. Particularly difficult students were removed from the class, and behaviorist courses for teachers taught behavioral regulation. Teachers realized that if one or a few students were singled out—for example, by being scolded in class—it had a preemptive effect on the rest. They became compliant and obedient—like Rebekka and the 4-year-old. This phenomenon was referred to as the *ripple effect.*

A Norwegian study described the long-term ripple effect:

> [There is a] tendency, which is often seen in connection with the recall of negative experiences such as assaults, rejection, violence, ridicule, etc.: Assaults on other, weak students occur just as frequently as memories about assaults etc. on oneself. Attacks on weak, defenseless individuals seem to be something that we remember for many years. (Dugstad, 1992)

Does this stem from the pain caused by one's inability to help the victim (powerlessness) or from one's identification with the victim (compassion) or from one's fear for one's own safety caused by the punishment? The story about the girl whose mother punished the dog demonstrates that the effect can be very powerful indeed.

Dugstad (1992) relates an incident of her own experience:

> During a lesson, I was admonishing one of these troublemakers very loudly. The troublemaker looked slightly concerned, but suddenly the girl next to her, a blonde girl, burst into tears: "I get so scared when you talk like that. I am vulnerable and sensitive, says my mother."

So, scolding has a double effect: It affects both the scolded child and the child bystanders—"the silent observers, " as they were called in a project under the Welfare Program (Højlund, 2001). Højlund seems to think that the effect on the bystanders may even be stronger than the effect on the targeted child.

Scolding and Stress

In recent years, stress in schools and institutions has received a great deal of attention. Useful considerations have been brought forward concerning the link between stress on the one hand and the noise level, the cramped space, the struggle for adult attention, and the tightly scheduled format of the day on the other. But it is also possible that the psychological climate itself may play a key role. The acclaimed British educator A. S. Neill was very aware of this. When there were visitors to the Summerhill School, he told them to walk around and sense the atmosphere, the air, and the climate. The key thing to him was the way people treat each other, that intangible quality; much is forgotten, but the learning that all students take with them when they leave the school will always stay with them and transfer to new settings.

A small incident from a kindergarten highlights the stressful aspect of scolding: An early childhood educator asked the children what they would do if one day the adults just weren't there. "Jump on the tables" and "Bring water into the doll corner" were some of the first suggestions. But when she asked one of the most frequently scolded children, he thought for a while, and then he said, "I would relax, for there would be no one there to scold us."

Noise studies often highlight the fact that children sometimes cover their ears or retreat into remote corners or shrubbery. Judging by what the children tell us, this behavior is not just about the decibel level—it may have more to do with the quality of the noise, the anger, the reproach, the tone, which can boost adrenaline levels and cause a physical restlessness, a condition of stress. This may lead to new clashes and conflicts, which in turn cause even more scolding. In this way, too, scolding is a self-fuelling process.

On the other hand, if scolding levels can be brought down, with the resulting reduction in stress levels for children as well as adults, the institution or classroom will appear less cramped.

This is not to say that space in itself means nothing. If preschools, kindergartens, and schools were to suddenly, by magic, get 50% more space, the amount of scolding would probably be reduced—but there would still be places where scolding was commonplace and places where scolding was rare or nonexistent. Moving play and learning outdoors to a greater extent would probably also have a beneficial effect on the amount of scolding. The same would be the case if more children experienced more time, calm, joy, and love in their families. But there would still be major differences in the mental environment created by the adults from one institution to another.

CHAPTER 9

Adults' Perception of Scolding and Children's Rights

This chapter examines how adults feel about scolding.

This was already briefly touched on in Chapter 2, where we wrote that all the adults in the project kindergarten felt slightly bad after a great amount of scolding. We also wrote that the "veterans" felt a special responsibility for the spirit and culture of the place and were therefore especially aware of any transgressions requiring a reprimand. "Newcomers," however, had a harder time figuring out the norms and rules and were therefore sometimes more reluctant to scold than the veterans felt was appropriate. This topic is explored in more depth in the section below from a learning perspective: The veterans teach the newcomers to scold.

We are also going to look at changes in the perception of scolding during the project period and the consequences this had for the children's rights.

"SCOLDING IS NASTY"

Let us first see how the adults in the project kindergarten replied to the question, "How do you feel after you have scolded someone?"

L: I consider whether it was reasonable, and I check how the child is doing, whether the child is upset. I feel a little bad. Sometimes I find a colleague or someone else to discuss it with, and I guess I do that because I don't feel so good about it.

G: On days when I feel that I have done a lot of scolding, I don't feel good; I might go over it in my head even after I get home. It depends how harsh it was. The harsher, the worse I feel.

M: It depends on the harshness. I don't feel bad afterward. I try to do something nice, like stroke the kid's hair or something.

B: Generally, I am a little upset afterward. Other times, I'm not, because it was deserved, most times it's deserved. But the more worked up I get, the more upset I am afterward; if I'm very upset afterward, I may even need a cigarette break.

F: Sometimes I am sad, but sometimes I forget about it, because I don't take it so seriously.

F: I don't like to scold, but sometimes you have to. If I haven't scolded anyone, then it's like I haven't been at work, then I've just been enjoying myself.

S: It depends how the child takes it. If the child is very upset or is mad at me, then I wonder if maybe I went too far. But generally, I don't like to scold.

T: I get irritated. If it is a "conflict" that was resolved successfully, then I can smile at it. When you look at it from a distance, it's often sort of amusing.

The staff feels "a little bad," "not so good"; they are "upset," "sad," and "irritated," at least if the scolding was severe. Only one person says, "I don't feel bad afterward." No one expresses relief or joy after scolding, as in, "nice to get it off one's chest," "letting it out," and certainly not "getting even." It may be that such feelings are less prominent than the reported discomfort, but it may also be that they are unacceptable and therefore unmentionable, perhaps practically unthinkable. The early childhood educators' active choice of scolding as a development focus, however, makes it unlikely that such proscribed feelings play any major role.

The staff is also asked whether they like to be scolded. No one does.

At the conclusion of the development project, some of the adults were asked again how they felt about scolding:

L: If I have done a lot of scolding, I don't feel good immediately afterward. It's not nice, but pretty soon I begin to analyze what I said and did, and then it soon blows over. . . . It's not okay if it turns into a bawling-out, but I have found an approach that works for me.

G: I certainly don't feel like it's every day I do any real scolding. I think it's that most of it happens through dialogues that don't make one's stomach clench up; it's a more equitable contact. For example, with the fruit the other day; some of the kids took a bite out of some fruits. So we get the kids together and we do a little funny play about how you're not supposed to that . . . I think in the past we would have wanted to find the culprit, but what's the point? And the new kids, the younger ones, they might have been scared . . . that is the effect of a collective bawling-out.

The adults feel better. There is less scolding, and it does not take the form of a bawling-out, but works more like a dialogue.

> G is asked, "So, the children's thesis about saying it in a normal way instead of scolding actually works?" G replies, "Yes, in most cases it does, if you take the time to think and count to ten." "But does it have the same effect on their behavior?" G: "Yes, I think so."

LEARNING TO SCOLD IS DIFFICULT

When the interviews with the adults were concluded, the staff debated them. It became clear that the newcomers felt that it was difficult to learn to scold, whether they had pedagogical training or not.

The staff had a long talk about why the "veterans" often had to do the scolding because the newcomers were reluctant:

— From what you've said, you don't really get to scold until you are no longer a newcomer?
— I guess that's how I've felt it . . . newcomers need to figure out how things work in this place . . . discover the style.
— We go in when no one else does. . . . I wait to see if someone else will do something, but no one does. (veteran)
— I still maintain that it's because you react differently, not faster, but differently. I am learning, but I react to the same things you do. (newcomer)

The phrase "I am learning" implies both that it is not easy and that it is a skill to be acquired—and one that the veterans master.

> I have had times when I have done a lot of scolding over something that I in fact think is okay, something that L [the director] might be upset over . . . I used to think of it as a rule, but with time I am getting more confident.

It is difficult to scold someone for violating a rule that one was not involved in making, but over time one gets more "confident": One internalizes and incorporates the rule. And as one becomes more immersed in the institutional culture, one may be able to put one's full weight behind the defense of that culture. Scold with conviction, for example.

This transfer of norms is a difficult process. The newcomers' uncertainty and reluctance irritate the veterans, and this irritation may be taken out on the children in the form of more scolding or more intense scolding.

The veterans often include the director or the deputy director. We will now look at some examples.

THE DIRECTOR AS THE "BAD COP"

In institutions with less internal agreement and a more hierarchical structure than the project kindergarten, conflicts may lead to increases in scolding, as illustrated by the following stories from the deputy director of an after-school center:

> In the kitchen I see a 10-year-old boy with diabetes stuffing himself with candy right in front of one of the early childhood educators. The early childhood educator does not notice that the boy is eating candy and does not attempt to have a dialogue with him.
>
> I feel that I need to talk with him about candy and what it does to him. I address the boy in a commanding tone of voice and tell him that we need to talk. The boy comes into the office with me. We get off to a bad start. I know that I only used that commanding tone of voice because I was frustrated with the early childhood educator's lack of contact with the boy. I think about how I would normally just have a normal, relaxed conversation with him in the kitchen. I think the visit to my office made the boy feel guilty rather than promote any understanding about why it is bad for him to eat candy.
>
> Sunday afternoon. Most of the youngsters are roasting bread on a stick over a campfire outside, and all three adults are out there with them. Inside are four 13- to 15-year-olds. At closing time, someone from the staff notices that someone tried to break into the candy cabinet. In the logbook, they write me a note, requesting that I talk to the four boys. In their opinion, the boys need to be suspended.
>
> I am against suspensions, and I don't agree with the way the staff planned that Sunday. I also feel that the staff was too conflict-avoidant in not talking to the youngsters themselves. I feel a pressure from the staff to act against my conviction.
>
> During our talk the boys maintain that they did not do anything, but I am not satisfied with their stories and tell them that they are not welcome in the center until they are able to come up with a better explanation. The next day one of them shows up and admits that he did try to fish out some candy. The staff still thinks the boy should be suspended. I feel that I am caught between a rock and a hard place, and I tell the boys that they can use the center while I take two days to figure out what should happen to them. I conclude that my decision

has to be based on a pedagogical rationale—not the pressure from the staff—and I have a talk with the boys about property rights and trust.

I resent the fact that I am unable to give the boys a straight answer right away, simply because I feel pressured into a situation where I don't agree with the rest of the staff.

An early childhood educator is having a fierce conflict with a 10-year-old in the main room. The boy is shouting and screaming and using bad language. She tries to calm him down, but instead he begins to kick and beat things around him. She now tries to hold him physically. I am very annoyed with her; she does not have a particularly close relationship with this boy, and it seems obvious, therefore, that she cannot possibly succeed.

I walk over and, in a very firm voice, tell the boy to stop. I must have been very angry, for in a split second I see actual fear in his eyes. I take him aside and discuss the incident with him. We end up on pretty good terms.

Afterwards, I felt bad because I had let my frustration get the better of me. I knew that my tone of voice would scare him. I also know that in similar situations, I am usually able to maintain a normal tone of voice.

An early childhood educator is sitting by the rabbits' cage, playing cards with a girl. Next to them, two boys are fighting. I observe the incident from my office. The early childhood educator gets up, and I think she is going to intervene, but she walks straight past them and asks me to come out and help. I am very annoyed that she did not take on the conflict herself, but I quickly move toward the boys. I am practically shouting; the boys stop, and I actually scold them.

Once I have calmed down a little, I talk to the boys and ask them why they didn't talk to the early childhood educator once the teasing began to escalate. They did, they say, but she didn't have time because she was playing cards.

Normally I would not have acted the way I did, but it was like a red flag to see the early childhood educator sitting there, right next to a fight, without doing anything. When she called me out, it was even worse. Later it turned out the early childhood educator thought—mistakenly—that she had a certain area of the playground to oversee, and that the fight was outside her territory.

The deputy director in this after-school center frequently feels pressured into imposing sanctions, including scolding, in a way that is too intense and irritated, where other reactions might have been more appropriate, and he does not feel good about it. And irritation scolding is not pleasant for the children. In a report on scolding, *Hvor tit skal jeg sige det?* (*How many times do I have to say it?*) (Jørgensen, 2000), the author distinguishes between

- Scolding due to rule violations
- Scolding because the adult has had a fright
- Irritation scolding

"Irritation scolding is by far the worst form of scolding, since we scold without any real (personally perceived) reason for doing so," he writes. He concludes, "One thing is for certain, long-term irritation is self-fuelling and, thus, wears both oneself and the children thin" (Jørgensen, 2000).

The lack of consensus within the staff group, the rather low self-esteem, the staff's tendency to get the deputy director to bail them out, and their belief in the necessity of punishment and scolding lead to more, and more severe, scolding than there appears to be in the project kindergarten, where the common understanding within the staff group, the professional self-image, the critical view of scolding and punishment, and the shared responsibility limit the amount and severity of scolding. When reading about rather intense scolding incidents from the project kindergarten, the reader should be aware that many, perhaps most, institutions have far more severe incidents—without any critical professional debate.

"YOU'VE GOT TO STEEL YOURSELF"

But the veterans in the project institution also have different opinions about scolding and, thus, different perceptions of it:

B *(to C):* Some of the children were playing with a model train. Joakim was mad—it was actually his train set, and Morten had taken it over . . . you took that conflict on in a very serious way, because it was so deadly serious to the kids . . . I think I might have brushed it off somehow. But you stuck to it, and you all found a solution to the problem. I was really impressed by that. That showed patience. I might have just said, hey, it's a train set, but you don't because you've got this empathy and patience.

G: But also gentleness, right? . . . I am sterner if the kids are suddenly crying. But with C, some of the scolding flies out the window if they start crying.

C: Oh, yes, I can't take very much crying.

G: Sometimes I feel that they're trying to shift the sympathy to the one who was making trouble.

L: That's the way it was with N, she was crying and said that her leg hurt, but she was the one who just bit Morten, and I just felt like, hey, don't you try that with me.

B: I don't think it affects me much either if the "sinner" starts to cry, but I do know that if I sometimes cry with rage or in an argument, then I am really, really upset and vulnerable.

L: Yeah, but that's different. If you were upset like that, I wouldn't talk to you like that. Then I would just hold you without saying anything.

The four early childhood educators steel themselves if their scolding causes the "sinner" to cry, but not if he or she is truly upset. The fifth early childhood educator is gentle and empathetic and cannot handle much crying. Instead, she is more patient than the others and sticks at it with the train set, until the situation has been resolved.

Why do the others steel themselves?

If one considers the question "Why don't the early childhood educators punish the victims?" it becomes clear that the scolding aims at punishing the "sinners" by removing any sympathy they might enjoy, making them uncomfortable, and—temporarily—expelling them from the community, all in order to make them improve their behavior. The punishment loses its effect if the "sinner" is comforted. Therefore, the early childhood educators must steel themselves. If they are unable to this—perhaps because they do not believe in the effects of punishment or do not find it ethically justifiable—scolding becomes a burden, and the children's crying becomes hard to handle.

This aspect of punishment grew ever less prevalent in the project institution during and after the development project. When it goes away completely, perhaps scolding is no longer scolding?

WHEN SCOLDING BECOMES A PUBLIC ISSUE

One day Lillian, the director, scolded Christina, an early childhood educator.

The individual talks with the three children who had been chasing the chickens and immersing them in cold water had just ended. Lillian was leaving the staff room, and there was Christina, who said that it looked like she and Lillian were supposed to have a chat. "Yes, I would like to talk to you," said Lillian, and she took Christina with her into the staff room, just as she had done with the three children. They sat down, facing each other, close. Another early childhood educator, Malene, was sitting by the computer in the same room, and Karina, one of the children, stood in the doorway, looking in.

> *Lillian:* I guess it's that we should talk about what we do in this house, and the pedagogical approach . . .
>
> *Christina:* . . . mm . . .
>
> *Lillian:* . . . and . . . when you're so enthusiastic and really keen, then you also use a lot of energy, well, I don't know if it's really nagging, but maybe sort of uptight . . .
>
> *Christina:* Hmm.
>
> *Lillian:* I wrote in my journal the other day: nag, nag, nag . . . and I guess I want to say . . . you shouldn't feel that you're solely responsible for everything being just superdandy all the time, no matter what we do . . . 'cause sometimes things go well, and some times they don't go so well.
>
> *Christina:* Sure, sure.
>
> *Lillian:* So don't spend all this energy on going around being irritated; instead get people to help you . . . like with cleaning the filter . . . you said to me, "Now it's fine, but it was completely clogged up," and I take that as a sign that you were irritated . . . and I can understand that, but instead of being irritated, you should say to someone: "Clean the filter!"
>
> *Christina:* Mm.
>
> *Lillian:* If people don't notice it themselves, they have to be told.
>
> *Christina:* I guess I tried that.
>
> *Lillian:* Yes . . . but you've just got to say it.
>
> *Christina:* Yes . . . but I guess you're right, Lillian, about much of it . . . *(Christina coughs a little.)*

A little later, Malene is talking to Christina:

> *Malene :* Did you think that Lillian scolded you?
>
> *Christina:* No, I don't think she did.
>
> *Malene:* What did you think she did?
>
> *Christina:* I guess I thought it was a, err, a reprimand, and at the same time it was a sort . . . a . . . err, well, like, how she thinks things are going right now.
>
> *Malene:* Isn't a reprimand a form of scolding?
>
> *Christina:* Well, yes, but I didn't feel it was like scolding.
>
> *Malene:* You didn't think it was unpleasant, done in a stupid way. You didn't feel like punching her?

Christina: No, because I guess I had sort of requested it . . . wanted her to talk about what wasn't going so well, and I know that I probably am a little negative . . . taking some things too personally . . . I didn't see it like that, so not like a reprimand, but as criticism of what I am doing . . . and for me, criticism can be both negative and positive . . . this one sounded negative, but it was positive because I can use it. It's not something that I can change here and now, but I am going to go home and think about it.

Malene: Were you aware that there were other people present?

Christina: No, not really.

Malene: It didn't bother you?

Christina: No, because . . . if it had been an actual review, then I probably wouldn't have liked it.

Malene: Do you think that she is angry with you now, or irritated?

Christina: No, I am sure Lillian would tell me if she were.

Malene: Okay . . . so you feel okay inside, and you're fine?

Christina: Yes, I think so . . . I am thinking about it, and I am going to try and change, but I know it's hard, 'cause I'm the sort of person who . . . I am very good at getting all worked up and irritated instead of saying: "Help me."

Malene: Yeah, I know what you mean.

Christina: Yes, that's it, then I get really pissed off instead.

It is not easy to be reprimanded or scolded, but it's easier when the reprimand is closer in character to constructive criticism. The reprimand or criticism is not aiming at degrading, shaming, or bawling anyone out. It aims at achieving change through dialogue and explanation, but it is also not an equitable talk unmarked by power relations. This is the director trying to use her authority to change relations within the kindergarten.

Such talks often take place behind closed doors, but not here. A colleague listens in and takes notes, and a child is listening in the doorway.

What does the openness mean for Karina?

Malene: Karina, you were in the doorway, listening, when Lillian was talking with Christina. Was Lillian scolding Christina?

Karina (uncertain): No, I don't think so.

Malene: Was Lillian angry?

Karina: No . . . *(laughs, not certain)*

The experience may give Karina the courage to do what 6-year-old Ask did:

> *Ask:* Lillian, I would like to see you in the staff room. *(Lillian and Ask go into the staff room and sit down, facing each other.)* When Anders went to this kindergarten, he told me that he had heard you using swear words. And I don't get that, 'cause you made a rule that says no one can use swear words.
>
> *Lillian:* That's not good. But sometimes I use swear words, that's if I'm really angry or really happy, but Ask, if you hear me cursing, can't you come up and say, "Hey Lillian, aren't you forgetting something?"
>
> *Ask:* Sure, I can do that. . . . That was all. *(Gets up and leaves.)*

Lillian writes in her journal:

> Now, afterward, I am thinking about all the times we said that children should be taken seriously. . . . Children are much more likely to let us know if they are mad at us these days. Ask comes to me, he feels that he is being taken seriously; he chooses to talk to me in the staff room. I can tell from his voice that he feels that I am taking him seriously. I also feel it among the staff; we are much more open with each other, closer; we have much more open discussions after conflicts with the children. It is not just *your* scolding, *your* conflict, it becomes an open discussion. Before it was like one's personal scolding, it was a right that we had, that we could scold the children; that was never questioned, but now it is like, you're not alone with it, it is made public.

Focusing on the touchy, often taboo topic of scolding has fostered an open and critical atmosphere, which in turn has fostered a sense of security rather than insecurity and created an openness that enables the children to make the adults change. The background for this is improvements in the children's rights. Adults used to be able to scold at will, without being held accountable.

Lillian clearly enjoys this critical openness and the reprimands that she may receive from the children as a result—reprimands, not scolding. Ask is not bawling Lillian out, he is not shouting, he is "saying it in a normal way," and that is why he is able to get his message across.

In another kindergarten, which had not previously focused on scolding, the staff was asked to answer 11 questions on the topic. Question 10 was, "Is there a need for raising this discussion (in this kindergarten)?" No one thought so. Question 11: "Is there a need for a more uniform agreement concerning when and how the children are scolded?" The conclusion was, "No one sees a need for a more uniform agreement concerning when and how the children are scolded."

This staff agrees to reject any discussion or criticism and, thus, increased openness. Thus, the children will continue to be without any rights in the face of the adults' exercise of power.

Perhaps the staff members in this kindergarten are afraid that a focus on scolding might get them in trouble. As we have seen, the experiences from the development work in the project institution point to the opposite: The critical public eye on scolding serves to democratize the situation, often to the extent that scolding ceases to be scolding and may not even count as a reprimand.

The burden is lifted from the shoulders of the adults (and the children), the children's rights improve, and the oldest of the children are now able to criticize and intervene with those in power.

CHAPTER 10

What Is the Relationship Among Scolding, the Pedagogical Approach, and the Physical Setting?

As we have seen, scolding has some unfortunate effects in both the short and the long term. We have also seen that neither children nor adults feel good about scolding. No one goes to college in order to get a degree that ensures the right to scold children. On the contrary, a study shows that early childhood education students have far more liberal attitudes toward childrearing than the average population (as measured in a questionnaire survey involving 1,200 people; Sigsgaard & Varming, 1996).

Attitude Toward Childrearing
Which is most important?

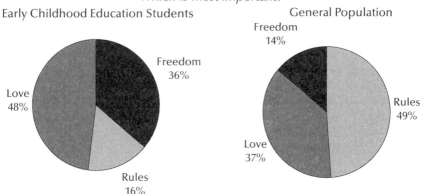

Early Childhood Education Students

Freedom 36%

Love 48%

Rules 16%

General Population

Freedom 14%

Rules 49%

Love 37%

With trained early childhood educators and teachers, however, the opposite is the case:

The number of consistent "boundary-setters" is higher among teachers and early childhood educators than in any other group. And they are slightly more in favor of rules and control values and slightly less in favor of love and emotion values than government employees as a whole.

In addition, early childhood educators and teachers, together with independent business owners and senior citizens, are the groups least likely to take the children's point of view when asked what can be done with regard to children who are in trouble (Sigsgaard & Varming, 1996).

So, it appears that early childhood educators and teachers change their views as a result of their work and come to favor values of freedom and emotion less and less in favor of rules and control values. The study is a strong indication of a link between the practitioners' pedagogical practice and their childrearing values. It also documents a relationship between childrearing values and the tendency to employ sanctions in childrearing. We therefore have to assume that scolding is related not only to child–staff ratios, the amount of space available, and how the children feel about themselves, but also to pedagogical practice and the early childhood educators' values.

It is this relationship between pedagogical approach and scolding that is the topic of this chapter.

SCOLDING AND THE VIEW OF HUMAN NATURE INHERENT IN THE PEDAGOGICAL APPROACH

The French philosopher Jean Paul Sartre has argued that people have two basic ways of relating to each other. They have either an *entreaty–demand* relationship or an *appeal–help* relationship. While the appeal–help relationship is characteristic of open communities that the members join by choice and are free to leave, the entreaty–demand relationship is the prevailing type in closed power systems, where some members are *placed* while others are *employed,* or where some act as employers for others, whom they have hired and may fire at will.

In principle, an institution is a closed power system, while children playing in a backyard form an open and elective community. A club—for example, a sports club—is an intermediate form, where relations are characterized by entreaty–demand as well as appeal–help. As we have seen, children and young people prefer appeal–help relations to entreaty–demand relations. The club's ability to attract children and youth therefore depends on its ability to maintain appeal–help relations and not let them give way to entreaty–demand relations.

To illustrate:

Open communities	Clubs	Institutions/schools
Predominantly appeal–help relations	Appeal–help relations compete with entreaty–demand relations	Predominantly entreaty–demand relations

That is the bird's eye view. If we look closer, we see a number of exceptions: open communities characterized by entreaty–demand relations, clubs that are so institutionalized that the appeal–help relations have almost been pushed aside by entreaty–demand relations, and institutions/schools with plenty of room for appeal–help relations.

What do we mean by entreaty–demand and appeal–help? An entreaty means bowing to the superior power ("May I please be allowed to go outside to play/to go to the bathroom/to eat?"). The demand aspect highlights the superiority ("Let's eat," "You're going to bed now," "Everybody into the playground—you, too").

Key concepts in the power-based entreaty–demand relationship are demands, duties, restrictions, replies, boundaries, conflicts, reward, and punishment.

Key concepts in the appeal–help relationship are help, openness, desire, responsibility, obligation, questions, mutual dependency, trust, and democracy.

> Sometimes her son does not want to put on his jacket. Then she takes his hand and talks to him about the day—not about the fact that he didn't come when she first called him. By taking his hand and helping him, she demonstrates that she is *with* him and beside him. Their relation is *cooperative*. If she were to insist, instead, that he obey her and put on the clothes himself, and if that were a common occurrence, he would see her as being *against* him and above him. Their relationship would be *hierarchical*. It would be a struggle about his *volition* and his *self-esteem*. (Sigsgaard, 2001)

Thus, the entreaty–demand relation is a power relation where both submission and demands cause conflicts. In these conflicts, the exercise of power will take place partly through scolding. Here, scolding is the rule. In the appeal–help relation, however, scolding signifies a violation of the trust and openness. Here, scolding is the exception.

As the adults in the project kindergarten became better at asking what was going on before they scolded, they began to move away from the entreaty–demand relation and toward relations characterized more by help–appeal. A teacher, Kirstine Sort Jensen, says, "If we bawl out the children, degrade them, and use irony, it's no wonder if they bully each other: We are, after all, their teachers" (Jensen, 2000).

So, if teachers bawl some of the children out, these children will bully or bawl each other out. Critical insights like this concerning the link between teacher–child relations and the child–child relations will also help to make teacher–child relations more oriented toward appeal–help:

> At assembly time, 16 children and 4 adults sat in a sort of circle on the floor. Not sitting so much as lying down or sitting, as each per-

son preferred. There was little control. When the children's internal chatter died down, an adult would comment on something that had been said, and then everyone would listen until the unstructured chatter took over once more. If things became a little too rowdy, an adult would help a child, with a pat on the arm, a stroking of the back, or a smile, to direct his or her attention toward the adult who was heading the assembly. The adults intervened in a manner that was quiet but firm. At the outset, one little boy was lying under a table next to the circle. An adult told a boy, who was sitting on her lap, that she needed to help the boy. She helped him, but did not force him, to join the circle. Everything happened almost without a word, and the adults expressed no irritation.

Throughout the assembly there was not a single scolding incident.

Drama session with the youngest children: An adult enters the world of fantasy together with the children who choose to join, while another adult helps the less focused children be less disturbing and helps them return to the drama session after a break. One little girl was running around, having trouble understanding what was going on (her Danish is not very good yet). By and large, she was allowed to drop in and out of the activity. When the adult wanted to include her from time to time, she was encouraged with a smile, a "come on!" or a "yes!" as well as positive facial expressions and body language. There was nothing even close to scolding throughout the drama session.

Overall, we can say that the more the entreaty–demand aspect dominates relations in an institution, the more scolding there will be, all things being equal. And vice versa: If an institution/school has a great amount of scolding, relations between the staff and the children are probably hierarchical in nature and characterized by entreaty–demand dynamics.

THE EARLY CHILDHOOD EDUCATOR AS A HELPFUL CONFIDANT— AND AS A PERSON IN CHARGE OF CHILDREARING AND RULE ENFORCEMENT

As mentioned earlier, the amount of time that a child spends in institutions/school throughout childhood has just about tripled in a generation, and consequently the socializing processes that used to take place mostly at home and in the local community now take place at least as much in institutions.

All children are disciplined and punished in institutions and schools as well as helped along and praised. Some children are disciplined and punished more, while some receive more help and praise. Just as some schools and institutions do more disciplining and punishing, while some spend more time on help and appreciation.

Here are a few examples, the first from an intern at a Copenhagen institution:

A trip to the open-air history museum

On the train to the museum, a 3-year-old boy kicks and bites one of the aides. An early childhood educator intervenes and sends him back to the institution, saying, "Now you're going back, and it serves you right. Maybe then you'll learn not to kick or hit an adult!" The other children are standing around the early childhood educator and the scolded child, watching.

Throughout the remainder of the trip, the other children are threatened with the same treatment if they don't do what they're told.

Here, the emphasis is squarely on childrearing and punishment. The following story was told by the early childhood educator involved:

A shoulder to cry on

I was on an excursion with six 5-year-olds. As we were walking, Malene, who was holding my hand, said, "My dad scolds me so much when I don't want to eat."

Me: Don't you want to eat?
Malene: Yes, but I don't like salad.
Me: Does your mom scold you too?
Malene: No, only my dad.
Me: Do you eat your salad, then?
Malene: I cry, but I don't eat it. (*Pause*) A dad doesn't hit his wife and kids! A dad doesn't!

Afterward, the early childhood educator said, "There was so much being said between the lines. The whole thing was said with great intensity and in the deepest confidence. She probably would not have said anything if the occasion had not arisen like that: the two of us alone—outside the institution."

The relationship between the educator and the child is characterized by trust and acknowledgment. There is no disciplining, let alone punishment. The child may be seeking the early childhood educator's help with something that is almost unbearably difficult; and the very fact that she dares confide in someone and has a chance to do so is helpful to her.

Many children today grapple with serious problems on their own. They have no siblings or close adults, besides their parents, to share them

with. It may be vital for these children to have access to the early childhood educator as a fellow human being, not just as a government em-
ployee in charge of childrearing.

Malene probably is not scolded much by this early childhood educator.
If she were, she probably would not confide in her. When early childhood
educators act more as helpers and confidants than as persons in charge of
childrearing and rule enforcement, there is less scolding, and when scolding does happen, it hurts less because of the trust and close confidence.

CHILDREARING NORMS CAN LEAD TO SCOLDING

An intern in a Danish kindergarten told this story:

> A group of kindergartners were eating, while they took turns telling
> everyone about their weekend. One girl was stuttering, as she ea-
> gerly tried to tell her story. "Don't interrupt; you have to wait!" says
> the early childhood educator.
> But the girl stutters on, eagerly.
> "SHUT UP NOW! DO YOU TALK THAT MUCH AT HOME, TOO?
> NOW SIT DOWN AND SHUT UP AND EAT YOUR FOOD! Now, does
> anyone want to tell us about their weekend?"

Spontaneity is as characteristic of childhood as the demand for delaying
gratification is to institutions in their most common incarnations. One has
to wait one's turn, even if one is ready to burst.

The norms that we have focused on here—sitting still and awaiting
one's turn—cause scolding, as the stories have shown. The norms are
widespread, but there are institutions that allow the children to eat their
food in what others might consider nonregulation positions and to eat in
smaller groups, where they can talk spontaneously to each other.

Generally, institutions tend to require the individual to adjust to the
greater whole. This might be seen as basic to the nature and concept of
institutions. It often requires power-based interventions toward the individual, which is legitimized with positively charged social concepts such
as "social behavior" and "showing empathy."

Another norm that causes scolding is "justice." Everyone has to have
one, and only one, piece of fruit, regardless how hungry they are. When
the others have to go outside, you have to go outside, too, even if today
you really, really want to stay inside and play. Children resist being treated as if they were all the same, and then they may be scolded.

Most norms are not debatable, but essentially taken for granted. If
they were examined, some might be modified or abandoned. That would

make life somewhat easier for the children, who would not have to consider changing kindergartens in order to be able to enjoy the tolerance awarded the "new kids."

It would be impossible to eliminate all conflicts between children and adults, but if there were fewer conflicts concerning norms that are less essential, there would be more time and energy to devote to more important conflicts, and scolding might be a less prominent feature of conflict management.

WHEN POVERTY COMES IN THE DOOR, LOVE FLIES OUT THE WINDOW

This old adage expresses the common experience that lovers and others have fewer conflicts when there are no shortages. Does this hold true for institutions and schools, too? And what might be in short supply here?

Above, we illustrated the need for a shoulder to cry on if dad scolds and, perhaps, hits his wife and children. This requires that shoulders be both available and accessible. But Danish institutions today have a shortage of shoulders. The child-to-staff ratio is higher than ever before. The budget for temps is often cut so far back that there are not sufficient funds for hiring temporary staff when someone calls in sick. Thus, today's children, who are already suffering from the increasing absence of adults from the home due to the increase in the family workload outside the home, are also suffering from the increasing absence of adults from the institution. If there are only one or two adults present in the institution after 2:00 in the afternoon—who, as studies show, only spend half their time with the children—there is less time to ask questions, look after, and simply be available; consequently, the staff resorts to scolding more often.

In addition, most places also have a shortage of space. Our homes are often spacious, but they are empty all day. Our institutions are cramped, with no possibility of finding a quiet corner.

As for the child-to-staff ratio, schools often have the worst conditions. Compared with preschool, it is not uncommon for 25 children to have to share one or one-and-a-half adults. (This means that public authorities stand to reap substantial savings by lowering the age for starting school!)

So, there is a shortage of time and space in institutions and schools.

Several of the intern observers in the project mentioned this problem spontaneously (they were not asked to pay attention to problems concerning time and space). One report from an after-school center in the Greater Copenhagen area says:

> I have noticed a big difference between days with good versus bad
> weather. Naturally, there is more scolding when mainly the indoor

facilities are used. The reason is that the children have much less space to move around in when they spend most of their time indoors, which of course leads to more noise and more fights and confrontations among the children.

The precise impact of this factor was not uncovered in the Scolding Project.

However, a Norwegian study suggests a link between the size of the school/institution on the one hand and welfare and climate on the other. In the study, parents of schoolchildren were asked to talk about their own schooldays in groups. This produced a number of negative memories, which proved difficult to discuss. The memories were still quite sensitive, even 20 years later. And they were most common among those who had attended larger schools:

> A woman in her 30s said, "I went to a large school in Oslo, and I was bullied and tormented so much that if I hadn't been allowed to change to another school in fourth grade, I probably would not be alive today."
> At the opposite end of the scale, another participant had attended a school where the two teachers were with the children all the time. They planned their own distribution of recess, playtime, and work, and "it was just as natural for the adults to be with us during recess as during classes." (Dugstad, 1992)

In-depth studies might tell us more about these connections, but we know enough to say that more adult time, more space, and more outdoor activities would reduce conflicts and scolding.

The fact that Sweden has far less bullying (experienced by 1 child in 16) today than Denmark (1 child in 4) may be attributable to a more dedicated fight against bullying, but it may also be related to the fact that Swedish children have up to 50% more space in preschool institutions and schools than Danish children.

TALKING, SITTING

Recently, Norway had a public debate on "sitting pedagogy" in the playground. The children sit in the sandbox, they sit on the swings, and they sit on the seesaw. They sit and sit and sit.

But what happens when they are indoors? Well, they often do even more sitting. Two boys talk about it:

— Do you like Children's Meeting?
— It's dumb.
— 'Cause we have to sit and talk. Sometimes it takes forever, and then we have to, then the adults have to sit and scold and stuff. And we don't want

GOOD IDEA: DON'T
HAVE THE CHILDREN
SITTING AROUND
WAITING FOR TOO
LONG—THEN THEY GET
SCOULDED TOO MUCH.

From Lis Andersen: *Børn og bevægelse*
(Children and movement), 1977

to listen to that. We'd rather wrestle. Me and Bjarne, we once got into a
fight during Children's Meeting.
— Why can't you change the way the meeting is run?
— 'Cause all the adults are stupid. They don't want us to change the Children's Meeting, and then we have to tell them, Why this, Why that, Why
splat! (Sigsgaard, 2001)

The Children's Meeting is about sitting around talking. Bjarne and his
friend do not like it, and then the adults begin to scold. Changing the
format seems an insurmountable task, which would require more talking,
even reasoning and arguing, an area where the children are no match for
the adults.

But sometimes talking is good. Christina from the project kindergarten
loves to be in charge of opening the kindergarten at 6:30 in the morning:

I made tea and breakfast. Soon there were 10 children there. One of
the children had brought a Mickey Mouse drawing, which I photo-
copied so that more of the children could color it in, cut it out, and
make a Jumping Jack. . . . It is also both fun and educational to talk
with the children, having a real conversation with them.

And toward the end of the day:

We talked about the new rabbits and the fact that soon they would
be going into the big cage together with the other rabbits. Later, the
children began to sing the Witch Song. The older boys started it, and
soon all the children sang along. They sang it over and over again.

But the middle of the day does not offer the same possibilities for talking
because there are so many activities going on. The children also like the
spontaneous conversation, but they don't much care for "sitting around
talking."

One day, Morten is squirming more than usual at lunchtime, mostly
under the table. He is reprimanded and promises to shape up, but it does
not last. Lillian says:

I am fed up; it will take something else to get through to them. I choose to perform a little play where I eat the way he does. He watches and pays attention. I choose this approach because there are so many people who tell him what to do and what not to do, all the time. He shuts it out; he doesn't want to hear it and builds his own little world inside himself, shutting out the world. He needs to see and feel things.

He needs to see and feel things, says Lillian. Perhaps Morten is not the only one who needs to see and feel things, but all of today's children, whose lives are more and more filled up with talk—not conversations—as their active life is more and more reduced.

The relationship is probably that the more active life and the more "activity-free" action time the pedagogical work allows, the more conversations will arise. And the less need there will be for scolding.

OFF TO SCHOOL

One day kindergarten is over, and this event occurs at an ever-earlier age. The children are off to school. Some come from a kindergarten where they have had to sit and talk a lot; others come from institutions with more action and more genuine conversations.

What is school like, then? Does it involve a lot of sitting? Waiting one's turn, sitting still, and listening to what the teacher says? Maybe 4, maybe 5, maybe even 6 hours a day? If that is the case, it may spell trouble, both for the children who are used to sitting around talking (they have just about had their fill) and for the children who are used to action and conversations (they are used to something better).

And how much conversation is there going to be room for in a class with just one teacher? Studies suggest that even teachers who seek to have conversations and set time aside for them may still wind up doing two-thirds of the talking. In other words, the teacher talks twice as much as all the children put together. The risk of scolding under these circumstances is considerable. The children are disappointed, and the teacher may be even more disappointed, as this was not what he or she wanted or dreamed of.

Some might think that schools in the past involved even more sitting and talking, and that is supposed to have worked out fine, but one must consider the huge changes in children's social life. Just 25 years ago, children led a much more active life outside the institutions. Today, many have only limited contact with their parents and other adults in their community, and they spend a great deal of time sitting in front of various screens.

It is children with this sort of childhood who are now sent to school at an ever-earlier age and who face ever-longer schooldays. That is a scenario that lends itself to scolding. Traditional classroom teaching may involve a very large amount of scolding indeed, as illustrated in the book *Barndom mellem børn og professionelle (Childhood Among Children and Professionals):*

> The students were having a science class; the topic was magnetism. The teacher, Jytte, walked around the classroom, handing out a large nail and a magnet to each child. Many began to experiment, which Jytte repeatedly told them not to do. "Don't touch the things yet; first you have to be told what to do." "Don't start until everyone's ready!" "Look up, you can only listen if you're looking up." The instructions came in an ever-sharper tone, since no one appeared to be paying any attention.
>
> While materials were being handed out, Mads was sitting with a magnet and a nail, trying to fit the two things together. Then he suddenly took his neighbor's magnet. He put one magnet up against one ear and the other magnet against the other and then let go of both magnets at once. They fell on the table with a great clatter. Jytte was now getting angrier, threatening to stop the experiment if the class did not settle down soon. Gradually, everybody put down the magnets, and Jytte went to the blackboard and began to draw a diagram of the intended experiment. At this point, half the class had already carried out the experiment she was outlining, and some went on to conduct experiments on their own while she was talking. A little later, when a girl dropped a magnet on the table in front of her, the teacher got angry and told everyone to interrupt the experiment, tidy up, leave the science room, and go back to the normal classroom, saying, "I guess you're just not old enough for this yet. You can't be allowed in this room if you can't follow the rules." (Højlund, 2001)

This description supports Susanne Højlund's claim that teaching and scolding/punishment/disciplining cannot be separated. The children are disciplined as an integrated part of their education. The teacher is enforcing the following rules:

- The rule of silence
- The rule of attention
- The rule of the power balance in the classroom

The rules "carry a coherent message: the notion that in school, children have to adapt to the group, not require too much attention, not stand out too much, not look after their personal interests, not draw attention to differences, but strive for equality" (Højlund, 2001, p. 211).

Several disciplining strategies are employed: correction, prohibitions, the spelling out of consequences, interruption, eviction, and scorn. In other words, of the 15 types of psychological disciplinary measures that we mentioned on page 43, the magnet incident involves 6. In a third categorization of verbal disciplinary strategies, Waksler (1991) distinguishes between *commands, statements, sarcasm,* and *threats.* All of these appear in the magnet incident.

Waksler (1991) offers a description of the ideal student — the one who adheres to all the school rules:

> When called upon by the teacher, they will answer immediately, briefly and pertinently. They will remain sitting. . . . They will follow all instructions. . . . They will always walk inside the room.

The more of these rules and norms schools impose and enforce, the more transgressions there will be, and the more use the teachers will make of sanctions, including scolding.

If one wanted to improve life for both teachers and children, there would be several options. The four most important options are: reducing the number of lessons, delaying school start, making school more action-oriented, and reducing the tendency to divide children into categories that reflect the adults' needs and perceptions rather than treating them as unique individuals. That would produce less scolding.

Instead, we see the opposite trend: earlier school start, more lessons, more requirements, more control, and more emphasis on book learning. This is bound to produce more scolding.

And Susanne Højlund has documented that certain categories of children bear the brunt of this: boys more than girls as well as a middle category of children who (according to the teacher) are "able, but not willing." She also shows that children are not perceived as individuals in the school that she studied, but rather perceived as belonging to a category: boy/girl, gifted/with potential/with limited potential.

Enough said. We have pointed out a number of connections between pedagogical approach and the use of sanctions, including scolding. The more hierarchical and entreaty–demand-oriented a school is, the more scolding there will be. And the more "liberal" the individual teacher or early childhood educator is, the less scolding there will be.

CHAPTER 11

Scolding—Why, That Simply Isn't Done!

ABOUT NONSCOLDING CULTURES
AND HOW THEY ARE DEVELOPED AND DEFENDED

In the previous chapters we have examined a number of issues: How much scolding is there, how is it justified, what and whom does it target, how does it work, how is scolding perceived and experienced, how does scolding at home relate to scolding in the institution or school, and how does scolding affect the child's self-esteem and social skills? We now know more about the nature of institutions and institutionalization.

What is left now is a closer look at the way that nonscolding cultures are developed and maintained, and how they may be understood.

This closing chapter provides a number of descriptions from pre-school facilities, schools, and other places that have rejected the scolding culture to a larger or smaller extent and taken steps toward something that we may call an appreciative culture.

The descriptions were developed as part of the Scolding Project, and we have not sought the involved institutions' approval of the presentations.

THE APPLE ORCHARD (ÆBLEHAVEN)

Our observers visited this combined preschool and kindergarten on several occasions and also interviewed some of the employees. The preschool has existed for 50 years; the kindergarten was added in 1997. First, a few glimpses from everyday situations that might have led to scolding in other places, but not here:

> A nursery school boy wants to do a jigsaw puzzle. He gets permission and is asked to sit at a table. He does not want to; the early childhood educator squats down next to him and says that if he sits on the floor, the pieces may get lost. He still does not want to sit on the chair. "Is it because you have doo-doo in your diaper?" asks the early childhood educator. "Yes," he says, and they go into the bathroom together.

The early childhood educator is not busy "setting boundaries." She assumes that the boy has a valid reason for saying "no."

A child (C) and an adult (A) are about to start an activity together when another child begins to cry.

> A: Hang on a sec, let me just deal with Oliver; he is upset.
> C: Yes, Oliver sad.
> A: There, there, Oliver, now I've picked you up, why are you so sad?
> C: Why Oliver sad?
> A: I think it's because he just woke up, and then he couldn't hear us.
> C: Mm.

Instead of interrupting the child's playtime with the adult, which might have resulted in frustration, tears, and scolding, the act of comforting Oliver becomes a part of the child's interaction with the adult.

> C: Woops!
> A: Woops, did you just knock the buttermilk out all over the table?
> C (concerned): Yes . . .
> A: Well, that can happen. I'll get a rag.
> C: Yes.

Small children will have plenty of "accidents"; their muscle coordination is not fully developed, and this may often lead to scolding. The child is prone to feeling guilty. That is exacerbated if the adult expresses reproach. This adult does not make a big deal out of the spilled milk, but simply treats it as a normal occurrence and takes care of practical matters. She helps the child.

> Two children are in the sandbox, crying and pulling on the same bucket. When one of them begins to cry more loudly, an early childhood educator comes over, squats down, and asks, "What's going on here?" The child who cries the loudest says something incomprehensible. The early childhood educator: "Do you want a bucket, too? This is Maria's bucket; you'll find another one in the sandbox—look!" She walks over to the other corner of the sandbox with the child and finds a bucket. "Here's a bucket for you!" She leaves, and the children soon go back to playing with their buckets and the sand.

The early childhood educator gets on the same level as the children physically. She does not shush them up or scold them, but asks what is going on, so that she can help the children help themselves.

> Amalie is wearing short sleeves. The early childhood educator looks at her, turns around, and gets a sweater. She takes a step toward Amalie and says, "Amalie, you should be wearing a sweater!" Amalie runs away from the early childhood educator, who looks at the sweater and puts it back where she found it.

The early childhood educator accepts the child's refusal. Shortly after this episode, she said, "It's not our attitude that we have to defeat the children. . . . If you're not sure you're doing the right thing with the children, then put yourself in their place and check whether this is something you would put up with. If the answer is 'no,' you're doing something wrong."

> In the kindergarten, a boy of 5 or 6 wants to paint. He is told to put some newspaper down first and wear an apron. He does not respond, but begins to paint. The early childhood educator again tells him to put down some newspaper, but as he does not respond she goes and gets him some. She puts it on the table next to him without saying anything, and the boy puts it under the drawing paper. The early childhood educator says that he also has to wear an apron. "Why?" "Because otherwise I'll be scolded." The boy: "Who will be scolded?" The early childhood educator: "I will." "How come?" "Your mom won't be happy if you have paint on your clothes, then she might get mad at me!" The boy looks at the early childhood educator and goes on painting. She leaves and returns with an apron, which she hands the boy—again without saying anything. He puts it on and continues to paint.

Little is said here, and the early childhood educator does not violate the boy's autonomy too much—she places the newspaper next to him but does not lift up his drawing to place it underneath, and she gives him the apron but does not put it on for him. He is a big boy and has heard plenty of orders and commands. Therefore, he is not really listening until the early childhood educator turns everything upside down by presenting herself as someone who risks scolding.

Let us conclude these observations with some of the observers' comments: "You often hear, 'What is it?' and 'What's the matter?' when someone is sad, angry or unhappy. No one raises their voice much, so there is a different sense of calm about this place than in most preschools. I never hear anyone saying 'NO!' or 'Stop that immediately.'"

Another observer: "I was so impressed with this place. We had discussed it before our visit—if they don't scold, what do they do? And we were surprised that they did not need to replace it with anything. They just told the children and helped them find alternatives. It was also clear that there were no power struggles. *It seemed as if children and adults were cooperating instead of working against each other.*"

Interviews with the Adults

Four staff interviews took place: with the deputy director, a "veteran" early childhood educator, a "newcomer," and the director. So what did they tell us?

About the pedagogical approach. The director: "The basis for our work today is 'the integrated background,' which aims at achieving coherence, documenting events, and using this documentation to improve our future efforts. And we aim for as much autonomy as possible." Everybody tries to include the children's point of view as much as they can.

The deputy director: "Now I always try to take the children's side. It's hard to do things any other way if one thinks that children have equal worth and deserve respect."

How did it all begin? The deputy director: "The new approach began when the kindergarten opened in 1997, and it spread to the preschool a few years later. In a way, of course, it had begun long before that. When I came here in 1997, I was surprised that the staff had no doubt that they were here for the children. Just a simple thing like lunch breaks, which the preschool had never been unable to fit in: One cannot leave the children alone. But that's intolerable, because then we never get to talk with the staff. Therefore, management has to tell them to take breaks; we tried, but it didn't work. And if someone on a team had called in sick, someone else would stay late, because they felt sorry for the children if they had to go and be with adults they didn't know. That is not viable."

The newcomer: "When I came here, in 1999, I said, 'I see that you don't scold?' Well, no, they might sometimes scold. I asked them, 'In what situations?' No one could think of any. And it turned out that the general consensus had been not to yell at the children. I found here what I have always wanted. But in some aspects they were lagging behind—bibs under the plate, stay seated until everyone's done, so that was a bit confusing. At that time, there were bowel movement schedules—maybe one team still uses them [November 2000]—dating back to the time of the preschool nurses. You'd think it was harder to change people's attitude about children, scolding, and punishment than about practical things, so that seemed a little odd."

The veteran: "In the 1970s children were simply there. They just had to be minded and looked after. There was no reason for scolding, for children didn't matter. In the 1980s, they developed personalities, and the reins were loosened; they became noisy and rambunctious. Adults had to sit on the floor, weren't quite able to cope, and had to resort to scolding. Today, children *communicate,* and they talk loudly. The situation is the opposite of what it was when I first came here. Back then it was a job. Now I am definitely here to receive what the children give me. It is an amazing gift to be a part of this. Back then, everything had to be planned and scheduled. Now we encounter open children and adults who know that children are busy exploring and developing. Adults no longer have to be the ones who decide, but the ones who help and support, and then there is no basis for scolding—although the children may scold us if there's something we don't get. A child used to be just one among many, but now there is a stronger focus on the individual. Children at 5 or 6 know their own needs. They are allowed to be selfish, but they are aware that there has to be room for everyone. The general outlook in this place has changed. There is more empathy, more room for diversity. And there is more humor among the staff members. And you can get just as far, if not farther, with humor as with bawling someone out. The children can tell that we adults have fun together. We may disagree, but it is never like seeing mom and dad arguing; therefore the children show great care and concern for each other—even if they yell at each other sometimes.

"We have no problem intervening with a colleague. If we're in doubt, we often ask a colleague for a second opinion or ask someone else to take over. We ask each other, 'How are you today?' If a colleague says, 'I didn't get any sleep last night,' we close ranks around her, sort of. We show our colleagues and the children the same degree of respect."

The background of the early childhood educators. The director: "In my family there were frequent discussions about childrearing. My mother's three brothers advocated strong discipline, but my father was very much against that. Then at my confirmation dinner, when I was 14, one of my mom's brothers got up and gave a speech in which he said that it looked like my dad had been right, after all. That meant a lot to me."

The deputy director: "I was often scolded, both at home and in kindergarten, where we were forced to eat these brown bread sandwiches. My parents were divorced when I was born. I was raised a Jehovah's Witness, but it didn't take."

The newcomer: "When I was at the after-school center, we had to sit with our hands under the table and wait to be served, and a towering adult would walk around the table, checking. I was afraid to be there. I only attended kindergarten very briefly. When we thought it was too tough, our parents took us out."

The veteran: "I was scolded at home when I was a kid."

Schooldays. The director: "When I was in second grade, one of the special ed kids had been to the baker's and bought some cake, which she offered the teacher. The teacher held the cake between the tips of her fingers and threw it in the garbage. I thought that was so mean. Otherwise, I was a model student in school and never got slapped. I loved debating with people."

The veteran: "In my school they promoted democratic norms—not so much scolding. I had new teachers, fresh from college; they made you feel like an equal."

The deputy director: "We had a very young class teacher who sat *on* the teacher's desk—even at PTA meetings. Some of the parents complained to the principal about that. I really liked her. She listened and treated you like a person. We actually had more respect for her than for the older teachers, even if she demanded less discipline, because we could tell that she took more of an interest in us than the others did. They just had a job to do. My class teacher was my ambassador, and every child needs an ambassador."

The newcomer: "Then we had this great Danish teacher who thought I was *ever* so gifted and talented. It wasn't just me; in fact, he liked the whole class. While I was in college, we often went to see him. We would smoke cigarettes in the teachers' lounge."

Own pedagogical experiences. The deputy director: "Shortly after I had started as an aide, at 17, there was first one and then another early childhood educator who came to mean a lot to me. They were the essence of harmony, always keeping things in perspective, aware of the individual child, and very caring. They meant a great deal to me, also later when I went to college.

"In this one place where I used to work, the deputy director was always scolding the toddlers. Then the children were sent to sit on their bench in the wardrobe; as soon as they heard her hoarse voice, they would just go out there and sit on the benches. She was extreme, but the others yelled at the kids, too. I was too cowed by their authority status. Even though I did not internalize it, I also didn't speak out."

The newcomer: "In my first internship they wanted me to learn that it was important to take conflicts on—to make sure the children did not win. That was so hard for me. She *had to* put on her own slippers, even if it might take 2 hours to make her do it. I could not understand why we couldn't just put them on for her. I was only 19."

The view of the children. The director: "Essentially, I think one should treat children and adults the same. Naturally, we don't just let go; we do regulate their behavior, but we don't make a big deal out of it—we leave that to the parents. We changed considerably when we abandoned the very structured pedagogical approach and tightly scheduled days; now we are much better equipped for dealing with the children here and now. That also made us consider how we might handle conflicts between children. I actually think that's when we first began to give up scolding."

The newcomer: "At my 10-year college reunion, we had many discussions about scolding. The general attitude was that the only way one can keep children under control is through punishment and scolding. That is actually a rather old-fashioned, reactionary view. I claim the opposite. It is not necessary to control them at all; the point is to see what the children are actually doing—and cooperate with them on what they need, help them."

The view of scolding. The veteran: "Scolding is very humiliating and degrading. When you have scolded someone you might have a bad taste in your mouth because you have abused your power. And the child is upset, begins to cry; that makes it hard to scold.

"Scolding that targets the personality is worse than scolding that targets the child intellectually. It is terrible to be scolded by the people you love the most."

The newcomer: "Scolding is humiliating, but sometimes I *do* scold my own kids. They can be such a pain in the neck that I just can't help it. But I wouldn't dream of scolding anyone else's children. My husband never scolds. Never ever! He asks—wants to understand. I don't have the patience."

How to Maintain the Spirit

When, as part of the Scolding Project, we suggested to 50 early childhood education students that they work with scolding during their internship in various types of institutions, most came back and said that it was almost impossible to avoid adopting the scolding culture of the host institution. The expectation for the intern to do so was in the air. Some places did criticize the interns for being too soft or wishy-washy. They had to learn to "set boundaries." Only one person had been told directly that she had to scold more. Apparently, "setting boundaries" sounds more acceptable. Thus, the scolding culture appears to be extremely widespread, which puts the emerging nonscolding cultures under pressure. They have to constantly maintain and develop their line. How do they do tackle this at The Apple Orchard?

Critical practice. One must expect the traditional perception of children to rear its head all the time and be ready to challenge it. As it happens here, for example:

Lucas, who is 1½, is drinking milk, wants more, but does not want to eat. An aide, Trine: "Lucas is so stubborn." An early childhood educator: "He is not stubborn, he is just thirsty." The early childhood educator's comment to the observer: "She might as well have said that he was 'testing boundaries.' We were raised to think the way that Trine does—therefore we need someone who can point out other possible views."

The deputy director: "If we get a temp who raises his or her voice, it is noticed straight away—she'll find out."

The institution is not a quiet place. It cannot and should not be, with so many people present. But noise from full-blown conflicts is rare, and there are no yelling adults. Therefore an unfortunate temp will immediately be aware that he or she has just acted as the proverbial bull in the china shop. A nonscolding culture is self-perpetuating, just as a scolding culture is.

Ongoing development. One early childhood educator said, "In some of the teams we have agreed to try to avoid saying 'no' or 'not.' That is in the Troll Kids and the Peanuts groups." So the staff in two of the groups had arranged to go one step further than the rest of the institution.

Not everybody is always prepared to go equally far, and the ones who want to push ahead are allowed to do so.

Here lies one of the keys to keeping up the enthusiasm. Development often falters because not everyone is ready and willing, and because everything is supposed to be based on consensus. This institution allows for different developmental tempos, as long as the overall developmental direction is maintained.

The adults with the Peanuts and the Troll Kids want to avoid saying "no" and "not." One might almost think that they had been reading Katherine H. Read's *The Nursery School* (1950/1960), which was studied in nearly all education colleges in the 1950s. An excerpt:

> A positive suggestion is one which tells the child what to do instead of pointing out what he is not to do. . . . By emphasizing the positive we reduce the attention and thus the importance of the negative aspect of his behavior. We usually help rather than hinder when we make a positive suggestion. . . . A positive direction is less likely to rouse resistance than a negative one. It makes help seem constructive rather than limiting and interfering. . . .
>
> In addition, when we make suggestions in a positive way we are giving the child a sound pattern to imitate when he himself directs his friends. . . . One can tell something about the kind of direction that a child has received as one listens to the kind of direction that he gives in play. . . .

> To put directions positively represents a step in developing a more positive attitude toward children's behavior inside ourselves. . . .
>
> At first, it is wise to allow oneself no exceptions to this rule, to discard negative suggestions entirely.

This may sound simple, but it is in fact rather radical. We do not know what impact Read had on pedagogical practice in the 1950s and 1960s. Read's book must have influenced early childhood educators at the time, however, for no book was more widespread in courses on pedagogical practice. It is therefore conceivable that there is more scolding now than 50 years ago. We have certainly established that there is a great deal of scolding.

But the director of The Apple Orchard says, "It is important that the one or two children who keep making trouble . . . that we look at them. What do we do to change the situation? Are we making sure that we give them attention for positive things, too?"

Management. The staff meetings are crucial for maintaining the line. The director says, "Essentially, I think one should treat children and adults the same. . . . That is also something that we have discussed at great length among the staff." The newcomer says, "When we have discussions in staff meetings, M [the director] may sometimes put her foot down and say, 'You have to believe that people say what they mean and mean what they say.' That attitude spreads throughout the institution and affects the relations between children and adults." So, opinions should be brought into the open and tested in honest and respectful debate. And the director provides an example. At the same time, the director takes good care of the staff.

An early childhood educator: "I have never before worked in a place where management has been so caring."

The newcomer emphasizes that it is crucial to have leadership with the necessary will, ability, and courage: "It is crucial who the director and the deputy director are. Good early childhood educators are important, but if management lets us down, it all comes to nothing."

The director says, "I invest a great deal of energy in helping the staff to let the children sort out their own conflicts. As adults, we often think that the children's solutions are unfair. Seen from the outside, it may appear that one side loses out, but the children seem to be fine with it. It is also important not to expect to be able to introduce morals and ethics in preschool; the children simply don't get it. We do begin to touch on it in kindergarten, though."

Hiring and firing. "Why did they hire you?" we asked the newcomer. "Because I said all the things I've told you today. And I accepted the job because they never seemed taken aback by what I said."

The deputy director: "The difficult thing with recruitment is: How do you manage to make clear what you think is essential?"

The institution had been through a series of turbulent years. In the deputy director's description: "The staff that were here back then [1997] could not cope and were not happy with the changes. They were paralyzed by the lack of structure and by having to include the children so much, and in response they did nothing; they thought that was the idea. Some of the early childhood educators were very, very structured in their way of thinking, and very controlling toward the children. One early childhood educator thought that she would be able to change, but she did not understand how big a change that would be to her personality. Neighboring institutions and parents also thought it was chaotic. It has been difficult to get things on track, and we had high turnover in staff for a few years."

The director: "I have had to let a few early childhood educators go because they used an inappropriate tone with the children. First, it was brought up by some of their colleagues, then I had talks with them, but it did not work out, and I had to let them go. I think that they may have had emotionally deprived childhoods."

So, management is strong and competent and has the courage to make tough decisions. It is child-centered, but also very caring toward the staff.

To RECAP: What were the conditions that made it possible for The Apple Orchard to introduce a nonscolding culture? They were about to set up a kindergarten section. To head the kindergarten, a deputy director was brought in who was interested in a nonauthoritarian style, as was the director. Staff members with an authoritarian approach had to change; some were not able to. They quit or were let go. Instead, new early childhood educators were hired who had a very different view of children and their work with them. The new nonscolding culture was able to build on an older culture in the preschool, where the job was considered a calling. At the same time, remnants of the old ways survived in parts of the preschool. They did not clash directly with the new paradigm, and they provided a sense of continuity for the "old" staff in a time ripe with change. Another supporting feature was newly developed, closer relations among the staff members: People looked out for each other, closed ranks around colleagues who were having a tough day, received help from the new members with adopting the new paradigm—for example, in terms of handling conflicts. Two teams were able to go farther than the rest of the place. Diversity kept the dynamics alive.

A common feature among the four staff members who were interviewed was that their approach to the care of young children had become an integral part of their view of other people and the very direction of their life.

But why do some early childhood educators choose this direction while it seems completely alien to others? Part of the explanation may lie in early life experiences: parents who insisted on interactions with their children that were not based on power, or teachers who became "ambassadors" for their students. An early childhood educator that one encounters during one's first internship may take on a similar sort of importance. All four relate this type of experiences. But they also all relate very negative experiences: the constantly scolding deputy director, the early childhood educator forcing a little girl to put on her slippers. Perhaps the negative experiences made it necessary for these four to act differently, while the positive experiences gave them the personal strength to carry it through?

NØRHOLM SCHOOL

In this chapter, we move from one part of the country to another, and from one type of institution to another. In fact, we even move outside the institutional area altogether. We do this to demonstrate that not only is the scolding culture omnipresent—so are critical views of it and alternatives to it. Currently, the differences between school and preschool institutions and between teachers' and early childhood educators' cultures are diminishing. This section will therefore show that a kindergarten may have more in common with a school than with the kindergarten next door—and vice versa.

Nørholm School, which covers kindergarten through tenth grade, is situated in Aalborg Municipality in the northernmost part of Jutland, which, along with Skive Municipality, is one of the places in Denmark that has done most to integrate school and after-school and expand the schoolday. Nørholm, however, has developed an approach of its own. In December 1999 the school board and school management presented a "Proposal to Protect the Children in the School Disctrict of Nørholm School." Some of the aims of the proposal:

1. To ensure that the children have a good childhood by ensuring their freedom to play in the hedgerows and space where they can be themselves, alone or with other children.
2. To contribute to a debate about children's education time from pre-primary class through second grade with the view of ensuring that it does not expand beyond its current duration.

3. To contribute to a debate about Learning Through Play with a view to preventing a development toward a suspension of children's freedom.

Background:

It is our claim that it is perceived as a problem, from an adult point of view, that children have a different perspective on the world than adults. Whatever the cost, we adults are intent on creating a sense of continuity in the children's time that they do not in fact require. Through the tyranny of good intentions we adults wish to create order in the children's day due to the completely flawed belief that children cannot handle a shift from a "*must*-section" to a "*can*-section," from school to leisure. The magic phrase in this concept of the all-day institution is "time for concentration and immersion." At Nørholm School, we consider it our duty to ensure that the children have the time and the peace to concentrate on and immerse themselves in the social mechanisms and democratic processes that are automatically engaged in the kids' unscripted play and activities.

The proposal also states that all adults in the institution are to ensure the necessary conditions for concentration and immersion and avoid the tyranny of tightly scheduled plans by working on the basis of a set of common values, "without thereby suspending the children's right to autonomy and self-determination." To insure this, it includes a number of "protective measures":

§ 1. Nørholm School hereby states its right to be constantly critical and to reject, as much as possible, any pedagogical approaches that are primarily based on adult perceptions.
§ 2. The children at Nørholm School are hereby secured the right to freedom from excessive adult supervision and at the same time maintain their right to contact with adults.
§ 3. The children at Nørholm School are hereby secured the right to be themselves, either alone or in the company of others.

The declaration concludes by stating, "This proposal was drafted by Nørholm School and set forth without basis in any existing legislation." This part of Denmark was the scene of a major peasants' revolt in 1534; it is old rebel country where a school—itself a part of the system—can choose to challenge the system head-on.

Scolding is not mentioned in the proposal. Still, it deserves mention in this chapter. For if children's right to self-determination, free time, contact with adults, unscripted play, and privacy are given priority over the needs of the system, then the basis for much scolding will crumble. Scolding often springs from situations in which the needs of the system come before the children's needs. Most institutions do not even mention children's rights, so the simple act of seeing children as *humans with basic human rights* will serve to reduce the use of sanctions against them.

If one asks a 6-year-old to describe what a good adult is like, it might be someone who "was able to think pretty well in their head . . . how children should be treated" (Sigsgaard, 1993b). Maybe this is the kind of adults that are in charge at Nørholm School? Some early childhood education students involved in the Scolding Project arranged a spontaneous excursion to Nørholm as soon as they heard about the place, in order to experience life here firsthand. But all classes had been suspended on the day they arrived. A child's father had passed away, and the adults in the school were busy talking to the children in the school about this difficult thing, the loss of a father. They apologized to the guests, who initially were disappointed that they did not get to see the school properly but realized on the way home that they had in fact seen the school the way it really is.

Most of the institutions portrayed in this chapter have been characterized by intense efforts to change their pedagogical practice, but not the world around them. In this respect, Nørholm School differs. The mission statement says that the school wants to "contribute to a debate" about the expansion in the number of lessons and Learning Through Play. The goal is to change the practice at Nørholm School and through this change contribute to a change outside the school walls.

PEDAGOGICAL WORK IN THE STREET

It has been said that a pedagogical approach that is not based on scolding, punishment, and "boundaries" may work with ordinary children, but would not stand a chance with troubled children and teens. They require a firm hand. Recently, there has been a heated debate in Denmark about crimes committed by young people from ethnic minority groups. Some politicians propose strong authoritarian measures based on fear and punishment. No more bleeding hearts—instead the youngsters were to be handled by "broad-shouldered types" with "rock-hard boundaries."

In this context, two Danish journalists set out to examine the pedagogical work on the frontline.

They produced a series of excellent reports on the practical reality of pedagogical street work in different towns. Below is an excerpt from one of the articles:

> "I never scold," he says for a start. It has no effect on these young criminals. They have been scolded their entire lives. He says, "We are going to the skating rink, and Poul is late. Should I be strict and leave without him? No, that has no effect. He has been left behind all his life and kicked out of five schools.

Instead I drive out to his place and pick him up. . . . If suddenly an adult is willing to invest in him, maybe he can still make something of himself. He has been given up on by all other adults, and I may be the last one that bothers. . . . . Normally, one would be required to make a contribution to society before one could expect to enjoy the benefits, but with these kids it's the other way around. They have to enjoy some benefits before they are able to make a contribution, for they have no basis for contributing. . . . First, we need to instill in them the belief that they are capable at all." Later he says that the teens have no shred of compassion, and that if they do not get "a small slice of the normal world into their world," they will just continue a life of crime. His comment on some politicians' call for harsher punishments: "But that simply doesn't work. When they come out from a prison filled with large, tattooed guys and boundaries, they're on speed, coke, pot, have built up massive debts and are extremely hard to reach." (Elkjær & Christiansen, 2001)

How do children and young people develop a feeling that they are capable, and how do they develop a sense of compassion? By seeing someone else show compassion for them and by building confidence through an active life together with people who believe in them. That is the opposite of scolding, punishment, and "rock-hard boundaries," something which any street worker knows.

Research bears this notion out. Consider the project (p. 137) that showed that a childhood characterized by frequent and severe scolding was a common feature among most violent men.

"Desperate times call for desperate measures," says an old adage. And it is still universally claimed that "difficult" children and youngsters require especially firm hands and boundaries. The experiences of the street workers, however, suggest that times have grown desperate precisely because of measures that are much too desperate, and that more of the same would only make things worse.

One might add that if the street workers scolded, the kids would just walk away. Children in preschool facilities and schools do not have that option. Or to put it another way: Continued scolding from teachers or early childhood educators is only possible because the children do not have the possibility of choosing their own teachers and early childhood educators (which they do in some place; see the description of The Clover Field later in this chapter, p. 202).

THE CHILDREN'S HOUSE AND GARDEN (BØRNENES HUS OG HAVE)

This kindergarten is located in Ballerup, close to Copenhagen. As in other kindergartens, the children were not free to simply wander off and leave the place, but they were free to choose whether and when they wanted to be indoors or outdoors. This changed the power relations between children and adults considerably. The adults no longer decided where the children had to be. Rather, the children decided where the adults had to be: If all the children were outside, most of the adults had to be, too. So although the adults decided that the children were not allowed to leave the premises of the kindergarten between early morning and late afternoon, it was mostly up to the children to decide where, within this territory, they and the adults had to spend the day. The children were also able to decide when, where, and with whom they wanted to eat. It was almost as free as if they were just playing in their own backyard or garden back home. This helped to reduce the number and the severity of traditional conflicts drastically, and there was more time for social-izing and for immersing oneself fully in an activity. This situation was not accomplished without strife. Initially, some parents felt that it was all a big mess, and some employees were not prepared to relinquish control, but after a while it came to seem natural and good to live and work in this fashion.

The "Organization Plan for 1999" provides the following description:

> Life in this kindergarten should be characterized by sharing and equality between children and adults and by the recognition of di-versity. The individual must have access to being heard and taken seriously. . . . Democracy is an essential concept. . . . Therefore, we want to create a kindergarten where life is full of diversity . . . to enable the individual child to seek out the challenges and the inter-action with other children and adults that the child desires. . . . The children in fact know what they want, and they will in time seek out all the different activities available in this kindergarten. We know that kindergartners primarily do what they see the adults close to them doing—rather than what the adults say. Therefore, we adults must have the courage to stand up with the full scope of our person-alities to function as role models for the children, and, metaphori-cally speaking, invite the children inside Danish culture.
>
> Days in this kindergarten should be rich and varied. We are going to sing, read stories, play, go on excursions, laugh, support the children's formation of friendships, and teach them to be around other children and adults. The kindergarten should help the chil-dren get to know the world and learn various skills—as well as teach them common norms for behavior in this society.

"Diversity," "democracy," and "helping the children" are key concepts, far from the laissez-faire attitude that is often presented as the only con-ceivable alternative to adult control and schedules.

Things went well, and it was even possible for the director to take a leave of absence in order to take a 1-year course. While he was away, however, a number of problems arose. "Many children are fragile . . . sometimes they get frustrated and overwhelmed and take it out on the other children or on toys or equipment . . . the speech therapist monitors the language development of 8 of our children (out of a total of 25). . . . It has not been possible to do the usual things with the children, for example, the large-scale games . . . very soon, one of the children will break down, and the game is ruined for everyone, while the adult talks to/comforts/cuddles the unhappy child." These problems became so pressing that the director noticed a marked change when he returned from his leave of absence: "You don't talk nicely to the children!" As mentioned, the staff had been aware of the problems. The annual report stated, "It has not been possible to create an acceptable everyday life for the children and adults in the kindergarten." When the director returned, he put his finger on the sore spot that provided the incentive for renewed action. Additional staff were hired. The Organization Plan established as a "required result" that "the staff return to addressing the children in a pleasant tone and manner," and arrangements were made for outside observers to come in 6 months later to observe and talk to the children—not the staff—to determine whether the efforts had succeeded.

This kindergarten has put in a more sustained and more qualified effort than most kindergartens in Denmark to achieve a freer and more democratic institutional life. The story shows that this sort of work is vulnerable. If the odds against it are stacked too high—here in the form of too many children with special needs without a corresponding increase in resources—the work can become so stressful that setbacks occur. Fortunately, the director returned and was able to take an outside perspective and diagnose the problem. And renewed efforts were made to bring the ship back on course.

In the meantime, however, the local government had decided to restructure the childcare area. The Children's House and Garden was not able to continue as a kindergarten. Thus ended one of the most promising attempts to develop an approach to early childhood education based on a greater degree of democracy and equality.

The outside observers never got the chance to assess whether the staff had been able to get back to using pleasant language with the children.

THE FREE SCHOOL (DEN FRIE SKOLE)

Recently, a private independent school was established that mentioned scolding in its brochure. Since such occurrences are so few and far between, it was tempting to take a closer look at the brochure. It states that the top level of decision making is the School Assembly, where children and adults take part on equal footing.

> One of the committees under the School Assembly is the Judicial Assembly, which is headed by a changing group of students and one adult. In the Judicial Assembly we address any problems that have arisen. We call it a Judicial Assembly because the purpose is to tell right from wrong. The adults do not have a unilateral right to "scold" and determine consequences. Everybody is held equally accountable for violations of the rules drawn up by the School Assembly.

These few lines describe a complete break from the common institutional legal system, where the teachers hold all legislative, judicial, and executive powers. In this school, the School Assembly holds the legislative power and sets up the rules. In the normal system, the teachers enforce the rules, while this school lets both students and teachers handle enforcement. Matters are not settled on the spot by a teacher— for example, through scolding—as in the normal system. They have to be brought before a "court," the Judicial Assembly, where they are heard by a group of students and a teacher. This provides the students with legal protection. Transgressions are reviewed and discussed from different angles.

Previously, in Chapter 7, we showed that what the children resent the most is unfair scolding, situations in which the adults did not, in their opinion, understand what actually had happened. That potential bias is addressed in this school.

This has turned the institution into a community governed by law.

The idea is not really new. After World War II, it was a common perception that society had to do anything possible to avoid another world war. Many saw education as a key. In kindergartens and schools, the children had to be raised to appreciate peace and democracy. Some felt that this could be achieved only if the institutions not only taught peace and democracy, but also practiced it. The best-known advocate of this approach was the British educator A. S. Neill, who introduced democracy and a legal system in his Summerhill School in a way that was somewhat similar to what The Free School has done. The Summerhill School exists to this day, but the idea has not spread—despite its obvious appeal—to many other schools. The Freinet Schools (named after their founder, the French educator Celestin Freinet), however, are influenced by it. Perhaps the ideas of Neill and other educational reformers will once again draw interest in a time when democracy is proving to be less firmly rooted than we may have thought.

THE CHILDREN'S HOUSE (BØRNEHUSET)

Where The Free School started out with a legal system to prevent or at least reduce the teachers' spontaneous scolding in class, The Children's House has no such established systems. But the staff members do plenty of experimenting!

After hearing about the Scolding Project, the adults here decided to abstain from scolding for a month. That went well, so they decided to continue. Perhaps they are still at it?

The staff worked with the question "Whom do I remember most clearly from my childhood?" Most found that their clearest memories were of their grandparents. They discussed the possible reasons for this. Was it because the grandparents had more time for the children?

Grandparents are often accused of spoiling their grandchildren. The staff tried to replace the institutional justice with spoiling. The sinner was not scolded, but instead offered a piece of cake.

The director describes the process:

> We have also tried putting *fruit* out. Immediately someone will ask, "How many pieces for each?" We say, "As many as you want!" Sometimes we have to peel more apples. There has to be plenty to go around. The children get a totally different look on their face when they are free to eat as much as they like. It is *amazing* to them.
>
> We also did a survey among the children, asking, "What do you think is the biggest drag here?" Typical replies were, "When we *have to* go outside, *have to* come along, when the parents are late or early, when someone takes your stuff, when we have to eat." That was clear enough: have to, have to, have to. So we loosened up: "You don't *have to*." Then they want to.

The issues the staff addressed are not randomly selected. They address some of the fundamental issues inherent in institutionalization:

- The meaningless scarcity (of apples or hugs)
- Arbitrary justice
- Irrational force
- Humiliating scolding

And yet the reason that this institution has been included in this chapter lies somewhere else: in the staff's willingness to experiment. They are like children: inquisitive, experimental, exploring. They demonstrate all the wonderful qualities that characterize thriving children but often disappear in adulthood, replaced by disillusioned conformity. They experiment in a professional manner, helping each other reach back to their childhood memories to find the answer to a question that they as professionals know is crucial: What characterizes a loving and well-loved adult? They ask the children to help them discover where the chains of institutionalization feel the tightest (knowing that they must feel tight indeed). They do not ask the children to pinpoint when they learn or develop the most, or what is the best part—only what they consider a drag. And when one's questions are straightforward and direct, one gets clear, specific answers that one can act on. And act they do.

They probably would not have been able to agree to simply stop scolding. That would have been too far-reaching. And some staff members will always be reluctant, wary of making too many changes. But a proposal to stop scolding for a month is hard to oppose. Just for a month! So that idea can be supported. And if it works out, the experiment can continue, as it did in this case.

The stronger the staff's ability to safeguard their progress in times of tribulation, the better their ability to explore these crucial questions in depth and on an ongoing basis: Why do we scold? What bad effects might it have? What was it like to be scolded as a child? What do children learn from it?

THE JOY (GLÆDEN)

We will now look at The Joy, a kindergarten whose primary pedagogical principle is "Save the child!" First a few notes on the staff's thoughts when they first heard about the Scolding Project. According to Jeanette, the director:

> After I told you that in principle, we don't scold at The Joy, I had to run out and ask the others if it was okay for me to say that, 'cause we never use that word. "Scolding," said Eva, "that's funny, it's such an old-fashioned word." We pride ourselves on the fact that we never scold!
>
> We talk a great deal about the importance of using a good tone with the children, for it is everyone at the table that is scolded if one person is scolded.
>
> If children are very mean to each other, if they have done severe and humiliating things to other children, we pull them aside and go somewhere where we can talk with the child in confidence; but by the time we get there, the scolding has evaporated, and we simply *talk* about it.

During the conversation with Jeanette and Mie, who is the deputy director, we managed to pin down the key principles concerning the care of
young children:

If a child and an adult disagree about the factual aspects of an event,
the child gets the benefit of the doubt. The basic principle is that everybody has an intention with his or her actions, but that sometimes the adult
cannot discern the intention and may therefore act unfairly.

The children eat when they are hungry. Since the adults do find it important for everybody to eat together as often as possible, they may *ask* a
child to join the others at the table. If the child says no, "In some situations,
we may tell them that they have to. But as a general rule . . . if they have
something they would rather be doing, they are allowed to do that." It is
the norm, then, to *ask* the children to do what one would like them to do.
An actual demand is the exception.

A third principle is "Save the child." That means that if an early childhood educator sees a colleague being too harsh with a child, he or she is
obliged to intervene on the child's behalf. Jeanette brought the seeds of
this principle with her when she arrived. She was hired partly on the basis
of her notion that children should never cry alone, and that they have the
right to be upset if an adult has been "stupid"; they also have the right to
be comforted by another adult.

> A child is crying, and I go up to him and say, "What's up, Morten?"
> And then there is an adult, with her back turned, who says, "I'm
> handling it. Those two were having an altercation, and this is the
> punishment. Please do not interfere!" That really makes me angry;
> I mean, if I'm talking with a child, I don't want anyone to interrupt,
> same as I don't want anyone to interrupt if I am talking to an adult.
> Morten has the right to say that Bodil is being a jerk. That's where
> it began, and then maybe it turned out that, "it's because I'm not
> allowed to do this or that." Then I might turn to this adult and say,
> "Why not, actually?" And then it got to the point where it was also
> considered okay to interfere even when the adult was still dealing
> with the child. And of course it's more difficult to get involved in a
> situation when someone else is clearly involved. But we did away
> with the loyalty toward the adult and asked ourselves, "Who is most
> important here, in fact, and what does that entail?" That is how we
> ended up with "Save the child." We couldn't stand having to turn
> our back on a kid out of regard for an adult; we had to save the child
> from the clutches of this adult.

When I brought up the common norm that if an adult wants to criticize
another adult, it cannot happen in front of the children, Jeanette replied,

"That's the old notion that adults are only credible if they stick to their 'no' once it's out there. And that mom has to say 'no' if dad said 'no.' We don't agree with that. One is only credible if one can change one's mind, if one is able to have second thoughts."

Mie illustrates with an example: "I suddenly realized that I had said something to someone that was not right, so I had to go and say, 'Hey, I was wrong.' Then he proudly gathered his friends around him and said, 'Mie was wrong in bawling me out—I didn't do it after all!' Then they sort of laughed at me, but that was okay. 'You can sit with us anyway.' And then I thought that being able to admit a mistake actually increases one's credibility."

Jeanette: "The worst thing is when the adults stick to their 'no,' no matter what. Then they make children stupid. That is bound to make children feel different, dumber than . . . because they don't feel that way. Their needs change all the time."

Another principle is "Speak for yourself":

— We have a climbing tree, and some of us don't think it's so cool when they reach the top branches, and then you might say, "Climb four branches down, won't you. But Eva will be out here shortly, and then you can climb back up 'cause she's not as worried as I am."
— And then you might be back out a little later, and then the kid has to keep climbing up and down the tree because one of you is more worried than the other?
— Yes, but the alternative is that the most timid gets to decide.
— And after all, that's life, isn't it. Mom and dad also have different sensibilities, and at grandma's you get to do a lot more, and in school, it's another story again. We learn from that, and we don't lose our integrity. I think that authenticity is more important than consensus!

This brings us to the guiding principles of the institution, which are described in the Organization Plan: self-esteem, confidence, and independence. Taking these principles seriously makes it impossible to scold: "If self-esteem is to be the guiding principle for the relations, in principle it is impossible to scold, for scolding will always be damaging to a person's self-esteem."

Children's Rights at The Joy

As we have seen, one of the guiding principles in the care of young children is to treat children the way one would treat anybody else. A discussion of rights is still necessary, however, because it is an inherent aspect of any institution's purpose and nature to view children as subordinate to the staff, who therefore have the power to treat the children as "subjects." To establish and respect children's rights means giving up some of that power. We will now look at the rights of the children at The Joy:

- *Children have the right to self-determination, as long as this does not infringe on anyone else's rights.*
  One boy did not want to go on the excursion that his friend had gone on the day before.
  "We used to try to manipulate them, because we thought it was really important that they see the Vikings at the National Museum. And we did go to him in the pillow room four times to convince the boy how cool it would be, until his friend said, 'There's no need for him to go, he can just ask me; I've been there already!' Put that in your pipe and smoke it! He will live, even if he does not see the Vikings, but maybe he won't be very happy if he has to go without his best friend. But if we think that a child refuses to do something because he or she is afraid of trying new things, we might infringe on his or her right to self-determination and say, 'You can hold my hand when we get there, but I want you to try!' But that hardly ever happens."
- *Children can go into the playground anytime they want (but there have to be at least two children out there).*
  — What happens, then, if two kids go out at 8:00 in the morning and play there until 4:00 in the afternoon?
  — They get to do that.
  — But they have to eat?
  — We'll bring them their food. In winter, too, if they prefer.
- *Children have the right to eat when they are hungry.*
  Many would expect rights like these to lead to chaos. They forget that when children are at home, it is quite normal for them to go out and play when they want to. They also forget that most children are hungry around lunch and like to eat together. If a few children eat outdoors or eat later, that is not going to bring down the system. If children who are not hungry are forced to sit in, perhaps even forced to eat, that may just lead to a lot of scolding, and where does that leave the cozy mealtime?
- *Children have the right to be upset and to be comforted by an adult of their choice.*
  If a child has been scolded by A, he or she may seek comfort from B. We recognize the fact that conflicts with and perhaps scolding by an unfamiliar adult are very tough on a child; especially in situations like that, the child may require a safe haven. The fact that adults can

be chosen or spurned probably also goes a long way toward preventing scolding.

- *Children have the right to change their mind.*
    - How close to the summer party can you still change your mind about whether you want to be a lion or Batman? Even on your way out the gate?
    - Yes, as long as there are still dress-up clothes left over.
- *Children are allowed to argue in order to stick up for themselves.*
  Even children under 2 can argue for a long time, even without a comprehensible language. This right is related to the more general right:
- *Children are entitled to an opinion.*
  This right would be somewhat flimsy if one did not also have the right to fight for that opinion.
- *Children are entitled to leave the kindergarten area—if an adult goes with them.*
  "One afternoon, some kids came up to me because they wanted to walk outside the kindergarten area. They asked I don't know how many adults and eventually came to me. And I said, 'Can't you ask one of the others, I am in the middle of something here in the kitchen, and I won't be able to watch you.' 'Yes, but we did ask the others, and they said "no."'' So, I had to stop what I was doing and go with them."

  As the story illustrates, this right is rather pointless unless the adults agree to say "yes" whenever possible.

  It is also an important right. The fundamental restriction in young children's freedom is the forced daily placement in a place that they did not choose. The right to leave the kindergarten premises makes this—necessary—restriction more tolerable.
- *In principle, anything is allowed unless it is expressly forbidden.*
  Many early childhood educators have stories about children who ask permission for every little thing. "Yes, naturally," they reply. But to the children, nothing is natural. From their home or from previous institutions, they are used to having to ask permission for everything. If it is not expressly permitted, it is forbidden. They are no longer able to do anything without permission from an outside authority. They have acquired an external locus of control and have lost power over their own lives.

  Many might fear that children who can do anything that is not expressly forbidden would become ruthless, spoiled, and selfish. They believe that children who get used to doing what they are told, receiving a collective order, and respecting the "boundaries" that the adults have set develop a social conscience, become well adjusted and considerate.

But how do children turn out when they are free to do what they want? We don't know, for no children are. Even in a place like The Joy, there are plenty of things that are forbidden. That is why it is so important to consider whether a prohibition or a rule is in fact strictly necessary. For if life is controlled and regulated by others, how are children supposed to be able to maintain and develop their ability for self-regulation? In this paradigm, children become social beings by living a life that is as autonomous as possible together with others that they develop attachments with of their own choice. They develop their will by pitting it against other people's will.

Children who live under conditions where everything that is not expressly permitted is forbidden will experience many of the restrictions as arbitrary. A boy who attended an after-school center where the adults had prohibited computer games on Wednesdays found it crazy: "It's the same as if the adults weren't allowed to scold the kids on Fridays!" he said.

Freedom is a big word. And they did not use the word at The Joy. Nevertheless, the key concepts in their pedagogical approach are freedom and equal worth. From these concepts springs the most striking principle, "Save the child," which, in recognition of the unequal power relations and the child's weak position, rejects the darker sides of collegial loyalty.

THE ZEALAND SCHOOL

A few years ago, the teachers in a school on the Danish island Zealand had become so tired of all the rules and regulations that something had to give. The result—as at The Joy—was children's rights. A teacher tells the story:

> We had grown so tired of spending all our time scolding and enforcing rules that we established a committee charged with creating fundamental changes. We used to have a whole battery of prohibitive rules. They have now been abolished by the teachers and students together and replaced with may-if-you-want-to rules.

One of these may-if-you-want-to rules states, "You may run in the hallways if there are only a few children around." One can almost imagine the discussions in the committee. The children explaining how hard it is not to run in the long hallways. The teachers, acknowledging this, but also pointing out the problems of children careening through a crowded hallway. And then the synthesis, which turns the rule into a right, but a right that recognizes the typical institutional situation of scarce resources, here the scarcity of space in relation to the number of children. The phrasing of the right even goes beyond the traditional dichotomy whereby the teachers lay down and enforce the law, while the children just have to obey. If a teacher stops a child who is running in the hallway while six other children are also present, it is up to the teacher and the child to determine whether six children make up more than "a few" children—math discussions in the hallway! The judicial power has ceased to be the teacher's exclusive domain. The children are gradually assuming joint ownership of the school.

The introduction of may-if-you-want-to rules instead of prohibitions codifies a new fundamental attitude in the school: Rights or may-if-you-want-to rules are desirable assets, while the traditional prohibitive rules are liabilities that should be abolished whenever possible.

There is a striking similarity between these may-if-you-want-to rules and the principle "anything is allowed unless it is expressly forbidden" at The Joy, yet the two institutions have no knowledge of each other.

Another noteworthy aspect of the reform is that its success stems from at least three features:

- It was those in power, the teachers, who acknowledged the need for change.
- The changes happened where they were most sorely needed.
- Teachers and students decided and carried out the changes together.

A few years later, a class and their teacher spent a night at the school. There were many interesting things to do, but the children's choice was clear: running in the hallway. The parents were slightly puzzled when they heard about the activity of choice.

THE NORWEGIAN KINDERGARTEN

As mentioned earlier, a group of Norwegian early childhood educators tried to address the issue of scolding around 1985. They began their efforts in their own institution in Oslo, where "the many rules of the institutionalized approach to the care of young children were replaced with one rule: 'Scolding a child is not allowed.'" This developed into a situation in which early childhood educators would interfere if a colleague was being negative toward a child; thus, it became acceptable to intervene in each other's work. The alternative to scolding was not other forms of sanctions, but a stronger involvement with the children. Instead of scolding the unruly child who is unable to sit still, the early childhood educator now thought, "What can I do to make this child comfortable?" Children and adults developed a closer relationship, and this was especially important to the most disadvantaged or troubled children. In describing the traditional institutional approach, one of the early childhood educators involved, Torgun Allgot, said, "The children who have the greatest need for positive attention from adults are the ones who receive the least."

There were attempts to expand this rejection of scolding through articles in the debate series of the Norwegian periodical *Pedagogisk Forum*. One of these articles was entitled "Stay in line, boy," and the introduction read, "Today, kindergartens are ruled by an institutionalized pedagogical approach, claim the three preschool teachers behind this article. They would like to see a debate about our rules and systems." The articles did spark some debate, but later the debate died out. In an article entitled "Can I get mad at you?" the authors, Taiet and Algot (1986), propose a set of alternatives:

- Have positive expectations of the children, and discover their good sides.
- Establish what the child ought to work with, but stick to one thing at a time.
- Adults must help children make choices, and adults have to assume responsibility.
- Poor child–staff ratios cannot be used as an excuse for scolding. Good child-staff ratios do not necessarily mean less scolding.
- If a child's request is turned down, the child has a right to know why.

This Norwegian kindergarten imposed a direct ban on scolding. The Danish institutions discussed in this chapter do not have such a ban, but, as we have seen, many of them do have a norm of avoiding scolding.

THE SPECIAL NEEDS INSTITUTION SUNGARDEN (SOLHAVEN)

In the previously mentioned debate on juvenile delinquency, in which many politicians called for tougher sentences and a more authoritarian pedagogical approach, a critical eye was directed at institutions advocating what one might call "pedagogical work with a human touch." One of them was Sungarden, whose staff were called on to defend their approach in the press on numerous occasions. The traditional pedagogical approach, based on tough rules and sanctions, was not called into doubt to nearly the same degree.

In one of these interviews, one of the employees at Sungarden said, "If a youth has stolen something at the football club, we don't scold them, 'cause we know that doesn't do anything; we take them back to the club— again and again" (Lihme, 1999).

Again and again. It has taken 15 years to break down this young person's spirit, confidence, and hope. No one can expect scolding, being banned from the club, being grounded, or other forms of sanctions to do any good—on the contrary. As we saw in the project kindergarten, even young children are able to articulate what the alternative ought to be—as they see it: "to say it in a normal way." When asked what the adults are supposed to do if that does not work, they say, "Say it again." That is what the staff at Sungarden is doing: saying it again and again.

Furthermore, they *accompany* the young person to the club. Instead of putting themselves above the youngsters, scolding, they stand at their side as they confront the people they stole from and admit what they did.

That is the only way that these young people can go on using the club, and this openness between club and institution is a necessity. The door to the club is the door to the society that the youth has been expelled from and is now trying to reenter.

An approach based on sanctions would slam that door shut.

THE AFTER-SCHOOL CENTER THE PLUM (BLOMMEN)

This after-school center had asked to be evaluated after they had abandoned a pedagogical approach partially based on "setting boundaries" in favor of a "value-based approach." One of the things they wanted to evaluate was whether an adult who had to turn down a child's request managed to refer the child to another adult who was willing or able to grant it. The director: "Saying 'no' is not the point. Finding out how to say 'yes,' that is the point." As an after-school center they wanted to help the children do what they wanted to do—rather than engaging them in activities that the adults had picked. The children were to receive qualified help. Therefore, the adults wanted to know if they actually remembered to say, "You should ask Christian instead, he's better at that."

If adults are to be able to help children resolve their conflicts—and that is a crucial point for the staff at The Plum—they have to be able to listen to the children. Therefore, one of the evaluation issues was, "Are we good enough at listening?" And, in fact, they did appear to be good at listening. Take, for example, this observation:

11:50 A.M.: Trouble in the wardrobe. Bente: "Hey, what happened?" She sat down on the floor with two children. She did not place herself above or across from the children, but sat down *with* the children.

The following observation demonstrates that the adults do not always manage to live up to their goal:

12:58 in the staff room. Seven-year-old boy: "Yo, Birgitte!" Adult *(curtly):* "My name is not Birgitte, it is Carina." The boy *(proudly):* "I'm the one who wrote 'football'!" (On the blackboard it said *football* in big, bold chalk letters). No response from the adult.

Compare this with an observation at 1:38 P.M.:

Katrine (the child, addressing the observer): "What is my name?"

Why does Katrine say, "What is *my* name?" not the more common, "What is *your* name?" and why is it so important for the boy to let everyone know that he was the one who wrote *football*? In general, everybody wants to leave their mark; more specifically, these children are institutionalized along with scores of other children in cramped rooms, and therefore constantly at risk of disappearing in the crowd. Therefore, heavily institutionalized children have to work harder to be seen, heard, and acknowledged. Being ignored is therefore a severe punishment for an institutionalized child.

In the two observations above there is no listening and no asking. At The Plum, as in the other institutions we visited, the staff certainly do not always do what they say they want to do. Still, it is vital for the staff to discuss what direction they want to aim for and to reach a degree of mutual trust and confidence that will enable them to criticize each other and help keep each other on track. That is the only way to stay on course. But even in outstanding institutions there will be slip-ups, mistakes, and, occasionally, abuse.

The generally nice and liberal atmosphere at The Plum is evident in the diversity of activities taking place all at once, which demonstrates some of the key differences between schools and after-school centers.

The ambience is abuzz and alive. There is playing, jumping, and singing, but no deafening noise. There is a great deal of adult attention. The adults help, inspire, support, but they do not sanction, regulate, or teach. Still, there are many spontaneous activities that provide good literacy preparation: lots of language, storytelling, rhythm, and physical activities.

A comparison between schools and after-school centers may make some of the characteristics of The Plum stand out:

In the traditional school, the children are often required to:	At the after-school center, the children are allowed to:

Sit still
Keep quiet
Raise their hand if they want to speak
Limit singing to music class and
   jumping to PE
Postpone playing till recess
	Work with their hands
	Talk when want to
	Sing as they play or cut paper
	Choose what they want to do
	Choose the adults and children
	   that they want to be with

In the traditional school, the body is silenced most of the time. In the after-school center, the body takes the floor. A physical *"can*-life" is certainly not without its conflicts, but it avoids the conflicts that spring from *musts* and restrictions. This means that fewer sanctions are necessary.

What happens, then, if recreation time is reduced, to ensure that the children learn more Danish and physics? Do children learn more Danish if they speak, sing, and play less? Do they learn more physics if physical activity is disciplined? And what happens to self-esteem and joy?

But not all schools are traditional in their approach. So, in a more optimistic tone, one may say that the stronger the *can*-aspect and the emphasis on bodily expressions, the less the damage from restricting the time spent on dress-up games, spontaneous talking, and singing.

Let us return to The Plum and see how the staff describe their goal.

The overall goal is: "We want to develop a culture for the children where we all address each other nicely and respect the other person's right to be who he or she is."

The staff's motivation for abandoning the rules, restrictions, and boundaries in favor of a value-based approach is described in the Organization Plan for 2001:

> To a child, rules are related to a particular location and a particular situation. That makes it difficult to transfer rules to other contexts. We want to expand the children's possibilities by teaching them things that they are able to transfer to contexts outside of The Plum. This includes basic values and personal attitudes to right and wrong. . . . We are now used to having fewer rules. That puts us in a good position to accept and approve the children's initiatives and requests, because our task now is to create the possibility and the setting for the children to "be able to . . ." For us, the point is to back the children's ideas.

Is there scolding at The Plum? During the time we spent there as observers and interviewers, it only happened in one of the teams. It is our general impression that The Plum is a very friendly institution with a good ambience and lots of activity. *Pædagogik 2001* (the Plum's project on value-based work) states, "We want to direct our energy toward responding to the good, positive, and valuable events and choices rather than directing it at reprimands and scolding." It is rare for a place to set up regulations for the behavior of the adults. Typically, norms are only set up for the *children's* behavior.

This presentation of The Plum will conclude with a brief, perhaps seemingly insignificant, observation. A girl to an observer: "Who are you helping?"

Other observations point in the same direction: The children perceived the adults as people who helped the children. Child–adult relations appeared to fit a typical appeal–help format, not an entreaty–demand format.

We have previously seen that appeal–help relations produce less scolding than entreaty–demand relations.

"THE VILLAGE SCHOOL"

Now we go from this after-school center in a Copenhagen suburb to a school in a small village, which today is part of a medium-sized municipality in the western part of Denmark. Here it appears to be the school's special function as a combined cultural center, assembly hall, and overall heart of the community that gives the teacher–student relations their unique character.

After the grocery store closed down, the church and the school were the only institutions left to keep this small village together. The church congregation was divided into two warring factions, so it was all up to the school. The school enacted major changes both to open itself to the community and to ensure open communication internally. Baptism parties often take place in the school lobby, which means that teachers and students are not able to use the lobby for the day. Anyone needing to use a computer can use the school's computer lab, which also offers free telephones. The school stays open until 10:30 P.M. every day, and there are no locks on the cabinets. There have been no incidents of theft or vandalism, but of course the locals look after *their* school.

If a schoolboy falls down and hurts himself he may run into the kindergarten section and receive care and a bandage from an early childhood educator. "They are better at handling the care thing than we are," says a teacher. And the boy may visit the kindergarten from time to time—a treat for the kindergartners, who are keen to spend time with the older children.

The hedgerow around the school includes a number of large trees, where the children have constructed forts where they can have some privacy.

The basic principles permeating the school are openness, involvement, and trust, unlike the general principles of institutionalization, which are closure, division of labor and functions, and control. One might say that the school is involved in an ongoing attempt to deinstitutionalize itself.

What does all this have to do with scolding? First of all, there is less reason to scold if most things are open and permitted. Second, its integration into the community gives the children a sense of the school as a big place belonging to them and their families, among others; this sense of shared ownership leads the children to take better care of the school. And third, the teachers come to see the children as more than just the parents' private domain. When the walls between home, school, and community are broken down, the walls between people also begin to crumble. The class teacher may take part in the party in the lobby to celebrate the baptism of a student's little sister. Thus, the teacher also sees the student as a big sister, and the child sees the teacher as a good acquaintance of her parents'. If a conflict occurs the following day, the two do not have the hierarchically determined relationship of an authority figure versus an institutionalized child.

Perhaps this is part of the explanation for why the teachers in this school have developed a nontraditional approach to conflict management. Instead of scolding, they try to set up a talk between the involved parties. Instead of administrating a set of fixed rules, they pride themselves on not proposing prepackaged solutions. Instead of looking at problems and barriers, they look at competencies. "Do you never scold anyone?" we asked. "No, we gave that up," answered the principal.

This statement—"We gave that up"—may reflect a relationship between the change in the school's view on scolding and its practice in general, perhaps even suggesting that the general practice caused this change. The order of events was not that the teachers stopped scolding, and then the school became an open part of the community. Rather, certain conditions favored a development whereby the school became the assembly hall and general center of the village. This in turn led to changes in the relations between adults and children. The teachers were more than just teachers. The students were more than just students. And scolding gradually disappeared. With the gradual change in practice, the teachers were in a better position to put the changes into words.

Naturally, parents, children, and former students alike love their school. But they are in a constant struggle with the municipality to keep it, because the municipality favors large, rational units.

THE CLOVER FIELD KINDERGARTEN (KLØVERMARKEN BØRNEHAVE)

The Clover Field Kindergarten does not have very much room indoors. But it does have about 5 acres of land for the children to roam. A schedule shows where the adults are currently working—one is with the farm animals, one is working in the garden, a third is in the kitchen, and so on. *It is the adults' time that is scheduled here, not the children's, as it is in most places.*
   Late in 2000, the staff had picked three focus areas for 2001:

- They were going to stop yelling or scolding.
- They were going to get better at appreciating and really seeing the children.
- They were going to attempt to ensure that every child in the kindergarten had at least one friend.

People who know the kindergarten might wonder about the choice of these three areas. The Clover Field has the reputation of being a great place to be, with a high degree of freedom, empathy from the staff, and a friendly tone. But in fact it is characteristic of the institutions and schools that have tried to limit scolding that they are places that already do less scolding than most other places. And still, they are aware that they do far too much.
   The staff initiated a process to change and document their practice, experiment, and take a critical look at each other's work. Let us illustrate the process with this little rabbit story, told by Ulla, the deputy director:

> Together with the children, the adults on the farm have just finished mucking out all the rabbit cages and mixing the feed for the rabbits. All is in order.
>   It is my job to handle the afternoon feeding. I see a boy and a girl at the rabbit cages. They have just taken two liters of feed mix and distributed it among all the cages. "Damn kids," is what I hear in my head, and at the same time, "How do I handle this?" I am angry: "Please leave now, I want to talk to you in a little while."
>   I clean up most of the mess and then find the two helpful young people, because that is in fact what they are. I take both of them by the hand. "I want to show you something." I take them to our scheduling board with pictures of all the adults and explain the system to them, keeping it as simple as I can. I tell them that I am at the farm when my picture is up there. I tell them that if they want to feed the animals, they have to do it together with an adult. "Would you like to help feed the rabbits?" They do. We all go and feed the rabbits.

The adults also intervened in each other's work if they saw a colleague scolding. In staff meetings scolding, appreciation, and friendships were addressed on an ongoing basis. The expectation was that if the staff could avoid scolding, the children would be more helpful toward each other and have a friendlier dialogue with each other. The children (as well as the adults) would also have less trouble accepting a "no."

Until April, the project was not very different from the other projects described in this chapter. But in April, the staff and board gathered all the notes and documentation they had assembled about their initiative and took it with them to a PTA meeting, where the staff and the parents agreed to adopt it as their common work papers. This implied that the parents were going to attempt to scold less at home, be more appreciative, and leave more room for friendships between the children.

Here are excerpts from an interview with the parents of three boys:

Parents: It often happens when we come home tired—everybody wants the couch, and the trouble begins.

Interviewer: And previously, you would have scolded them?

Parents: Yes.

Interviewer: So what do you do now?

Parents: We try to break it up a bit, and maybe one of them will go to his room instead.

Mother: Recently, we have been trying to do stuff together when we get home, before we cook or clean. We bought some glass paint and some board games. Then everybody settles down a little. It is easier if you just manage to count to ten first.

Father: While I was at home, recuperating from my illness, I was able to drop the kids off later and pick them up earlier. That gave us more time together and made things more relaxed—and there was less scolding. You calm down instead of blowing up.

. . . .

At first, I thought the project was a load of bull. Am I going to have spend even more of my time? I thought, "Don't do this, don't say that," but I think it only took 3 weeks, then I was past that. . . . You get tired, after all, of being the guy where the kids say, "Dad is always scolding us."

Two other parents were asked for examples of instances in which they would have yelled or scolded in the past but would find a different solution now:

— We haven't made any plans for it. We are just a little more aware of it.

— When we eat, and once again they don't want to taste the vegetables, at one point one of us will raise their voice, but then the other person gives you a look, and you know you have to pipe down.
— Getting dressed, that's where we may sometimes take some time, and I'll say, "Don't you see, they don't go together!" I guess I feel that he should look nice. That's an area where maybe I should get better at saying, "So what"—but he often thinks his clothes are lame, and then I might get stubborn and think that he has to learn to wear those pants.

One year later, parents and teachers held another meeting, at which they decided to continue the project for one more year. There had been great progress. When parents complained that their children did not want to come when they came to pick them up in the afternoon, the early childhood educator would say, "How about having her bring a friend home?" and the parents do this more and more frequently. For 5 or 6 years, the institution had had the tradition of a communal trip to the swimming pool on Friday afternoons—including parents and grandparents. After the swim, many plans are made on an individual basis, and this has increased after friendship became an explicit topic. The institution plays an important role in the development of the parental networks that used to develop on their own, and the early childhood educator see this as a responsibility they should take on.

VOGNMANDSPARKEN KINDERGARTEN

The preparations for the work described in this book began in 1994. As mentioned, the point of departure was a development project in Vognmandsparken Kindergarten, which aimed at developing more appreciative child–adult relations.

Chapter 2 presented the development project and its methodology, and data from the kindergarten have been presented and analyzed along with other data throughout the book.

We will now return to Vognmandsparken. We will provide a few glimpses from the place and try to draw out some of the most important general features of the development in order to outline the contours of a nonscolding culture.

Vognmandsparken Kindergarten after 7 years of Development Work and Research

A graduate student working on her final thesis, with no knowledge of the Scolding Project, visited Vognmandsparken Kindergarten recently to take a closer look at the 6- and 7-year-olds in the kindergarten. For many years, most children have remained in the kindergarten until they were old enough to go directly to first grade. During her visit, she was so fascinated with some of the general features of the kindergarten's approach that she described them in her report:

> I spent some hours watching the children while they played. They all seemed to be having a great time. They were immersed in their play with each other, and they moved freely, both indoors and outdoors. The staff has the declared intention of letting the children lose themselves in the things that hold their interest. If some children are in mid-play when it is time for lunch, they are allowed to eat where they are or wait until they are done. It is the staff's general aim to avoid interrupting the children when they are involved in something, simply to have them do something else. I saw no adult interference, only adults who stepped in if the children needed help. The adults addressed the children in a friendly and respectful way, and the atmosphere was very positive. Suddenly, some children wanted to take a bath, so a tub was filled up, and they were given some bubble bath. Perhaps even a tad too pedagogical for my taste!! Later, when I wanted to talk to the director over a cup of coffee, a boy came in and also wanted coffee; he wanted to sit with us while we talked. Nothing appeared to be out of the question.
>
> The place itself was warm and friendly; it looked like a cozy home, not an institution. The furniture was not like standard kindergarten furniture; instead the furniture and décor made it look more like a private home. There was even a piano room, and I heard someone who was actually able to play the piano, probably one of the early childhood educators, which provided a nice atmosphere. The fireplace was lit, and there was an atrium with lots of plants. The rooms were nice and sunny, and there were cozy nooks where the kids could withdraw and find some privacy. In the playground there was an apple tree with lots of red apples, and the playground was full of hiding places and possibilities; some chickens strolled about. "We think of the kindergarten as the children's house," said the director.
>
> The kindergarten seemed like an oasis in the midst of the concrete housing blocks.

What has happened in the course of the project years? Two episodes that resemble each other may provide a partial explanation. The first incident occurred in August 1996, the following happened:

Assembly time in the Red Group. All the children sit together, except Lisa and Nana. "Are you coming?" asks Lillian. "We are going to talk about where to go on our outing." Nana: "But we went
yesterday." Lillian: "Well, maybe you did, but yesterday we went
to the zoo, and today we are going to the beach." Lisa comes along,
but Nana puts her chin on her chest so that her hair falls down and
completely covers her face. She says nothing but just sits there, sort
of frozen. Lillian considers for a while, then walks over to Nana
with quick, determined steps. She grabs Nana's arm and moves her
away from the chair. She sits down on the chair in exactly the same
position as Nana had before: "What would you think if you had to
say something to me, and I sat like this?" Nana: "Nothing." Lillian:
"Nothing! I think may be we should try that some day, for I can tell
that I getting damn irritated. Now go sit down with the others!"
Nana sits down and says nothing.

Three or four years later, things were different:

Lillian was sitting in a circle with the children, but Jannik did not
want to join. Lillian stretched an arm out behind her while she kept
talking with the children. She said, "Jannik is angry, so he does not
want to join in right now." The boy gradually moved closer, and
a few minutes later, he had joined the circle. Lillian had her arm
around him.

This story, which we examined in a different context earlier, is very
different from the story about Nana. While Jannik is helped to join the
circle, Nana is ordered to join. Jannik's right to be angry is validated, and
he is allowed to stay outside the circle until he is ready to participate.

It probably would not be true to say that there is no use of force in
the kindergarten today, but over the years there are considerably fewer
confrontations and much more help.

Another change has to do with the staff's perception of the amount
of scolding in the institution. Initially they did not think that there was
very much scolding, but already after 1 year they realized that there was
actually a fair amount. Later, the nature of the scolding changed rather
quickly. No one scolded without having first inquired about the events,
no one scolded a child that they were not close to, there was no scolding
in front of everybody, and after a scolding the early childhood educators
always told the child that they were not angry with the child anymore.
But the staff still felt that the amount of scolding was unchanged and that
scolding was necessary. The change was strictly qualitative. Only a few

years after the end of the Scolding Project did Lillian and Gitte reach the point of view that the children are always right. It is not necessary to scold. One may, as the children had hoped for, "say it in a normal way."

At the same time, there have been many changes in the approach to the care of young children, large and small, that have reduced scolding—for example the previously mentioned introduction of a tablecloth to reduce the amount of noise that bothered Gitte so much. In an interview, Lillian and Gitte say, "The children are nicer to each other after the Scolding Project." Perhaps, if the adults are nicer to the children, then the children will be nicer to each other, too. This means fewer clashes requiring adult intervention, which has reduced the need for scolding even more. The child–adult relations have entered a good cycle.

This experience from Vognmandsparken Kindergarten supports the assumption in The Clover Field Kindergarten that less scolding will make the children be kinder and more helpful toward each other.

The Children's Social Skills

Overall, it seems that changes in child–adult relations help the children develop their social skills. At the end of the development project, Gitte, the deputy director, said, "The children come to us on their own initiative now, to ask us for help to resolve a conflict. Sometimes we send them back with suggestions for what they might say. That lets them practice their communicative skills."

In a conversation with three children on their last day in the kindergarten, Lars said, "I don't mind being scolded by Lise, 'cause she isn't very harsh." Sara: "I feel the same way." Later, Lars says in reply to a question, "No, I'm not sure what she will say, but I know that she won't be angry with me."

The children are not free to choose whom to get a reprimand from if they are to be reprimanded, but they can imagine the possibility. They have learned to take a critical look at scolding, and they are familiar with scolding that is not accompanied by anger. Scolding is no longer just a given that simply hits a person. Some staff do more scolding, some do it less or more mildly, while some do none at all.

As previously described, the children have learned to defend themselves against scolding: "I just don't listen." "I just walk away, I don't want to hear it." "Sometimes I just let it go in one ear and out the other." That is what three children said when they were asked what one might do when one is scolded. To be able to protect oneself from "attack" would have to qualify as a social skill.

Later in the conversation, Sara said to the director, Lillian, "One time, Lillian, you were scolding me in the office, and then I scolded you."

The fact that Sara is able to speak in that way to Lillian reflects that the kindergarten is well on its way to developing a nonscolding culture. It is not normal for a child to scold an adult. The fact that Sara dares to do that and even has the courage to bring it up—proudly—in the farewell conversation may be taken as a reflection of the long-lasting openness about scolding. The oppressive atmosphere and the taboos surrounding it are gone. Sara is equipped to face the potential abuses of power that she may experience in the next installment of her long institutionalized life.

Perhaps it should be added that if an adult scolds a child in a climate where the child has the ability and the courage to talk back, if necessary, the scolding will do far less damage than it would otherwise. The child is not left defenseless and humiliated.

Younger children also criticize scolding. In the incident in which some children had immersed the chickens in cold water, they were scolded, and another group of children, who had witnessed the events, were interviewed by Lone:

> *Lone:* How could you tell that the adults were angry?
> *Child:* They were upset . . . the children were upset.
> *Lone:* Was it right or wrong for the adults to scold them?
> *Child:* It was right.
> *Lone:* Was there anything the adults could have done instead of scolding the children?
> *Child:* They could have just said "no."

And from another child:

> *Lone:* What might Jan and Gitte have done instead of scolding?
> *Child:* They could have just said "no."

Just say "no," say the two children, but they still thought it was right for the children to be scolded. This probably implies that they felt that some intervention was necessary—but not anger, simply an authoritative interference with what was going on.

So, most of the children in Vognmandsparken Kindergarten no longer just accept scolding, and they may protest it when they think it necessary. They are able to imagine alternatives. Some may on occasion even scold an adult, but they may also ask adults for help with resolving their conflicts. By turning scolding into an issue that can be questioned and debated, the adults enable the children to imagine alternatives to scolding and to interfere with a scolding adult in the kindergarten or perhaps at home, as we saw in an earlier example. And if children dare stand up to those in power, they may also dare to do the same as adults.

WHAT COMES IN WHEN SCOLDING GOES OUT?

Until now, the critical debate on punishment has focused on the use of physical force. Verbal punishment has gone largely unnoticed, and it has been the object of little or no critical thinking. The common perception of an alternative to scolding would be reward, usually praise. Many early childhood educators have worked with "punishment and reward," a dichotomy that points to rewards as the opposite to punishment. That misses the point that punishment and reward have many features in common. In both cases, an external authority evaluates and grades the child. In both cases children learn that their own self-opinions are of no importance, and in both cases the long-term effects may be personal insecurity and a dependence on praise or punishment from others. The child may eventually be unable to take pride in achievements until these achievements have been praised by an adult. The child is no longer guided by his or her own desires and volition, but by a search for praise or fear of punishment. Both praise and punishment, therefore, have the potential of damaging the child's self-regulation, confidence, and self-esteem.

So it is not praise that comes in when scolding goes out. What is it then? One answer might be that the opposite of scolding is appreciation: Appreciation of the other—the child—as a person, not just as "my" student or "my" child; "the other" in his or her own right, not just subject to the rights of the institution, and with the right to be *oneself* with one's own thoughts, feelings, and opinions. Like praise, scolding invalidates the child's own opinion and experience and replaces them with the adult's opinion and assessment. But if the child's opinion, experience, and intention are to be recognized and validated, they must be expressed. And they can be expressed only by the child.

If appreciation is the true alternative to the praise and punishment of a pedagogical approach based on adult assessment and evaluation, its most salient feature is that it helps give the child "a voice." Where praise and punishment tend to silence the child, an appreciative culture values the child's own expressions.

FROM ASSESSMENT TO APPRECIATION

So, what do they have in common, all the very different institutions, schools, and other places presented here? Their practice varies a great deal, but they share a number of common features, which are outlined below:

- They have given up the traditional notion of adults standing across from and often in opposition to the children. The notion that adults are the ones who know, who are able, and who are right. The notion that children do not know, are not able, and are not right. The notion that the adults therefore have to rear the children and provide them with knowledge and skills. In The Joy they give the child the benefit of the doubt and assume that children always have a reason for doing what they do. In The Apple Orchard the adults learn from the children. In The Free School children and adults have equal say.

- All these places are in the process of discarding a normative child-rearing philosophy. While most people find it natural that adults sometimes scold children, "our" institutions are coming to find it equally natural that scolding is nonexistent or rare. "We gave that up," they say in The Village School.
- When children cease to be seen as objects for the adults to rear and educate, the path is prepared for them to be seen as human beings in their own right, of equal worth, and with their own desires, volition, and direction. This enhances the adults' understanding of the children and their ability to put themselves in the children's place.
- The changes in the adults' attitudes make institutionalization more tolerable and turn it into an experience that is often rewarding and even enjoyable for the children, who in practice are able to develop such equality with adults that they may even scold the adults or intervene on behalf of a child who is being treated unfairly, as happens in Vognmandsparken Kindergarten.
- The tradition of making demands on children is increasingly replaced by a helping attitude, as we saw in The Plum ("Who are you helping?") and in Nørholm School when a child's father had passed away.
- Pedagogical norms and duties are supplemented with or replaced by the rights of the institutionalized. We saw this clearly in The Joy, which had listed eight rights, including the right to have arguments in order to stick up for oneself and the right to be comforted by an adult of one's own choice, and in The Zealand School, where children have the right to play in the hallway when there are not too many other children around. And we saw it most clearly in Nørholm School, where the children's right to be free from learning and scripted play and from expansions in school hours and their right to play in the hedgerows were laid out in a protection declaration. But the children also have a strong position in The Children's House and Garden, where they decide when to go outside to play and when to eat, and in The Clover Field, where they choose which adult they want to go to, if any.

- In many places, the parents visit the institution often, most clearly in The Clover Field, with the communal swimming on Fridays and the parental involvement in a 2-year scolding project, and in The Village School, where the parents use the school as a venue for family parties, a computer lab, and many other functions.
- The staff are characterized by an experimental attitude as in The Children's House, where they temporarily suspended *must,* introduced bottomless fruit trays, and offered the sinners cake—or in The Apple Orchard, where two teams decided to try to avoid saying "not" or "no."
- All the institutions are permeated by a critical attitude. Established truths are open to debate. Even colleagues are subject to criticism, most pronounced in The Joy, where an early childhood educator who sees a colleague being too hard on a child is obligated to intervene on the child's behalf, to "save the child," but also consistently and powerfully in Vognmandsparken Kindergarten where early childhood educators record their colleagues' scolding episodes for subsequent discussion in staff meetings.
- Documentation is generally not the strongest feature in these stories. More documentation, and more systematic documentation, would provide a stronger basis for the critical debates and the processes of change. One early childhood educator says, "We had a little girl with massive problems. We decided to describe them in order to provide a better basis for action. As soon as they were described, the girl got much better."
- A few of "our" institutions hardly even mention scolding. The reason for including them anyway is that they, like Nørholm School, have carried out consistent efforts to address the causes for scolding. More room for self-determination, more free unstructured time, and freer contact with the adults are bound to reduce the amount of scolding. Scolding—like bullying—is a symptom of underlying problems.
- The adults are good at thinking "both–and" instead of "either–or." The angry child who cannot cope with being in the circle may sit close to it, holding Lillian's hand and gradually moving closer. Hungry children can help themselves to food from the fridge without compromising the communal meal.
- Laissez-faire practices are often presented as the only alternative to a pedagogical approach based on training and adult assessment. All "our" institutions are characterized by adults who are active, help the children along, walk ahead of or are helped by the children. They dare to be intense and to immerse themselves,

including in their own adult activities. This is most evident in the preschool facilities. But the special-needs educators also say how they try, over and over again, patiently and persistently. The failing youths are so damaged that that they have to enjoy some benefits before they are able to contribute to society, enjoy the care that others enjoyed while growing up, but that they were deprived of. Here, "broad-shouldered types" with "rock-hard boundaries" will only make matters worse.

- Only the Norwegian kindergarten and Reventlow's Brahetrolle-borg School from 1784 have a written ban on scolding. This may be reflection of the fact that, unlike spanking, scolding is not yet perceived as violence against children, but perhaps also of the fact that the change in schools and preschool facilities from child-rearing and education facilities to life arenas has only just begun. And perhaps it is a reflection of the fact that a critical view of institutionalization is a new and emerging area.

What is best for the children, then: an emphasis on grades, academic skills, early literacy training, the integration of school and after-school programs, boundaries and restrictions—or the approach described in this book? Well, this book has documented the probability of the claim that children from the project institutions and schools will emerge with fewer scars, more confidence and joy, and better social skills than children from more traditional institutions or schools.

Whether they also develop superior academic, intellectual, and practical skills has to remain a matter of faith for now.

It would seem self-evident, however, that "our" institutions and schools are better adapted to the modern world, which requires independence, communicative skills, and flexible and creative thinking.

After all, children are at the mercy of institutions and schools for a massive 25,000 hours of their childhood. If they experience scolding, reprimands, and the like for upwards of 25% of that time, as the previously mentioned Icelandic study (Sigurdardottir, 1997) suggested, that means 6,000 hours of reprimands, reproach, and scolding during childhood—not including any scolding within the family. These 6,000 hours correspond to at least 3 of the 15 to 16 years that an average modern child spends in schools and institutions.

Even if the children did not come out one iota better in terms of academic or human competencies by being met with appreciation, it would still be really nice for them—and for the adults in their lives—if the scolding could be turned down a notch or two.

References

Allen, R. M., & Casbergue, R. (1997). Evolution of novice through expert teachers' recall: Implications for effective reflection on practice. *Teaching and Teacher education, 13* (7), 741–755.

Alvestad, T. (Ed.). (1999). *Utfordringer og muligheder i barnehagen.* Oslo: Pedagogisk Forum.

Andersen, L. (Ed.). (1977). *Børn og bevægelse.* Them: Dixit.

Bae, B. (1996). *Det interessante i det almindelige—en artikkelsamling.* Oslo: Pedagogisk Forum.

Bae, B., & Waastad, J. E. (Eds.). (1992). *Erkjennelse og anerkjennelse.* Oslo: Universitetsforlaget.

Barn och misshandel—en rapport om kroppslig bestraffning och annan misshandel i Sverige vid slutet av 1900-talet. Statens offentliga utredningar 2001:18. (2001). Stockholm: Fritzes.

Bettelheim, B. (1988). *En god nok forælder—En bog om børneopdragelse.* Copenhagen: Schønberg.

"Den Blå betænkning." Undervisningsvejledning for folkeskolen: betænkning afgivet af det af Undervisningsministeriet under 1. september 1958 nedsatte læseplansudvalg (1960–1961). Copenhagen: The Danish Ministry of Education.

Botor, C. O. (1987, July). *Mother–child relationships in early childhood: Japan, Philippines and Thailand. The Philippine report.* Paper presented at the Biennial Meeting of the International Society for the Study of Behavioural Development, Tokyo, Japan.

Brahetrolleborg skolevæsens instrux. (1784). Retrieved August 30, 2004 from http://www.reventlow.dk/skoleinstrux.php.

Bronfenbrenner, U. (1979). *The ecology of human development: Experiments by nature and design.* Cambridge, MA: Harvard University Press.

Cherryholmes, C. H. (1988). *Power and criticism: Poststructural investigations in education.* New York: Teachers College Press.

Coopersmith, S. (1967). *The antecedents of self-esteem.* San Francisco: Freeman.

Dollard, J., Doob, L., Miller, N., Mowrer, O. H., & Sears, R. (1950). *Frustration and aggression* (8th ed.). New Haven, CT: Yale University Press.

Dugstad, B. S. (1992). Sanksjonsformer i skolen. In *Rapport nr. 6.* Trondheim: Norsk Senter for Barneforskning.

Dutton, D. G., van Ginkel, C., & Starzomski, A. (1995). The role of shame and guilt in the intergenerational transmission of abusiveness. *Violence and Victims, 10* (2).

Elever der forstyrrer undervisningen for sig selv og andre i folkeskolen. redegørelse til Folketinget 1997. (1997). Copenhagen: Danish Ministry of Education.

Elgin, S. H. (1980). *The gentle art of verbal self-defense*. Englewood Cliffs, NJ: Prentice-Hall.

Elkjær, J., & Christiansen, F. (2001, March 20). Utilpassede unge: Militærstribet bolchepædagogik hjælper unge. *Politiken*.

Endo, Y., Yoshikawa, S., & Sannomiya, M. (1991). A study on types of parents' scolding utterances. *Japan Journal of Educational Psychology, 39*, 85–91.

Etaugh, C., & Harlow, H. (1973). *Behaviors of male and female teachers as related to behaviors and attitudes of elementary school children*. Paper presented at the biannual meeting of the Society for Research in Child Development, Philadelphia.

Foucault, M. (1979). *Discipline and punish: The birth of the prison*. Harmondsworth, UK: Penguin Books.

Giddens, A. (1992). *The transformation of intimacy: Sexuality, love and eroticism in modern societies*. Stanford, CA: Stanford University Press.

Giddens, A., & Held, D. (1982). *Classes, power and conflict*. Basingstoke, UK: Macmillan.

Gissel, S., Tølbøll Mortensen, J., & Juul, S. (2000). Høreevnen hos danske skolebørn ved ind- og udskolingsundersøgelsen. *Originale Meddelelser, 42*.

Habermas, J. (1987). *Samtalens fornuft*. Copenhagen: Rosinante.

Halse, J. Aa. (1998). *Omsorgssvigt—hvorfor, hvad gør vi?* Copenhagen: Børns Vilkår.

Hart, C. H., DeWolf, M., & Burts, D. C. (1993). Parental disciplinary strategies and preschoolers' play behavior in playground settings. In C. H. Hart (Ed.), *Children on playgrounds: Research perspectives and applications*. Albany: State University of New York Press.

Hind, A. (Ed.). (2001). *PGU'erens Grundbog*. Frederikshavn: Dafolo.

Hong, S. M., & Page, J. (1989). A psychological reactance scale: Development, factor structure and reliability. *Psychological Reports, 64*(3), 1323–1326.

Honig, A. S. (1992). *Prosocial development in children*. New York: Garland Publishers.

Honig, A. S. (1994). Comforting babies in public spaces. *Early Childhood Development and Care, 97*, 165–173.

Honig, A. S., & Lally, J. R. (1988). Behavior profiles of experienced teachers of infants and toddlers. *Early Childhood Development and Care, 33*, 181–199.

Howes, C., & Hamilton, C. E. (1992). Children's relationships with caregivers: Mother and child caregivers. *Child Development, 63*, 859–866.

Højlund, S. (2001). *Barndom mellem børn og professionelle*. Århus: Århus Universitet.

Ingen slinger i valsen, parts 1–2. Program on Danish TV-channel DR 1, December 27, 1998.

Jensen, K. S. (2000). Børnene viser os voksne hvordan vi er. *Liv i Skolen, 2*.

Jeppesen, K. J., & Nielsen, A. (2001). *Tosprogede småbørn i Danmark. Rapport nr. 4 fra forløbsundersøgelsen af børn født i 1995*. København: Socialforskningsinstituttet. Retrieved from http://www.sfi.dk/graphics/SFI/Pdf/Rapporter/2001/0106Tosprogede_boern_i_Danmark.pdf

Johnson, D. W., Johnson, R., Dudley, B., & Burnett, R. (1992, September). Teaching students to be peer mediators. *Educational Leadership*.

Johnstone, M., & Munn, P. (1992). Discipline in Scottish secondary schools. *Research in Education, 50*.

Joubert, C. E. (1992). Antecedents of narcissism and psychological reactance as indicated by college students' retrospective reports of their parents' behaviors. *Psychological Reports, 70*(3).

Juncker, B. (1998). *Når barndom bliver kultur. Om børnekulturel æstetik.* Copenhagen: Forum.

Juul, J. (1995). *Dit kompetente barn.* Copenhagen: Schønberg.

Jørgensen, P. S., Christensen, E., & Ertmann, B. (1995). *Børn og unge på tværs.* Copenhagen: Hans Reitzels Forlag.

Jørgensen, S. S. (2000). *Hvor tit skal jeg sige det?* Internship report on scolding. Glostrup: Højvangseminariet [unpublished manuscript].

Kato, S. et al. (1998). Untitled paper on children's rights and violence against children presented at the OMEP world conference in Copenhagen.

Kragh-Müller, G. (1997). *Børneliv og opdragelse.* Copenhagen: Hans Reitzels Forlag.

Lidegaard, B. (2002). *Jens Otto Krag* (vol. 2). Copenhagen: Gyldendal.

Lihme, B. (1999). *Det er så fucking træls: Solhaven og de unge.* Copenhagen: Forlaget Børn og Unge.

Løkken, G. (2002). Goddag, goddag, tag masken af. *The Journal 0–14, 2.*

Luhmann, N. (2000). *Sociale systemer.* Copenhagen: Hans Reitzels Forlag.

McNeil, L. M. (1988). *Contradictions of control, school structure and school knowledge.* New York: Routledge.

Merrett, F., & Whelldall, K. (1992). Teachers' use of praise and reprimands to boys and girls. *Educational review, 44* (1).

Mikkelsen, M. (2004). Forældre afviser fysisk afstraffelse. *Kristeligt Dagblad,* July 27, 2004. Retrieved August 30, 2004 from http://www.religion.dk.

Miller, A. (1991). *Banished knowledge. Facing childhood injuries* (rev. ed.). London: Virago Press.

Moos, H. (1995). *Hvad har dit barn lært i dag? Rationel børneopdragelse.* Copenhagen: Borgen.

Nilsson, U., & Eriksson, E. (1983). *Lille Søster Kanin eller fortællingen om den fede nattergal.* Copenhagen: Gyldendal.

Nygaard Christoffersen, M. (2002). *Children and adolescents' life conditions in the Nordic countries. Social predictors of children's life conditions.* (Children and adolescents life conditions in the Nordic countries, No. 564). Copenhagen: Nordic Council of Ministers.

Paul, J. (1991). *Forældre og børn.* Copenhagen: Schønberg.

Perris, C., Jacobsson, L., Lindstrom, H., von Knorring, L., & Perris, H. (1980). Development of a new inventory for assessing memories of parental rearing behaviour. *Acta Psychiatria Scandinavica, 61,* 265–274.

Pfiffner, L. J., & O'Leary, S. G. (1989). Effects of maternal discipline and nurturance on toddlers' behavior and affect. *Journal of Abnormal Child Psychology, 17* (5).

Qvortrup, J. (1994). *Børn halv pris.* Esbjerg: Sydjysk Universitets Forlag.

Rasmussen, K., & Smidt, S. (2000). Institutionskritik er ikke det samme som kritik af institutionerne. *Arbejderhistorie, 4.*

Rasmussen, K., & Smidt, S. (2001). *Spor af børns institutionsliv.* Copenhagen: Hans Reitzels Forlag.

Read, K. H. (1960). *The nursery school: A human relationships laboratory.* Philadelphia: Saunders. (Original work published 1950)

Respekt for læreren. (1997). *Folkeskolen,* 14/15.

Sabillón, J. C. T. (1999). Kommunikasjon og grenser—i Norge og Honduras. *Barnehagefolk, 3.*

Salzinger, S., Feldman, R. S., & Hammer, M. (1993). The effects of physical abuse on children's relationships. *Child Development, 64,* 169–187.

Sartre, J. P. (1992). *Notebooks for an ethics* (D. Pellauer, trans.). Chicago: University of Chicago Press.

Serbin, L. A., O'Leary, K. D., Kent, R. N., & Tonick, I. J. (1973). A comparison of teacher response to the preacademic and problem behavior of boys and girls. *Child Development, 44,* 796–804.

Sigsgaard, E. (1993a). *Er opdragelse nødvendig.* Copenhagen: Tiderne Skifter.

Sigsgaard, E. (1993b). *Hvad er et godt seksårsliv?* Vejle: Kroghs Forlag.

Sigsgaard, E. (1995). *Om børn og deres virkelighed.* Copenhagen: Hans Reitzels Forlag.

Sigsgaard, E. (2001). *Børn i institutioner.* Copenhagen: Tiderne Skifter.

Sigsgaard, E., & Varming, O. (1996). *Voksnes syn på børn og opdragelse.* Copenhagen: Hans Reitzels Forlag.

Sigurdardottir, A. K. (1997). Disiplin i grunnskolen. *Nordisk Tidsskrift for Spesialpedagogikk, 75,* 4.

Skolen ved Sundet. (2003). *Handleplan 2003.* Helsinger: Skolen ved Sundet (www.svs.kk.dk)

Slee, R. (1995). *Changing theories and practices of discipline.* London: Falmer Press.

Stern, D. N. (1995). *Barnets interpersonelle univers.* Copenhagen: Hans Reitzels Forlag.

Sørensen, T. B. (1991). *Sociologien i hverdagen.* Århus: Forlaget Gestus.

Taiet, S., & Algot, T. (1986). *Kjeftepedagogikk.* Oslo: Debattserien for Barnehagefolk.

Tangney, J. P. (1991). Moral affect: The good, the bad and the ugly. *Journal of Personality and Social Psychology, 61* (4), 598–607.

Termansen, E. (1998). En bedre voksen er en bedre lærer. *Folkeskolen, 18.*

Thorup, K. (2001). *Bonsai.* Copenhagen: Gyldendal.

Tobin, J. J., Wu, D. Y. H., & Davidson, D. H. (1989). *Preschool in three cultures.* New Haven, CT: Yale University Press.

Vognmandsparken (the staff). (1997). *Skældud er ikke bare "skældud."* Copenhagen: Højvangseminariet.

Wagner, S., & Wagner, J. T. (2003). *Early childhood education in five Nordic countries.* Århus: Systime.

Waksler, F. C. (1991). Dancing when the music is over: A study of deviance in a kindergarten classroom. In F. C. Waksler (Ed.), *Studying the social worlds of children: Sociological readings.* London: Falmer.

Weber, M. (1992). *Den protestantiske etik og kapitalismens ånd.* Copenhagen: Nansensgade Antikvariat. (Original work published 1920)

Young Voices opinion survey of children and young people in Europe and Central Asia (2001). Geneva: UNICEF.

About the Author

ERIK SIGSGAARD is a teachers' college lecturer and researcher at the Center of Institution Research at Højvangseminariet in Glostrup, Denmark. He is a well-known debater, lecturer, and author of a number of books on educational and political topics.